Pro SQL Server 2005 Assemblies

Robin Dewson and Julian Skinner

Pro SQL Server 2005 Assemblies

Copyright © 2006 by Robin Dewson and Julian Skinner

ISBN (pbk): 1-59059-566-1

Library of Congress Cataloging-in-Publication data is available upon request.

Printed and bound in the United States of America 9 8 7 6 5 4 3 2 1

Trademarked names may appear in this book. Rather than use a trademark symbol with every occurrence of a trademarked name, we use the names only in an editorial fashion and to the benefit of the trademark owner, with no intention of infringement of the trademark.

Lead Editor: Tony Davis
Technical Reviewers: Damien Foggon, Adam Machanic, Joseph Sack, Kent Tegels
Additional Material: Adam Machanic
Editorial Board: Steve Anglin, Dan Appleman, Ewan Buckingham, Gary Cornell, Tony Davis,
    Jason Gilmore, Jonathan Hassell, Chris Mills, Dominic Shakeshaft, Jim Sumser
Project Managers: Laura Cheu, Richard Dal Porto
Copy Edit Manager: Nicole LeClerc
Copy Editors: Ami Knox, Nicole LeClerc, Liz Welch
Assistant Production Director: Kari Brooks-Copony
Production Editor: Kelly Winquist
Compositor: Molly Sharp
Proofreader: Dan Shaw
Indexer: Julie Grady
Cover Designer: Kurt Krames
Manufacturing Director: Tom Debolski

Distributed to the book trade worldwide by Springer-Verlag New York, Inc., 233 Spring Street, 6th Floor, New York, NY 10013. Phone 1-800-SPRINGER, fax 201-348-4505, e-mail orders-ny@springer-sbm.com, or visit http://www.springeronline.com.

For information on translations, please contact Apress directly at 2560 Ninth Street, Suite 219, Berkeley, CA 94710. Phone 510-549-5930, fax 510-549-5939, e-mail info@apress.com, or visit http://www.apress.com.

The information in this book is distributed on an "as is" basis, without warranty. Although every precaution has been taken in the preparation of this work, neither the author(s) nor Apress shall have any liability to any person or entity with respect to any loss or damage caused or alleged to be caused directly or indirectly by the information contained in this work.

The source code for this book is available to readers at http://www.apress.com in the Source Code section. You will need to answer questions pertaining to this book in order to successfully download the code.

Contents at a Glance

Contents

About the Authors

 **ROBIN DEWSON** has been hooked on programming ever since he first saw a computer, a Commodore PET, at Glasgow University. He bought his first computer, a Sinclair ZX80, in 1980. His first main program was a Visual FoxPro application that could be used to run a fantasy league system. Realizing that the marketplace for Visual FoxPro was limited, he decided to learn Visual Basic and SQL Server.

Starting out with SQL Server 6.5, Robin soon moved to SQL Server 7 and Visual Basic 5, and became involved in developing several applications for clients in the UK and the United States. From there, he moved to SQL Server 2000 and Visual Basic 6. Currently, though, it is the .NET world that Robin concentrates on, using C# and VB .NET and, of course, SQL Server 2005. Robin currently is consulting at Lehman Brothers in London, where he has been for nearly nine years. Robin is also the author of *Beginning SQL Server 2000 Programming* (Apress, 2003).

JULIAN SKINNER is a freelance programmer and technical author. He studied Germanic etymology to the PhD level before joining Wrox Press as an indexer in 1998 in order to get a real job. He became a technical editor shortly after that, later working as a technical architect and commissioning editor. He moved to Apress in 2003 and then went freelance in 2004 to concentrate on writing code. He has consequently spent most of the last seven years reading books about programming, focusing in particular on Microsoft technologies and, since 2000, on C# and the .NET Framework.

Julian has contributed many sections and code samples—and often whole chapters—to the books he's worked on over the years, mostly hiding behind the relative anonymity of an "additional material" credit. He is also a coauthor of *The Programmer's Guide to SQL* (Apress, 2003) and *Pro SQL Server 2005* (Apress, 2005). You can contact Julian through his web site at http://www.JulianSkinner.com.

About the
Technical Reviewers

 **ADAM MACHANIC** is a database-focused software engineer, writer, and speaker based in Boston, Massachusetts. He has implemented SQL Server for a variety of high-availability OLTP and large-scale data warehouse applications, and he also specializes in .NET data access layer performance optimization. He is a Microsoft Most Valuable Professional (MVP) for SQL Server and a Microsoft Certified Professional (MCP). Adam is the coauthor of *Pro SQL Server 2005* (Apress 2005).

Adam contributed additional material to Chapters 1, 6, and 7 of this book.

KENT TEGELS is the database curriculum lead for DevelopMentor, where he is responsible for developing and teaching classes in database technologies, programming, and Microsoft .NET. Since 2004, Kent has been recognized by Microsoft with Most Valuable Professional (MVP) status in SQL Server for his community involvement with SQL Server and .NET. Kent holds Microsoft certifications in Database Administration and Systems Engineering. He has contributed to several books on data access programming and .NET, and is a well-known industry speaker. He lives in Omaha, Nebraska, with his fiancée, Janell, and pet cat, Jack. Kent and Janell enjoy making ale, cooking, and playing with Jack. Jack mostly enjoys sleeping.

 **JOSEPH SACK** is a database administration and developer based in Minneapolis, Minnesota. Since 1997, he has been developing and supporting SQL Server environments for clients in financial services, IT consulting, manufacturing, and the real estate industry. Joseph received his bachelor's degree in psychology from the University of Minnesota. He is the author of *SQL Server 2005 T-SQL Recipes: A Problem–Solution Approach* (Apress, 2006) and *SQL Server 2000 Fast Answers for DBAs and Developers* (Apress, 2005), and the coauthor of *Pro SQL Server 2005* (Apress 2005) and *Beginning SQL Server 2000 DBA: From Novice to Professional* (Apress, 2006). Joseph is also a Microsoft Certified Database Administrator (MCDBA). He can be contacted at joe.sack@gmail.com.

DAMIEN FOGGON is a freelance programmer and technical author based in Newcastle, England. He is the technical director of Thing-E Ltd., a company specializing in the development of dynamic web solutions for the education sector, and the founder of Littlepond Ltd. He started out working for BT in the UK before moving on to progressively smaller companies, until finally founding his own company so that he can work with all the cool new technologies and not the massive monolithic developments that still exist out there.

Damien is currently coauthoring books for Microsoft Press and Apress, and has acted as a technical reviewer for both Wrox Press and Apress. His first solo outing as an author, *Beginning ASP.NET 2.0 Databases* (also from Apress), will be arriving soon.

He can be contacted at damien@littlepond.co.uk or online at http://www.littlepond.co.uk.

Acknowledgments

As ever, there are millions of people to thank, and I apologize now for anyone I miss. I'll try to not make this one of those Oscar speeches that go on for hours.

First of all, thanks to Jack Mason, my boss, a very understanding and great guy to work with for so many years. Anthony "Jock" Jawad, my head trader, who kept me employed through thick and thin. I owe a deep debt that is regularly paid back when Rangers lose to Celtic. For relaxation, Debbie and Charlie Roberts at the cafe and amusements at Sea Palling in Norfolkshire, England. All at BBC's 6 Music (http://www.bbc.co.uk/6music), who get me through the day and weekend, with special mention to Phill Jupitus and Phil Wilding, Vic McGlynn and Liz Kershaw—great presenters with brilliant music. Also all those at Bedford Rugby (http://www.bedfordrugby.co.uk), including Bernie McGee, who makes me laugh.

Thanks also go to my brother-in-law Andrew Lockwood and my mate Paul Goodwin for keeping me company on those very early morning trains and prodding me when I snore too loud or when it's time to get off and change to the Underground.

A huge thank-you has to go to Tony Davis, Laura Cheu, and Richard Dal Porto at Apress, who must all be very bald by now with the worry over this book. Also to Gary Cornell for rescuing my writing career when buying up so much of Peer Information Group.

This book would never have been possible without my *very* understanding family: my wife, Julie (yes, we can now go out at the weekend); Scott (yes, this does mean I can now sort out your computer); Cameron (yes, this does mean I can now practice rugby with you); Ellen (will you ever want to do girl things and give up rugby?); my mother-in-law, Jean, who is wonderful; and my late father-in-law, David, who I still miss and was just so brilliant with the kids.

But this book is dedicated especially to my mum and dad, Scott and Laura, who cattle-prodded me down this great road in life. From letting me use the television with my ZX80 and ZX81 when they wanted to watch the news, to helping me find my two colleges and prodding me down that road, and supporting me every step of the way. Without them, I might have ended up a bored civil servant. Many thanks to them for helping me achieve the great life I have.

Up the Blues!

Robin Dewson (http://www.fat-belly.com)

Preface

The main aim of this book is to show you each of the different types of .NET assemblies now possible within SQL Server 2005. This is a major leap in technology for developers and database administrators alike. Knowing when, how, and why to use this technology is crucial in continuing to offer stable and efficient database servers and database solutions.

By the end of this book, you will not only be competent in building assemblies, but also know which assemblies are safe for your server, what expansions each can give your server, and how you can build and deploy your own assemblies.

We hope you enjoy this book.

Robin Dewson
Julian Skinner

Introduction

The ability to run .NET code in the database is arguably the most exciting development in SQL Server for years. Traditionally, if T-SQL did not meet your needs, then you could write the required logic in either an external business object or an extended stored procedure. With the former, you could often generate unnecessary network traffic, and you also would lose the advantages associated with encapsulating data-centric logic in a single location (i.e., the database). The latter were complex to write and notorious for decreasing the stability of SQL Server.

In SQL Server 2005, which hosts the common language runtime (CLR), all this has changed. You can now write modules such as stored procedures, triggers, functions, and custom types in a .NET language instead of T-SQL. These modules have access to powerful .NET Framework classes, so they vastly extend the processing and formatting capabilities available through T-SQL. They also allow access to custom data sources for which there may not be an ODBC driver or OLE DB provider.

What This Book Covers

The coding requirements for a SQL Server assembly differ somewhat depending on the type of SQL Server module the assembly implements—for example, writing a user-defined type requires a bit more work than writing a CLR stored procedure.

The bulk of this book consists of chapters that walk you through how to build each type of SQL Server assembly. In each case, we provide carefully chosen examples that demonstrate business problems where assemblies could be of true benefit. For example, we show how .NET greatly simplifies working with images and XML data, and accessing external data sources and web services. We also devote chapters to debugging and error handling strategies in SQL Server assemblies and to their security implications.

The following sections provide chapter-by-chapter overviews.

Chapter 1: Introducing Assemblies

We start by putting SQL Server assemblies in context and looking at what they are, why they're useful, and what we can do with them.

Chapter 2: Writing a Simple SQL Assembly

Now that we've covered the theory, it's time to get our hands dirty with a real example. Here we show how to create and deploy a simple CLR stored procedure, covering every step of the process and providing instructions for both Visual Studio 2005 and the command-line compiler.

Chapter 3: The SQL Server .NET Programming Model

In this chapter, we introduce the new .NET classes used to build SQL Server assemblies. These include the `SqlContext` class, which provides information about the context in which the assembly is executing, and the `SqlPipe` class, which allows us to send information back to the caller. We'll also show how to access SQL Server data from within a SQL assembly.

Chapter 4: CLR Stored Procedures

Once we've covered the basics, we can start to look in detail at the individual types of SQL Server assemblies we can build. We start with the simplest type: stored procedures. We'll also show how .NET can make image manipulation and working with XML much easier, and how we can use .NET to execute external programs.

Chapter 5: User-Defined Functions

User-defined functions (UDFs) come in two flavors: scalar-valued functions, which return a single value, and table-valued functions, which return a resultset of values. We'll demonstrate how to create and use both types, and along the way we'll also cover how to work with Active Directory and how to browse the file system.

Chapter 6: User-Defined Types

User-defined types (UDTs) have been around for some time in SQL Server, but the ability to create these types in .NET greatly increases their functionality. Unlike traditional UDTs, CLR UDTs don't need to be based on the standard SQL Server types, and they can also expose properties and methods. In this chapter, we look in detail at creating CLR UDTs and illustrate their use with types representing a time duration and an e-mail address.

Chapter 7: User-Defined Aggregates

As well as the standard UDFs we met in Chapter 5, we can also use SQL Server assemblies to define custom aggregate functions that work on a set of rows. In this chapter, we look in detail at building user-defined aggregates (UDAs) and also examine how to use UDAs in combination with UDTs by building a UDA that calculates the average for a column of the duration type we defined in Chapter 6. Finally, we look at a full implementation of the population variance statistical function.

Chapter 8: CLR Triggers

As well as the ability to write triggers in a .NET language, SQL Server 2005 boasts another major development on the trigger front: the ability to write triggers to react to DDL events, such as creating or dropping stored procedures or tables. In this chapter, we look at both DDL and DML triggers in .NET and show how to use DDL triggers to create automatic backups of source code.

Chapter 9: Error Handling and Debugging Strategies

Once we've covered each type of SQL Server assembly, we pan out again to look at a couple of more general issues relating to all assembly types. In this chapter, we consider two distinct but related topics: error handling and debugging. We start by looking at debugging SQL Server assemblies, both in the full version of Visual Studio 2005 and in the pared-down version that ships with SQL Server 2005. Then we examine how to handle any errors that occur, including sending e-mails from a SQL assembly and writing entries to an event log.

Chapter 10: Security

.NET provides two main security mechanisms: role-based security, which allows us to imper-sonate Windows users and restrict execution of code to particular users or groups of users, and code access security (CAS), which lets the developer or administrator restrict what actions a section of code can perform. In this chapter, we look at both these mechanisms and explore how to use them in SQL assemblies.

Chapter 11: Integrating Assemblies with Other Technologies

In this final chapter, we examine a couple of different applications of SQL assemblies. First, we look at integrating SQL assemblies and XML web services, and show how to access a web serv-ice from within a SQL assembly. Then we cover how to use assemblies with a completely new SQL Server technology: the Service Broker message-queuing system.

Who This Book Is For

This book is intended for SQL Server developers and DBAs who want to learn what SQL Server assemblies can do for them and want to know what the advantages and possible pitfalls are of allowing .NET code to run in the database.

You should have a working knowledge of the .NET Framework, and specifically of the C# language, as all the examples in this book are in C#. However, the code is explained in detail, so you don't need to have an in-depth knowledge of every class in the .NET Framework Class Library.

■**Note** All of the C# code examples for this book, along with their Visual Basic equivalents, can be down-loaded from the Apress web site, http://www.apress.com.

CHAPTER 1

■■■

Introducing Assemblies

SQL Server 2005 sees the integration of the common language runtime (CLR) and .NET technology into the SQL Server database engine. No longer is a developer or database administrator restricted to using only Transact-SQL (T-SQL) when working with data inside the database.

This chapter covers the following topics:

- Examining how data manipulation was performed prior to SQL Server 2005

- Understanding the basics of assemblies, their capabilities, and how they might affect the design and distribution of your application components

- Using .NET assemblies

- Examining the different types of assembly-based objects you can build, including CLR-based stored procedures, user-defined functions, and user-defined data types

Data Manipulation Prior to SQL Server 2005

Some data manipulation tasks are difficult to express in T-SQL, resulting in code that can be awkward to create and maintain. If T-SQL does not meet your needs, then you traditionally have had two options:

- Manipulate the data through a development language such as Visual Basic (using ADO). For example, if you need to perform some complex data validation (such as credit card validation) that requires you to connect to a third-party validation system, or if you need to format data such as tax codes or government insurance numbers, then you might do so outside of SQL Server.

- Perform the work on the sever side using an extended stored procedure written in a language such as C++.

In the former case, working outside the database is not always the optimum choice. The code is not under the control of SQL Server and possibly not even running on the physical server. Also, there can often be substantial overhead associated with fetching data from SQL Server over a network, manipulating it in a third-party language (such as Visual Basic), and then returning it to the database.

For server-side programming, C++ is the next step up from T-SQL—and it is a very large step. Developers have occasionally had to resort to processing data using extended stored procedures in order to allow them to perform more complex logical processing (often this involves overnight processing of data such as archiving, reconciliation, and validation). However, extended stored procedures are notoriously prone to instability and memory leaks, so processing data in this manner always has the attendant risk of server crashes. There is also no control over what the code can access outside of SQL Server, and therefore you are potentially exposing sensitive data to unrestricted resources, without the knowledge of the data owner. This is not only a major concern to database administrators, who lose the ability to ensure that a server is stable and secure, but also to corporate auditors.

With SQL Server 2005 and its integration with the .NET CLR and .NET languages, coding becomes more manageable, and you can build your server applications on a greatly extended architecture. This book will empower you as a developer or a DBA to build on this technology with database enhancements that were impossible previously.

Developers can now build code that can safely run not only *on* the same server as SQL Server, but also *within* SQL Server. This code is made up of *assemblies*, which are compiled sets of code modules written using any .NET-compatible language (although only C# and VB .NET are officially supported). .NET integration can be used to build upon the foundation of SQL Server 2005 and to provide enhanced data types, functions, and aggregations.

■**Note** Before we go any further, we should note that this book won't teach you the basics of .NET. Although all the code presented is explained in careful detail, if you're unfamiliar with the .NET platform and the .NET languages, you may want to first read a companion reference, such as *C# and the .NET Platform, Second Edition* by Andrew Troelsen (Apress, 2003).

SQL Server Assemblies Overview

As noted earlier, an assembly is usually written in C# or VB .NET. The code is compiled using the .NET language compiler, either through a specialized command window or Visual Studio 2005. Each different type of assembly requires you to implement a specific interface and the methods associated with that interface. For example, a user-defined aggregate (UDA) using .NET requires certain methods such as `Initialize`, `Accumulate`, `Merge`, and `Terminate` to be defined.

Once the assembly has been compiled, the `.dll` file can be moved onto the SQL Server system and loaded into the database. When loaded, the assembly's bits are stored within the database in a system table called `sys.assembly_files`. This means that the actual assembly file is no longer necessary; the database has all it needs and is not reliant upon external resources.

So quite simply, a SQL Server assembly is a compiled code module (or a set of modules) that results in a file that can be imported into SQL Server to fire on certain actions. An assembly is a not a stand-alone executable—it requires the .NET runtime on the server to execute.

Common Language Runtime Overview

The CLR is an environment within the Microsoft .NET Framework that allows code, whether written in VB .NET, C#, or any other .NET compatible language, to execute in a common fashion. The CLR is a *managed* environment designed with safety and stability in mind. "Managed" here means that memory and resources are automatically handled by the runtime, and it is very difficult (if not impossible) to write code that will cause a memory leak. "Managed" also means that SQL Server can control the runtime if something goes wrong. If SQL Server detects instability, the hosted runtime can be immediately restarted.

In the sections that follow, we'll briefly describe some of the key principles underpinning CLR-based code.

Compiling and Executing Assembly Code

When you build a .NET assembly for SQL Server, you will use a language-specific compiler to convert your code to Microsoft intermediate language (MSIL). This compiled code can be held in different formats for .NET applications, but for SQL Server 2005 it will always be held as a dynamic link library, or DLL.

■**Note** A DLL has no graphical interface, you cannot start running it by double-clicking it like an EXE, and it can be invoked explicitly only by another program or service on a computer.

At the same time as the DLL is built, metadata is also created and held inside the DLL alongside the MSIL. The CLR takes this MSIL code along with the metadata and compiles it to execution code at runtime using just-in-time (JIT) compilation. One of the main goals of the CLR is that it shouldn't matter what language developers use to develop their code. All the information about to how to store and retrieve type information is stored in a common format, as metadata. Thus, the CLR provides built-in support for language interoperability. It can manage execution of any .NET-compliant language, and it can ensure that your code is accessible from any programming language via the Common Language Specification (CLS), which defines a common set of language features and how they should be used.

■**Note** In reality, different MSIL code will be generated for different languages, which can lead to better optimization of code from language to language. For example, Microsoft is promoting C++ .NET as the most optimized language to compile to at the moment.

Code is compiled only as it is needed, but once it is compiled it will reside within SQL Server until the server completes the specific task. The code is then removed from memory and, when the task is run again at a later state, processed by the JIT compiler again. This is different from T-SQL code that produces a plan that is stored after first execution and can be used on future executions.

When an assembly is first called, the .NET CLR is loaded by SQL Server in the form of a Microsoft DLL called `mscoree.dll`, the Microsoft common object runtime execution engine. From this DLL other .NET assemblies that form the .NET Framework are loaded and executed as necessary. Once all .NET code within SQL Server has completed running, then the DLLs are cached. These will be unloaded from memory only when the server encounters extreme memory pressure.

Code Access Security

The CLR is not just a runtime engine; it also inspects your code to ensure that there are no security breaches or unauthorized actions occurring. It does this using a code access security (CAS) model that allows you to define what actions a specific block of code may perform, such as which Windows resources it can access, or whether it is permitted to access unmanaged code.

When an assembly is deployed to SQL Server, you must specify the CAS permission set for the assembly in the CREATE ASSEMBLY statement. We discuss permission sets in detail in Chapters 2 and 10, but we'll outline briefly here:

- SAFE: This permission set doesn't allow access to external resources (such as non-SQL data sources), calls to unmanaged code, or operations that break .NET's type safety rules and are therefore unverifiable by .NET.

- EXTERNAL_ACCESS: This permission set allows access to external data sources, such as file I/O, Internet, and e-mail access. It doesn't permit assemblies to contain unsafe or unverifiable .NET code, or to call into unmanaged code.

- UNSAFE: This permission set allows access to almost all the functionality of .NET, including access to external resources and unsafe and unmanaged code.

So, for example, if you want your code to access the registry or the Windows event log, the CLR checks its security via CAS to determine whether or not the assembly can perform the desired action.

Threading Model

Normally SQL Server uses a *non–pre-emptive* threading model, whereby SQL Server controls the threads running and determines when to yield one thread process to allow other threads to run. When SQL code is executing within SQL Server, each active query will have its own thread. As a lock is placed or removed on a row, a page, or a table, or the next leaf of data is being read in to the I/O buffers, that processing thread will enter a wait state. This thread will therefore yield execution back to SQL Server to allow it to process another thread or give more processing to threads currently running.

CLR assembly code *within SQL Server* offers a different, *pre-emptive* threading model, whereby the operating system schedules which thread to run. To allow these two models to coexist, the CLR will call *synchronization objects* within SQL Server to allow SQL Server to manage the threading of any CLR object that is being executed within the SQL Server.

For example, garbage collection is a function of CLR that cleans up memory allocated during your assembly execution that hasn't been explicitly deallocated. SQL Server will know that garbage collection is occurring and therefore can yield processing to another thread.

Once garbage collection is finished and the thread terminates, the SQL Server synchronization object will be notified and processing can continue. This is similar to when SQL Server places locks on tables, rows, and so forth. Also, any other threads within the assembly that are processing will pause to allow garbage collection to run exclusively for that assembly, avoiding possible memory corruption.

The main point to bear in mind is that, since the CLR uses its own threading model, it is probably wise to avoid writing assemblies that control their own threading or synchronization (and the same argument applies to memory allocation).

Memory Management

When creating your SQL Server installation, you can define how much of the server's physical memory you wish to allocate to SQL Server. It is possible to set minimum—and, more important, maximum—memory allocation amounts, thereby allowing more than one SQL Server instance on a physical server, for example. When CLR objects require memory, the space is requested from the SQL Server operating system (SQLOS) virtualization layer rather than directly from the operating system. This means that a CLR process's memory utilization cannot exceed the configured maximum for the SQL Server service. It is important to remember that SQL Server hosts—and controls—the CLR process, not the other way around.

Once memory has been granted by SQLOS, the hosted CLR runtime manages object allocation and deallocation within that memory space. It does this by managing the lifetime of any objects created within your code and performing garbage collection sweeps to periodically check the memory heap for any object that is no longer referenced. Any object dereferenced within your code will cause the deallocation of any memory set aside for that object. This means that the problems associated with working with unmanaged code (whereby an application reserves a pool of memory for objects and then does not release it properly) should be moot, providing you are not accessing resources that are not managed by the CLR.

Of course, this is no excuse for bad programming, and it is still highly advisable to do as your mother has always told you and "Clean up after yourself." Also, by implementing the IDisposable interface within your assembly, you can use the Dispose function to explicitly remove any unmanaged resources.

Application Domains

Another feature provided by the CLR to ensure code stability is the idea of *application domains* (AppDomains). A single CLR process can host many AppDomains, which can be thought of as virtual process spaces. Each AppDomain is completely isolated within the process space, which is referred to as *sandboxing*. By hosting applications in this way, the CLR can run many applications simultaneously in a single process, without allowing a single misbehaving application to destroy the entire process space. Should an application become deadlocked, leak memory, or otherwise enter an unstable state, its AppDomain can be reset by the CLR without affecting the other AppDomains loaded in the process.

AppDomains are especially important in the SQL Server–hosted CLR environment. Assemblies loaded into databases, like other database objects, are owned by a database user. All assemblies owned by the same user in the same database will run within the same AppDomain. Assemblies owned by a different user will run within a separate AppDomain. This means that the SQL Server process can reset any misbehaving AppDomain without affecting other users or the general state of the system. In effect, this goes a long way toward guaranteeing that enabling CLR hosting cannot bring down your database server!

Using Assemblies

You'll notice as you progress through this book that no matter what .NET object you're building, you'll have to take into account design and development considerations. To clarify one point immediately, just because .NET assemblies are available as an alternative to T-SQL for processing and validation logic, this does not mean that all (or even most) development will now take place inside a .NET assembly running in the database. T-SQL is still very much a valid method for solving database problems, and where the processing is set-based, T-SQL is by far the most effective solution.

The advent of assemblies does mean, however, that you now have alternative strategies available when you encounter tasks beyond the capabilities of T-SQL or tasks that stretch its capabilities too far, resulting in unacceptably complex code or poorly performing code.

■**Caution** Just because you can move all the processing or business logic to SQL Server does not mean that you should. There is an obvious processing overhead when you move your business logic to your SQL Server, and therefore doing so could result in degradation of performance on the server.

Not only does .NET perform certain tasks more efficiently than T-SQL, but also use of a .NET assembly provides your code with access to all the functionality within the .NET Framework, much of which is not available through traditional T-SQL.

So, you are probably now wondering when you should consider migrating business logic to an assembly, and when you should not. The following sections discuss some of the considerations surrounding this question.

Application Tier vs. Database

As technologies change and mature, so should the applications designed to use them. Keep in mind as you work with SQL Server's new capabilities that you are no longer constrained to the strict tiering models that have been popular in the database world for many years. This change, in many cases, is a good thing.

.NET assemblies running inside of SQL Server are running in the same process space, thereby reducing the overhead of marshaling data across networks and onto other servers. This will often be the greatest benefit when you consider switching logic from the application tier into the data tier. For instance, if your application is pulling 1 million rows from the database and filtering or aggregating them down to three rows worth of data, the savings in network bandwidth of only sending those three rows will be massive.

However, as with all things, your decision will be based on several factors. If the data traffic is light compared to the data processing the code is doing, then it probably doesn't make sense to risk dramatically increasing the processing load on the database server in order to cut back on a level of network traffic that ADO.NET may be more than capable of handling comfortably.

You also have to bear in mind the security setting that will be applied to the assembly. If you need your assembly to have access to any external resources or run unmanaged code, and therefore have an authority level of EXTERNAL_ACCESS, then your database administrators or your company policy may force you to take the processing out of the SQL Server process.

Many developers feel that if there is logic that is central to the data itself, and therefore central to the business itself, this logic should be encapsulated as much as possible within the database. The database is, in many organizations, a shared entity used by many consumers—be they legacy or new applications, reporting clients, clients doing ad hoc queries, and so on. Data consumers should not have to reproduce these rules every time, and many rules problems occur because one or more consumers either failed to or forgot to properly reproduce the rules.

However, embedding these rules in the database could have been difficult in the past due to complexity of the required logic; T-SQL is not as flexible as some might wish. If you subscribe to this "database-centric" philosophy but have business logic in the application tier (or in an extended stored procedure) due to the limitations of T-SQL, then you may well consider moving this logic into CLR objects.

T-SQL Code or .NET Assembly

T-SQL is a set-based language and therefore provides very fast and efficient data access and manipulation functionality. As previously discussed, if you already have a stored procedure or trigger working perfectly well in T-SQL, you need to think very hard about moving it to .NET. The advent of .NET programming within the database is certainly no reason to stop improving and refining your T-SQL knowledge.

EXECUTING T-SQL CODE FROM AN ASSEMBLY

Where possible, any T-SQL code that needs to be executed as part of a .NET assembly should be placed in a normal stored procedure and called from the assembly. This will ease the process with which CLR code can be moved between tiers. Very little needs to be done in order to move application-tier data access code into SQL Server or SQL Server data access code back out to the application tier. By using stored procedures, developers can ensure that best practices (i.e., using stored procedures for data access) can be easily maintained if code should ever have to move.

However, there may be times when you might consider migrating from T-SQL to an assembly. One example is when you've used T-SQL and cursors to perform extensive row-at-a-time data processing. You probably know of some large and cumbersome stored procedures with many, many lines of code, possibly with some GOTO statements, using cursors and some in-depth CASE statements. Maybe you even have stored procedures that call other stored procedures, that call more stored procedures, and so on. In both of these scenarios, error handling can become awkward and not foolproof, and maintenance can be complex. Altering these stored procedures to use .NET code might solve the headache of maintenance or upgrades.

There are some things that T-SQL just isn't meant to do. For instance, it's not known as a language that excels at accessing data from web services. Also, in T-SQL, there is only one data structure: tables. Tables work fine for most data needs, but sometimes you'll need something else—an array or a linked list, for instance. And although these things can be simulated using T-SQL, the process is messy at best.

A further consideration is that objects are somewhat "limited" in T-SQL, whereas user-defined functions (UDFs) and user-defined types (UDTs) have greatly expanded functionality in .NET. With CLR UDFs, you have far more powerful processing and formatting capabilities. With CLR UDTs, you are no longer restricted to the base (single, scalar) SQL Server data types such as varchar, int, and so on. It is now possible to create complex types that can expose their own properties, methods, and operators.

Entirely new objects are available in the form of CLR UDAs, whereas the number of aggregate functions available in T-SQL is limited (SUM, MAX, etc.). When no aggregate function existed for your task in T-SQL, you were often forced into row-by-row processing using cursors. With CLR UDAs, a whole new range of possibilities opens up. You can define your own custom aggregations, which can access the .NET Framework classes, thus extending their capabilities far beyond simple mathematics.

In summary, if you've "forced" T-SQL into situations for which it wasn't designed, then you may gain performance benefit from switching such T-SQL objects to assemblies.

Migrating Extended Stored Procedures

Probably the most commonly heard exclamation of relief upon the announcement of CLR integration with SQL Server 2005 was "No more extended stored procedures!" Migrating extended sprocs is probably the lowest-hanging fruit in terms of reaping the benefits of CLR integration.

Extended stored procedures (XPs), usually written in C++, give you more procedural processing power than is possible using T-SQL, and allow you access to operating system and other external resources. However, they are notoriously complex to write and are known for decreasing the stability of SQL Server, as there is no access control. An unwitting developer could easily write code that may overwrite some of SQL Server's own memory locations, thereby creating a time bomb that could explode when SQL Server needs to access the memory.

With the level of control available in the managed CLR environment, such scenarios are no longer an issue. XPs should probably be one of the first items on your "upgrades" list when moving to SQL Server 2005.

■**Note** Even when using CLR objects, it is prudent to limit the extent to which you work with the operating system (where problems might occur, such as disks filling up, log files becoming full, etc.) or with third-party APIs (that may hang or crash).

ADO.NET and SQL Data Provider

ADO.NET is the common platform that sits as the middle layer between client-side code and the data repository, and has the task of passing data between the two. Any code execution that passes data between these two areas goes through ADO.NET in some form or another.

The biggest change for ADO.NET 2.0 in relation to SQL Server concerns the new in-process data provider for SQL Server 2005. When a CLR stored procedure or function needs to access data in the database, it will do so via ADO.NET objects running in the SQL Server process space.

If you're accessing SQL Server data via ADO.NET 2.0 from an external client (such as a VB .NET client-side program), then you always have to create a connection to the data. However, the in-process provider will always have a connection to the calling context. In other words, if you're calling a CLR stored procedure, there exists a connection back to SQL Server so that you can send back information such as error messages without creating a database connection. However, if you need to retrieve further information, perhaps from a table, then you would need to explicitly open a new connection via the SqlConnection object, just as you would if you were running a client-side application. This connection will be with the server. Assemblies can also return data back via this connection.

SQL Server assemblies provide extended functionality with UDFs, UDAs, and so on. These can all make use of SQL data types that, as you know from previous SQL Server versions, can have a value of NULL. Therefore, these types have more features than the normal string data types that you find in VB .NET, C#, and so on, and as such need to be defined as their own data types. This is because they are nullable and support different levels of precision than the built-in .NET types. If you're looking at a SQL Server string, you would define a variable as SqlString, not as String.

■**Note** SQL data types are held in the System.Data.SqlTypes namespace.

Another enhancement is the support for notification when executing a SQL Server query that produces different resultsets using the same command. One example would be to send a query testing stock levels. If you place a mathematical function within your query that always returns the same value while you had enough stock, but returns a different value when stock ran low, ADO.NET allows a tag to be added that notifies SQL Server to generate a notification. Think of these capabilities as query callbacks, rather than you having to query the server for the information at a specified time interval.

Building Objects from Assemblies

Up to this point, we have discussed CLR integration, but we have not yet covered at what point we can hook into this new nirvana. Once you have created and compiled your .NET code, you can register that class as an assembly in the SQL Server database. Having done that, you can create CLR objects based on that assembly and register methods in the assembly as procedures, functions, and so on.

In the sections that follow, we'll briefly review some of the CLR objects that we cover in detail throughout the rest of the book.

CLR Stored Procedures

It is now possible within an assembly to build a CLR stored procedure in your preferred .NET language. A CLR procedure is able to encompass more functionality than a T-SQL stored procedure and is more secure than C++ extended stored procedures.

As when you create any CLR object, your first question should be, "Why should this routine be programmed using the CLR?" Remember that in most cases, T-SQL is still the preferred method for stored procedure programming, so give this question serious thought. As discussed earlier in the chapter, the most attractive use cases for CLR stored procedures are when the required task is simply too messy or difficult to achieve in T-SQL. Examples might include dynamic cross-tabulations, image handling, working with web services, and so on.

■**Note** CLR stored procedures are covered in detail in Chapter 4.

User-Defined Functions

When SQL Server 2000 was launched, it provided us with the ability to call UDFs to perform the same code on each row of data. UDFs were built using T-SQL code only.

Now that assemblies allow UDFs to be built with greater complexity, you are not restricted to performing only mathematical or textual processing with them. Performing logical processing, manipulating the file system using the .NET Framework's file access classes, and working with web services are just a few of the possibilities available to you. Scalar UDFs still work on a row-by-row basis when included with T-SQL, so be aware that every time you call a UDF in an assembly, the data included within the call will be marshaled across to the CLR. Therefore, you need to have a good processing justification to use a .NET assembly in this instance.

■**Note** UDFs are covered in Chapter 5.

User-Defined Types

Prior to SQL Server 2005, UDTs were based on predefined SQL Server data types such as varchar, nchar, and so on. Every user-defined data type could only derive from one of these.

It is now possible to build your own data type, and you are no longer restricted as you were in the past. For example, you can define a "circle" data type, which might have properties such as circumference and radius, or a "monitor-resolution" data type—there are no boundaries. Plus, you can define methods and properties on your new types and call them from T-SQL.

■Note UDTs are covered in Chapter 6.

User-Defined Aggregates

Aggregations such as SUM, MAX, AVG, and so on have been a great help for developers in many different scenarios, not just with mathematical functionality but also with logical functionality. Developers have been limited to these aggregations up until SQL Server 2005, but now any aggregation is possible. For example, with UDAs you can build an aggregation for calculating the median of a set of values if required—after all, there is a MAX and a MIN, so why not a MEDIAN?

■Note UDAs are discussed in detail in Chapter 7.

DDL Triggers

Triggers that fire when data has been modified in SQL Server have existed for a long time. They are still possible in SQL Server 2005, but now CLR and T-SQL triggers can fire on database and server events as well. The ability to trap and work with database or server events—such as when a stored procedure is created, modified, or dropped, or when a user is modified—will be a great boon for database administrators.

DBAs likely will use DDL triggers more than developers, as it will allow better auditing and monitoring of DDL actions as they occur. No longer will it be necessary to wait for a stored procedure that monitors system tables to fire at predefined intervals to inspect when a DDL action has occurred. With an event, notification of the action will occur instantly, allowing DBAs to see the action instantly.

It is also possible to roll back any DDL modifications, further enhancing the DBA's ability to lock down at what times of the day certain actions can occur.

■Note Triggers are covered in Chapter 9.

Summary

The advent of .NET within SQL Server 2005 provides developers with the ability to use this new functionality with SQL Server objects, actions, and services. As a result, the skill set required of developers is likely to increase.

T-SQL will still be the core requirement of DBAs and developers, but with the inclusion of .NET technology and new services within SQL Server, you may find that the distinction between the job functions of a DBA and a developer grow less well-defined. Tools used by DBAs will now expand to include .NET functionality, thus ensuring assemblies will be an all-embracing technology within the database world. This will, of course, mean that DBAs will also have to learn .NET. But developers will need most of all to embrace .NET more.

The main advantage for developers with SQL Server–hosted assemblies comes with the extended functionality that can be built. No longer is there a need for cursor-based, row-at-a-time processing using the limited functionality of T-SQL. Although CLR-based, row-at-a-time processing may not perform any faster, you will have the added functionality .NET brings to work with the rows.

The main decision to make is when to use T-SQL and when to use an assembly. In many instances, the choice will be simple and straightforward, as the need for extended logic processing is required. Although assemblies are in-process and server based—and therefore might process the data much faster than client-side processing or a stored procedure, which both transfer data across the network—this does not mean that assemblies are the ideal choice in all situations.

CHAPTER 2

■ ■ ■

Writing a Simple SQL Assembly

Before we go any further and examine in detail the new .NET objects needed to write SQL assemblies, we'll look at a simple example for an overview of the whole process. SQL Server 2005 supports assemblies that perform a number of different tasks within the database, and the process of writing these and creating the objects within SQL Server that we use to call the assembly can vary considerably. However, certain concepts apply to SQL assemblies in general, and the best way to understand these is to look at an example.

In this chapter, we'll cover the following topics:

- Understanding the basic steps involved in SQL assembly creation

- Writing and compiling .NET code

- Registering the assembly with SQL Server

- Creating a stored procedure

- Examining SQL Server projects in Visual Studio

SQL Assembly Creation Overview

Four steps are involved in creating a SQL assembly and preparing it for use within SQL Server:

1. Write the .NET code for the assembly.

2. Compile the .NET code.

3. Register the assembly as a database object within SQL Server.

4. Register the method within the assembly as a stored procedure, function, etc.

The first two steps are essentially the same as for any other .NET code used outside SQL Server, although there are some new classes and attributes that are used specifically for building SQL assemblies; we'll look at these in detail in the next chapter. There are also new project types in Visual Studio (VS) that help us build SQL assemblies quickly. In fact, VS can effectively perform all of the last three steps for you, so you only have to write the .NET code—and VS will even do some of that! However, we're going to show the process done the long way first, as it's vital that you understand completely every step. Then, when you hit problems (and you will), you'll stand a much better chance of solving them. If you don't understand how your project works in the first place, then when you encounter a problem your only option is going to be a lengthy phone call to Microsoft support. After you've digested the example, we'll show you the quick and easy way to accomplish the same thing.

Once we've created the assembly, we need to give SQL Server some way to access it. We do this using the new ASSEMBLY database object in SQL Server 2005. This gives us a way to refer to a .NET assembly within T-SQL code. However, it doesn't provide any way to call a specific method, and it doesn't distinguish between the different object types that we can now write in .NET. Therefore, to call .NET code from within SQL Server, we need to create a standard database object such as a stored procedure or function. To do this, we use the normal CREATE PROCEDURE statement, CREATE FUNCTION statement, and so on, but instead of including the code behind the module within these statements, we reference the code in a .NET assembly that we've already registered with SQL Server.

There are five types of objects we can create with .NET code in SQL Server 2005, based on the SQL assembly produced in steps 1 to 3:

- *Stored procedures*: Common language runtime (CLR) stored procedures are used in exactly the same way as T-SQL sprocs, but because they're written in .NET they can involve much more complex processing. We'll use a simple stored procedure as our example in this chapter, and we'll look at CLR stored procedures in detail in Chapter 4.

- *User-defined functions*: These can be divided into scalar-valued functions that return a single value and table-valued functions that return a whole table of values. We'll look at both types in Chapter 5.

- *User-defined aggregates*: These are functions that calculate values based on a whole series of rows, like built-in aggregate functions such as COUNT. Strictly speaking, these are a type of user-defined function (UDF), but since they are considerably more complex to write, we'll devote a whole chapter (Chapter 7) to them.

- *User-defined triggers*: As well as the ability to write triggers in .NET languages, we also now have the ability to write triggers that are fired by Data Definition Language (DDL) events such as CREATE TABLE. We'll look at CLR triggers in Chapter 8.

- *User-defined types*: SQL Server now allows us to create our own T-SQL types, so that we can store data in a custom format instead of being constrained by the built-in types or composites of those types. We can also define methods on those types. We'll examine these topics in Chapter 6.

Although the general steps outlined earlier for creating SQL assemblies apply to all these types, the actual .NET code contained in the assemblies doesn't necessarily have much in common. The simplest of these object types are stored procedures and scalar functions, which evaluate to a single method call in the .NET assembly, so we've chosen a stored procedure for our example.

Writing .NET Code

The first task, then, is to write the .NET code for our procedure. C# code can be written and compiled using either of the following:

- Visual Studio 2005

- A simple text editor (such as Notepad) and the C# command-line compiler

SQL assemblies must be written using version 2.0 of the .NET Framework, so if you're using VS, you *must* use VS 2005 (formerly known by the code name Whidbey). However, SQL Server 2005 ships with the .NET Framework 2.0 redistributable, which includes the Framework Class Library and the C# and Visual Basic (VB) 2005 language compilers, as well as the runtime itself, so it provides all the bare essentials for creating SQL assemblies. For this book, we assume that you don't have VS 2005 installed, but we'll provide instructions where necessary for VS users. For this first example, we'll provide explicit instructions for both environments.

Coding the Simple Stored Procedure

For this first example, we'll keep things very simple and just do some basic data access, returning a resultset to the caller of the procedure. In this case, we'll select all the data from the HumanResources.Employee table of the AdventureWorks database where the HireDate is after a supplied value. In a real application, you wouldn't use a CLR assembly to do this: T-SQL will always be more efficient for this type of data access. However, we want to keep the .NET code as simple as possible for this example so that you can see more clearly what's going on. SQL assemblies are generally best suited for situations where a procedure has to perform complex procedural logic (e.g., extensive string handling) or has to access some external data source.

As this is the first example in the book, we'll walk through it in some detail. Like the other examples in this book, we'll use C#, as this is the standard language of .NET. Also, because it's a completely new language designed specifically for .NET, it doesn't come with any "baggage"— there are no compromises made in the name of backward compatibility, and developers don't approach the language with preconceived ideas of how to use it.

So, let's begin and open up either Notepad or Visual Studio. If you're using VS, you'll need to create a new C# class library project called SimpleSprocTest in a new directory called Apress\SqlAssemblies\Chapter02. We'll write the code from scratch, so delete all the auto-generated code and rename the default source file SimpleSprocTest.cs instead of Class1.cs.

Now we're ready to write the code. As with all C# programs, we start with the using directives. These tell the C# compiler which namespaces to look in for any classes used in the code. In this case, we have three:

- The standard System namespace, which contains the core types used by .NET and which is used by pretty much all .NET programs

- The System.Data.SqlClient namespace, which contains the ADO.NET data provider for SQL Server, which we'll use to access data within SQL Server, just as we would in a normal .NET assembly running outside SQL Server

- The `Microsoft.SqlServer.Server` namespace, which contains the `SqlContext` and `SqlPipe` classes that we need to communicate with SQL Server from within a SQL Server assembly

We'll look at the classes in this namespace in more detail in the next chapter.

```
using System;
using System.Data.SqlClient;
using Microsoft.SqlServer.Server;
```

Next comes our own namespace definition. We'll place this example in the `Apress.SqlAssemblies.Chapter02` namespace:

```
namespace Apress.SqlAssemblies.Chapter02
{
```

Now we can define the class that will contain our code, which we'll call `SimpleSprocTest`. For this simple example, all the code will be defined within a single class (in fact, within a single method within that class). For a stored procedure, the class is no more than a container for the method, and there's no object-oriented programming going on at all. However, we still have to have the class:

```
public class SimpleSprocTest
{
```

Now we come to the meat of the example: the method that actually does the work of the stored procedure. As intimated earlier, a CLR stored procedure is contained basically within a single method. When the stored procedure is executed, SQL Server will simply call this method and return from the method. With some of the more complex SQL assemblies, things aren't so simple—a single call to table-valued function, for example, will result in many method calls being made to the SQL assembly.

Our method is called `GetEmployeesHiredAfter` and does pretty much what its name implies: it sends a resultset back to SQL Server containing all the data from the `HumanResources.Employee` table for employees who were hired after a certain date. This date is passed in as the single parameter to the method. Note that we're using the standard .NET type `System.DateTime` here, but the method will actually be called from T-SQL code, so it will be called with a parameter of the native SQL `datetime` type. This can be represented in .NET code using the `System.Data.SqlTypes.SqlDateTime` type; however, .NET can perform the conversion for us automatically, so we can get away with passing in the standard .NET type here.

```
[SqlProcedure]
public static void GetEmployeesHiredAfter(DateTime date)
{
```

Notice that we decorate the method with a `SqlProcedure` attribute, which just indicates that this method implements a CLR stored procedure. We define the return type as void. Methods that are used as CLR stored procedures must have a return type of either `void` or `int`, just as return values of a T-SQL sproc must be integers. Any other scalar values you want to return must be defined as output parameters. If the stored procedure generates a resultset of data (as indeed ours does), then that isn't returned from the method in the normal way, but must be sent directly to the caller. This is similar to the way we retrieve data from a T-SQL stored procedure: we use a SELECT statement to send it to the caller, rather than setting it as the return value. A return value from a CLR stored procedure will be treated like the return value of a T-SQL procedure, which is why if we return anything it can only be an integer.

Within the body of the method, we'll include all the code within try...catch blocks. If any runtime errors occur within the code in the try block, an exception will be raised and execution will pass to the first catch block associated with an exception of the same type or of a parent class. All exception types in .NET derive from System.Exception, so a block that catches System.Exception will catch any exception thrown in your code. For a discussion of exception handling strategies, please see Chapter 9.

```
try
{
```

Our first task is to get the data from the AdventureWorks database. We do this using more or less standard ADO.NET code, with a slight difference. Because SQL assemblies run in the security context of the caller, we don't pass in user credentials; instead, we use a special connection string that tells SQL Server we want to connect to it on the connection for the current context rather than to an external SQL Server instance.

There are five steps required to retrieve data from a SQL Server assembly:

1. Create a new SqlConnection object with the connection string set to "context connection=true".

2. Open the connection.

3. Create a new SqlCommand object using the SqlConnection object you've just created and the T-SQL query you want to execute.

4. Add and configure any parameters to the command.

5. Execute the command.

We start by creating and opening the context connection. This code is typically included in a using statement:

```
using (SqlConnection cn = new SqlConnection("context connection=true"))
{
    cn.Open();
```

This ensures that the connection will be closed when we're finished with it, even if we don't explicitly close it. The SqlConnection object will go out of scope when the block of code in braces following the using statement ends. At this point, its Dispose method will automatically be called even if an exception occurs, because the code within the using block is implicitly placed within a try block, and the call to Dispose within an associated finally block. The finally block is always executed after any code within the try and catch blocks, and is intended for precisely situations like this, where we need to perform an important action such as closing a connection regardless of what happens in the preceding lines of code. So our using statement implicitly compiles to the equivalent of this C# code:

```
SqlConnection cn = new SqlConnection("context connection = true");
try
{
```

```
        cn.Open();
        // Code that uses the connection goes here
    }
    finally
    {
        cn.Dispose();
    }
```

Next, we define the SQL code we want to execute and create the `SqlCommand` object that we'll use to execute this query:

```
        string sql = @"SELECT * FROM HumanResources.Employee
                       WHERE HireDate > @hireDate";
        SqlCommand cmd = new SqlCommand(sql, cn);
```

The @ symbol before the string allows us to include characters that otherwise we couldn't simply type into a string literal. It's very frequently used with file system paths, to avoid having to prefix every backslash in the path with another backslash. It also allows a string to break over multiple lines, so it's handy for keeping SQL statements readable within .NET code. You'll see a few examples of it later in this book.

Notice that we parameterize the query by including a T-SQL variable (with the customary @ prefix) in the `WHERE` clause. Instead of using parameters, we could have simply built the query using string concatenation to include our C# `date` variable in the command. However, parameterization has several advantages. First, it provides more readable code, as the SQL query is coded as a single string, instead of being broken up to include the C# variable. Also, it can provide a greater degree of type safety, because we can specify the type of the parameter at compile time (although we don't actually do that in this case). Finally, and most important, it can be more efficient, as SQL Server can prepare a single command for execution many times with different parameter values.

So, the third step is to add the parameters to the command. There are a number of ways of doing this, and we'll look at them in more detail in the next chapter. For now, we'll use the simplest method possible: we'll call the `AddWithValue` method of the `SqlCommand`'s `Parameters` collection. This method has two arguments: a string containing the name of the parameter (i.e., the name of the T-SQL variable we included in the `CommandText`, including its @ prefix) and the value for the parameter. Because this is passed in as an object, this method doesn't provide any compile-time type checking, but it does simplify our code as we can add the parameter and set its value in a single method call:

```
        cmd.Parameters.AddWithValue("@hireDate", date);
```

Lastly, we execute the command by calling one of the `SqlCommand.ExecuteXXX` methods. The exact method we choose depends on the type of the query and the object we want returned from the query. In this case, our query will return a resultset of data, so we'll call the `ExecuteReader` method. This returns a `SqlDataReader`, a forward-only, read-only resultset something like a fire hose cursor, and we store a reference to this in a variable called `reader`:

```
        SqlDataReader reader = cmd.ExecuteReader();
```

Now that we have the data, we just need to do something with it. Generally speaking, you'll want to perform some form of complex processing or external data access in a CLR stored procedure, or else you're most likely better off sticking with T-SQL. You'll see many examples of the new functionality that SQL assemblies permit in the later chapters, but for the purposes of this example, we're going to send the data right back to the caller. To do this, we have to use another object from the in-process provider—namely, the SqlPipe object. This object represents the communication channel between SQL Server and the calling application (e.g., Management Studio). We can get the SqlPipe for the current context from the new SqlContext class, which provides us with information about the context in which a SQL Server assembly is running (we'll look at this object in the next chapter):

```
SqlPipe pipe = SqlContext.Pipe;
```

The SqlPipe class has one particularly useful method: Send. This method has a number of overloads, and it can take, among other things, a string or a SqlDataReader object. So, to send our results back to the caller, we simply pass it into this method. We'll also send a message to the user to let her know that the command completed with errors:

```
            pipe.Send(reader);
            pipe.Send("Command completed successfully");
        }
    }
```

That completes the code that will execute if all is well, but if something goes wrong, execution will switch to our catch block. In this case, we'll use the one-size-fits-all approach and just have a single catch block that matches System.Exception or any type of exception derived from that class—or, in other words, any exception that .NET can throw at us!

In the code for this exception handler, we'll get a new SqlPipe object (the one we got within the try block is no longer in scope in the catch block, and with good reason: the exception may have been thrown before we created the SqlPipe). Once we have this, we'll send some data back to the user about what went wrong. We'll send the Message of the exception and the StackTrace, which represents the method call stack and lets us pinpoint exactly which method the exception was thrown in. In this case, the stack trace won't be too illuminating, as our GetEmployeesHiredAfter method only calls methods in the Framework Class Library, but even so, this information can be useful when debugging, and it's vital to include if your assembly has many methods called from within the stored procedure method.

```
        catch (Exception e)
        {
            SqlPipe pipe = SqlContext.Pipe;
            pipe.Send("Error occurred executing command:");
            pipe.Send(e.Message);
            pipe.Send(e.StackTrace);
        }
    }
    }
}
```

Save this file as `SimpleSprocTest.cs`, either in the main project folder if you're using VS or in the `Apress\SqlAssemblies\Chapter02` folder if you're using Notepad.

That completes the .NET code we'll be writing for this example, but there's still a lot to do before we can use it from SQL Server—we've completed only one of the four steps involved in creating a SQL assembly. The second step is to compile the source code into a DLL.

Compiling .NET Code

If you're using VS, compiling the .NET code couldn't be easier: you just select Build ➤ Build Solution from the main menu. Depending on the current build configuration (Debug or Release) and project properties, VS will compile the code and create `SimpleSprocTest.dll` in the `\bin\Debug` or `\bin\Release` directory under the main project directory. (Obviously, production code should be built using the Release configuration, but Debug is fine for this example.)

If you're using Notepad and the command-line compiler, there's a bit more work to do. First, you need to tell the system where to find the C# compiler and other files required by .NET. If you have the full .NET Framework 2.0 SDK installed, this provides you with a command prompt that's already configured with the correct values for the `PATH` environment variable. However, if you're using the redistributable that comes with SQL Server 2005, you need to set this up for yourself. The easiest way to do this is to create a new environment variable called `DOTNET2` and then set the path to this variable whenever you want to compile some code with this version of the Framework. Open up the System Properties dialog by double-clicking the System applet in the Control Panel and then clicking the Environment Variables button on the Advanced tab to bring up the Environment Variables dialog, as shown in Figure 2-1.

Figure 2-1. *The Environment Variables dialog*

To add a new system environment variable that's valid for all user accounts on the machine, click the New button in the System variables area in the bottom half of the window. In the New System Variable dialog, type **DOTNET2** as the name of the variable and the path for the .NET Framework directory for .NET 2.0:

```
<Windows_dir>\Microsoft.NET\Framework\v2.0.xxxx
```

for example (see also Figure 2-2):

```
C:\WINDOWS\Microsoft.NET\Framework\v2.0.50727
```

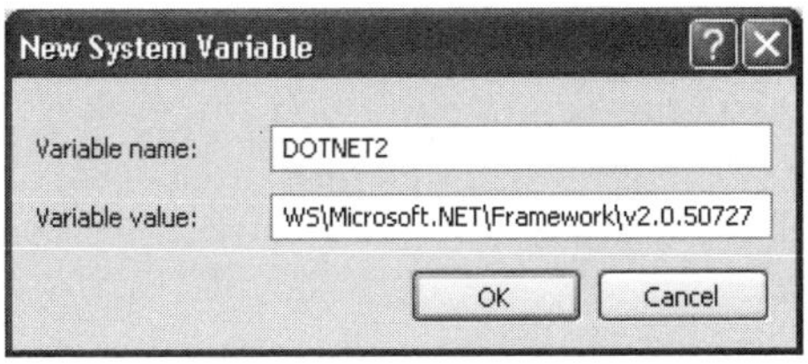

Figure 2-2. *The New System Variable dialog*

When you've added this new environment variable, open up a new command prompt and change to the directory where the `SimpleSprocTest.cs` file was saved. Now update the `%PATH%` variable for the command prompt by setting it to the same value as the `%DOTNET2%` variable you've just created:

```
C:\Apress\SqlAssemblies\Chapter02>SET PATH=%DOTNET2%
```

Now that Windows will know where to look for the C# compiler, we can compile the source code. The C# compiler, `csc.exe`, takes the following syntax:

```
csc [options] input_file
```

The C# compiler can take a fair number of options, but we need concern ourselves here with just two, as shown in Table 2-1.

Table 2-1. *Selected C# Compiler Options*

Option	Short Form	Description
`/target:`	`/t:`	Stipulates whether the compiler will generate a console application (exe), a Windows application (winexe), a DLL (library), or an assembly without a manifest (module)
`/reference:`	`/r:`	Specifies a list of assembly files that the compiler should import metadata from

In our case, we need to produce a DLL assembly that will execute within the SQL Server process, so we need to use the `/t:library` option. We won't use the `/r` option in this example, but we will see it in many examples later in the book, where our assembly calls into another assembly.

The full compilation command on his machine is

```
C:\Apress\SqlAssemblies\Chapter02>csc /t:library SimpleSprocTest.cs
```

The C# compiler will then print out its copyright information and, all being well, nothing else, before returning after a second or two:

```
Microsoft (R) Visual C# 2005 Compiler version 8.00.50727.26
for Microsoft (R) Windows (R) 2005 Framework version 2.0.50727
Copyright (C) Microsoft Corporation 2001-2005. All rights reserved.
```

If there are any compile-time errors, the compiler will print them out and the compilation will fail. In most cases, the error messages are fairly descriptive and compilation errors in C# are generally not too hard to solve. See Chapter 9 for information about debugging SQL assemblies.

Registering the Assembly with SQL Server

The final steps are to create the assembly and stored procedure as objects within the AdventureWorks database in SQL Server. We'll do this using Management Studio, so open that up and click the New Query button. You will be required to confirm your user credentials again, but these will already be auto-inserted in the dialog.

Now you can write the script to create the database objects. This is available in the code download as Chapter02.sql. The first task is to enable CLR integration within this instance of SQL Server. For security reasons, it is not permitted to execute .NET assemblies within an instance unless the DBA has specifically reconfigured the instance to authorize their use. To do this, you need to run the following reconfiguration command the first time you use CLR integration in a SQL Server instance:

```
sp_configure 'clr enabled', 1
GO
RECONFIGURE
GO
```

■**Note** You need the ALTER SETTINGS server-level permission to run this code. By default, members of the sysadmin and serveradmin fixed server roles have this permission.

Once that's done, we can proceed to install our assembly. First, we need to change to the AdventureWorks database, as our stored procedure must be created there:

```
USE AdventureWorks;
GO
```

Next, we create the assembly as a database object within SQL Server. To do this, we use the new `CREATE ASSEMBLY` T-SQL statement. This takes the following form:

```
CREATE ASSEMBLY <assembly_name>
FROM <assembly_file>
WITH PERMISSION_SET = { SAFE | EXTERNAL_ACCESS | UNSAFE };
```

The first two clauses are fairly straightforward. The `assembly_name` is the name that will be used to refer to the object from within T-SQL code. This *must* be the same as the assembly's actual name (in other words, the name of the assembly file minus the `.dll` extension). The `assembly_file` is the full path and filename of the DLL assembly file.

The last clause requires a little more explanation. One of the big advantages of SQL assemblies over old-style extended stored procedures written in unmanaged C++ is that the database administrator can have much more control over what rights are granted to the assembly code. The `PERMISSION_SET` option can have one of three settings:

- `SAFE`: Assemblies marked as `SAFE` may not access external resources (such as non-SQL data sources), call unmanaged code (such as using P/Invoke to call a function in the Windows API), or perform operations that break .NET's type safety rules and are therefore unverifiable by .NET (i.e., unsafe code in C#).

- `EXTERNAL_ACCESS`: Assemblies marked as `EXTERNAL_ACCESS` are also forbidden from calling unmanaged or unsafe code, but are permitted to access external resources (*if* the code to do this doesn't break either of the other two strictures—and this is a very big "if").

* `UNSAFE`: These assemblies may perform all three operations.

Clearly, assemblies that are given the `UNSAFE` or `EXTERNAL_ACCESS` permission set can perform actions that the DBA might not wish to allow. For example, if a stored procedure accesses an external data store, the DBA can have no control over what data is sent out of the database. `UNSAFE` is even more perilous; if .NET code calls unmanaged code, then that can effectively do anything at all, as .NET's security features such as code access security can place no restrictions at all on non-.NET code. While many SQL assemblies may need these less restrictive permissions, at least the DBA has a much clearer idea of the potential dangers of each assembly and the ability to limit the dangers as much as possible by granting the minimum permissions the functionality requires. One point to beware of, however, is that many of the .NET class libraries are at present only thin layers on top of existing Windows APIs, so any code that wishes to, for example, access a directory service will have to be given the `UNSAFE` permission set. We'll look at the security of .NET assemblies in detail in Chapter 10.

One final point to note is that when an assembly is installed into SQL Server, then SQL Server makes a local copy. If the SQL Server assembly calls into any other assemblies that aren't installed into the global assembly cache (GAC), SQL Server will also need to make private copies of these assemblies. If the called assemblies can't be found, the `CREATE ASSEMBLY` statement will fail. The CLR looks for private assemblies in the same directory as the executing assembly, so if your code calls another DLL that isn't installed into the GAC, you'll need to copy this to the same directory. Also, SQL Server implicitly creates an `ASSEMBLY` object for any private assemblies called by the SQL assembly, so if you make any changes to this private DLL, you'll need to drop it from the database and rerun the `CREATE ASSEMBLY` statement before the changes will take effect.

So, with those explanations out of the way, we can at last look at the CREATE ASSEMBLY statement for our simple procedure:

```
CREATE ASSEMBLY SimpleSprocTest
FROM 'C:\Apress\SqlAssemblies\Chapter02\SimpleSprocTest.dll'
WITH PERMISSION_SET = SAFE;
GO
```

Note that you may need to change the path to the assembly for your system, particularly if you're using Visual Studio. In this case, the DLL will be in the \bin\Debug or \bin\Release subfolder underneath the Chapter02 directory.

Otherwise, the only points to note here are that the assembly name *must* be SimpleSprocTest, because our DLL is called SimpleSprocTest.dll, and that we use the SAFE permission set, simply because we can. Our assembly accesses only SQL Server data and doesn't do anything dodgy like calling unmanaged or unsafe code, so we grant it the minimum permissions required.

Creating the Stored Procedure

We've now written the code for our stored procedure and created the SimpleSprocTest assembly in the AdventureWorks database, but we're still not quite there. There's one step left before we can actually call the procedure from within T-SQL code: we need to create a standard PROCEDURE object within the database, which we'll be able to call just like a normal T-SQL sproc.

Given that we're creating a standard PROCEDURE object, it follows that we use the standard CREATE PROCEDURE statement to create it. We won't go into this in detail here, because it's specific to creating stored procedures rather than .NET database objects in general, but the principal difference from a normal CREATE PROCEDURE statement for a T-SQL sproc is that where the latter would have the T-SQL code as the body of the statement, we now have an EXTERNAL NAME clause that references the method in the SQL assembly that will be executed when the sproc is called. The format for this varies slightly depending on the type of database object being created, but in each case we need to provide the name of the ASSEMBLY object in the database, the .NET type in the assembly to which the method belongs, and the name of the method. In our case, the CREATE PROCEDURE statement looks like this:

```
CREATE PROCEDURE uspGetEmployeesHiredAfter(@hireDate datetime)
AS
EXTERNAL NAME SimpleSprocTest.[Apress.SqlAssemblies.Chapter02.SimpleSprocTest].
GetEmployeesHiredAfter;
GO
```

And that's it! We finally have our first fully working CLR stored procedure. If you haven't already, run the SQL script to create the two database objects, and then test the new sproc by getting all the employees hired after January 1, 2002:

```
EXEC uspGetEmployeesHiredAfter '01/01/2002';
```

You should be rewarded with a table of data in the Results pane of Management Studio, as shown in Figure 2-3.

	EmployeeID	NationalIDNumber	ContactID	LoginID	DepartmentID	ManagerID	ShiftID	Title	Emerger
1	284	982310417	1013	adventure-works\amy0	3	273	1	European Sales Manager	1303
2	285	668991357	1025	adventure-works\jae0	3	284	1	Sales Representative	1315
3	286	134219713	1022	adventure-works\ranjit0	3	284	1	Sales Representative	1312
4	287	90836195	1027	adventure-works\tete0	3	268	1	Sales Representative	1577
5	288	481044938	1012	adventure-works\syed0	3	273	1	Pacific Sales Manager	1302
6	289	954276278	1023	adventure-works\rachel0	3	284	1	Sales Representative	1313
7	290	758596752	1024	adventure-works\lynn0	3	288	1	Sales Representative	1314

Figure 2-3. *The results of executing the CLR stored procedure*

SQL Server Projects in Visual Studio

Now that you've seen how to create a stored procedure assembly the long way, let's take a look at how to do it the easy way by taking full advantage of Visual Studio. VS now has a range of project types specifically geared to SQL assembly projects that allow us to create CLR modules such as stored procedures, triggers, and functions with the absolute minimum of effort.

To re-create the preceding example using a VS database project, create a new project in VS and select SQL Server project under the Database node in Project types, as shown in Figure 2-4.

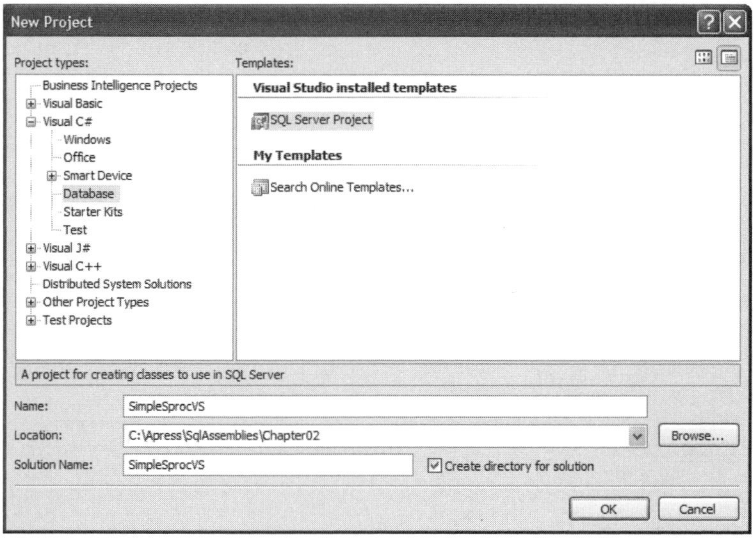

Figure 2-4. *Creating a SQL Server project in VS*

Next, you'll be invited to add a reference to the database where you want to install the CLR module. If you've already set up any database references, they'll appear in this list, in the form *servername.databasename.username*, as shown in Figure 2-5. If you don't have any references configured, you'll go straight on to the Add Database Reference dialog.

Figure 2-5. *Adding a database reference to your project*

You're going to be accessing the AdventureWorks database, so if a reference to that database doesn't already exist, click the Add New Reference button.

In the New Database Reference dialog, enter the connection information for your SQL server, as shown in Figure 2-6.

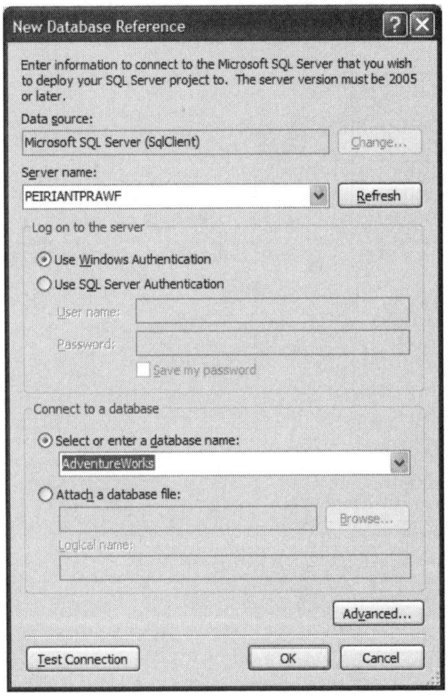

Figure 2-6. *Creating a new database reference*

After you've filled in the connection info and clicked the OK button, you'll be asked whether you want to enable debugging on this database, as shown in Figure 2-7.

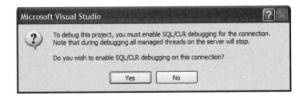

Figure 2-7. *Enable debugging*

As the dialog implies, and as you'll see in Chapter 9, enabling debugging has some serious implications and shouldn't be done on a production server. However, for this example click Yes.

VS will now create a new project, with no SQL Server module files. To add a new module, right-click the project name in Solution Explorer, select Add, and then choose the appropriate module type from the context menu (for this example, select Stored Procedure). This opens up the Add New Item dialog, as shown in Figure 2-8.

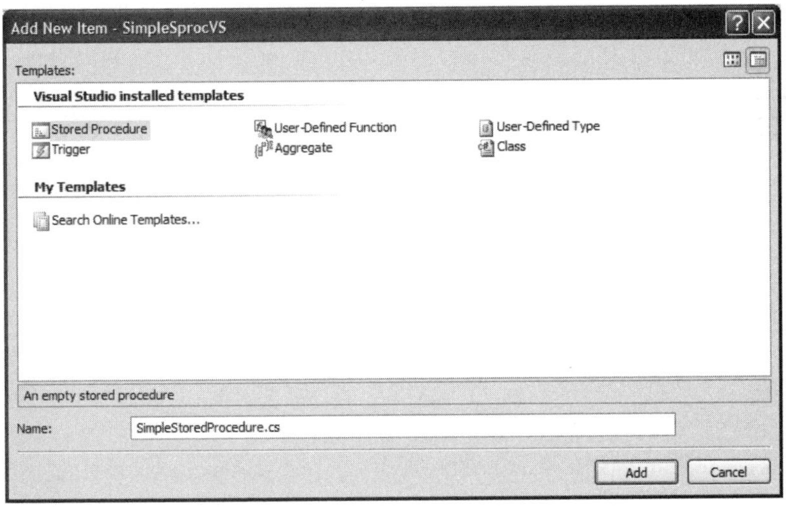

Figure 2-8. *Adding a new CLR module to a SQL Server project*

The stored procedure item should already be selected, so you just need to enter a name for the source code file (here, we've chosen SimpleStoredProcedure.cs) and click Add. This creates the skeleton code for a stored procedure method:

```
using System;
using System.Data;
using System.Data.SqlClient;
using System.Data.SqlTypes;
using Microsoft.SqlServer.Server;
```

```
public partial class StoredProcedures
{
    [Microsoft.SqlServer.Server.SqlProcedure]
    public static void SimpleStoredProcedure()
    {
        // Put your code here
    }
};
```

The autogenerated code contains using statements for the most common namespaces you'll need for SQL assembly projects, as well as a partial class and a method outline. Partial classes are a new feature of .NET 2.0 and allow a class definition to be spread over several source code files. The thinking here is presumably that you can have a single class named StoredProcedures that contains all your CLR stored procedures for a project without having to place them in the same file. However, some developers prefer to define different procedures in different classes, to rename the class to something more specific to the project, and to add a namespace, as in the code presented earlier in the chapter.

The generated method is given the same name as the source code file, but without the extension, so in this case it's called SimpleStoredProcedure. It's marked with the SqlProcedure attribute (you'll learn more about this in Chapter 4), but it has no body. We just need to fill this in with our code and add the parameter to the method signature:

```
using System;
using System.Data;
using System.Data.SqlClient;
using System.Data.SqlTypes;
using Microsoft.SqlServer.Server;


public partial class StoredProcedures
{
    [Microsoft.SqlServer.Server.SqlProcedure]
    public static void SimpleStoredProcedure(DateTime date)
    {
        try
        {
            using (SqlConnection cn = new SqlConnection("context connection=true"))
            {
                cn.Open();
                string sql = @"SELECT * FROM HumanResources.Employee
                            WHERE HireDate > @hireDate";
                SqlCommand cmd = new SqlCommand(sql, cn);
                cmd.Parameters.AddWithValue("@hireDate", date);
                SqlDataReader reader = cmd.ExecuteReader();
                SqlPipe pipe = SqlContext.Pipe;
                pipe.Send(reader);
                pipe.Send("Command completed successfully");
            }
```

```
    }
    catch (Exception e)
    {
        SqlPipe pipe = SqlContext.Pipe;
        pipe.Send("Error occurred executing command:");
        pipe.Send(e.Message);
        pipe.Send(e.StackTrace);
    }
  }
};
```

We're very nearly done, as VS does most of the rest of the work for us. There's just one thing we need to look at before we build and deploy the assembly. We saw when we deployed the assembly manually that we could assign it one of three different permission sets: SAFE, EXTERNAL ACCESS, or UNSAFE. To change this in VS, right-click the project name in Solution Explorer and select Properties. This displays the project properties in the main pane of VS, with the various settings available for the project on a number of different screens. The Permission Level setting is on the Database screen, as shown in Figure 2-9 (you don't actually need to change it for this example, so leave the level as Safe).

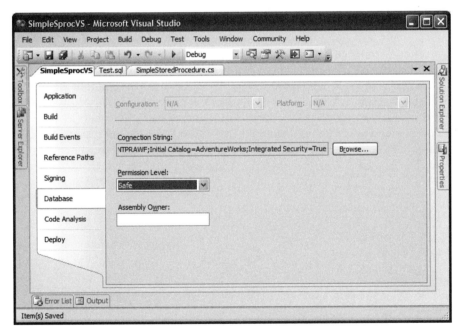

Figure 2-9. *Changing the permission set for a SQL assembly in VS*

When the stored procedure is created, VS adds a SQL script called test.sql to the project (you'll find it in the Test Scripts folder in Solution Explorer) that we can use to execute the procedure from within VS. Make this the startup script by right-clicking it in Solution Explorer and selecting Set as Default Debug Script. This allows you to run the project using this script from within the VS environment.

The script contains a number of commented-out lines to serve as template SQL statements, as well as one uncommented statement:

```
select 'To run your project, please edit the Test.sql file in your project. This
file is located in the Test Scripts folder in the Solution Explorer.'
```

But to be honest, these aren't incredibly useful. To test our simple stored procedure, delete or comment out the uncommented line, and add the following line to the test SQL script:

```
EXEC SimpleStoredProcedure '01/01/2002'
```

We're now ready to build, deploy, and execute the stored procedure. Simply click the Start button (the green arrow), and VS will take care of the rest. Once it has compiled the C# source code, VS will create and execute the appropriate CREATE ASSEMBLY and CREATE PROCEDURE statements to install the objects into SQL Server, and then finally it will execute the line that you added to the test.sql script. The output from the procedure will appear in the Debug view of the Output window; unfortunately, however, resultsets aren't displayed in the Output window in the current version of VS (they were in earlier betas), so we're afraid what you'll see is a bit anticlimactic.

```
EmployeeID  NationalIDNumber ContactID   LoginID
----------- ---------------- ----------- --------------------------------------------
No rows affected.
(1 row(s) returned)
```

When you build the project, it's deployed to SQL Server, so VS executes the CREATE ASSEMBLY and CREATE PROCEDURE statements for you. The name of the assembly follows the same rules as for manually deployed assemblies—it's the name of the DLL without the .dll extension, which is the name you gave the project when you created it (SimpleSprocVS in this case). The procedure is by default given the name of the method that implements it; when VS generates the skeleton code for the assembly, it gives this method the same name as you allocated to the C# file, or in this case SimpleStoredProcedure. However, you can change this behavior by setting the name property of the SqlProcedure attribute:

```
[Microsoft.SqlServer.Server.SqlProcedure(Name="uspGetNewEmployees")]
public static void SimpleStoredProcedure(DateTime date)
{
    // etc...
```

This allows you to call the SQL module something different from the .NET method, which is useful for enforcing different naming practices in T-SQL and .NET (e.g., it allows you to prefix all user stored procedures with usp, without forcing you to break with C# coding standards).

There's one final but very important point to make about SQL Server projects in VS 2005: you aren't allowed to add references to assemblies that aren't already installed in SQL Server. If you need to add a reference to a custom DLL or to one of the assemblies in the FCL that aren't preinstalled in SQL Server (the most widely used ones are, but this includes far from all of them), then you'll need to install it in SQL Server before you can reference it from your VS project. In several examples later in the book, some of the code is in a separate DLL assembly from the SQL Server assembly. To create these examples as VS SQL Server projects, you'll need to deploy that DLL manually to SQL Server using a CREATE ASSEMBLY statement before you can reference it from the SQL Server assembly.

Summary

This has been a short but important chapter. We've gone through the whole process of creating a simple SQL assembly in considerable detail because it's vital to understand how the whole process works before you move on to the specific assembly types, which makes up the core of the book.

Although the exact details vary, there are four steps involved in creating any CLR database object in SQL Server 2005:

1. Write the .NET code for the object.

2. Compile the code, using either Visual Studio (VS) or the command-line compiler.

3. Register the assembly as an object in SQL Server using the CREATE ASSEMBLY statement.

4. Create the database object such as the stored procedure or user-defined function that the .NET code implements.

You also saw how to get VS to do a lot of this work for you—but remember that it's important to understand fully how the CREATE ASSEMBLY and other statements work, even though you'll doubtless use these features a great deal if you have VS for .NET 2.0.

Now that you've seen how to create a simple SQL assembly, let's dig into the details. We'll start in the next chapter by looking at the new classes provided for writing SQL Server assemblies.

CHAPTER 3

■ ■ ■

The SQL Server .NET Programming Model

In the last chapter, we saw how to create and deploy a simple SQL Server assembly. This introduced us briefly to a couple of the new .NET classes that we use to create SQL assemblies: SqlContext and SqlPipe. These classes act as extensions to the standard .NET data provider that is used to access SQL Server data from .NET code, both from outside the server and from within a SQL assembly.

In this chapter, we'll look at the following topics:

- Using the SqlContext and SqlPipe classes

- Examining other classes that we use when creating SQL assemblies

- Using the standard ADO.NET provider for SQL Server from within a SQL assembly

The .NET Data Access Namespaces

Although data access in a SQL assembly basically uses the standard ADO.NET provider for SQL Server, there are inevitably some differences from data access from an external application, and therefore there need to be extensions. After some internal debate, Microsoft eventually decided to add the new classes to a separate .NET namespace (earlier, prerelease versions of SQL Server 2005 used an entirely different data provider for SQL assemblies, which closely mirrored the ADO.NET provider but contained a few extensions). In fact, the new combination of SQL Server 2005 and .NET 2.0 sees no fewer than four new namespaces added to the already sprawling .NET APIs dealing with data access. There are now eight .NET namespaces involved in working with SQL Server (not including the System.Data.SqlServerCe namespace used for working with the Pocket PC edition of SQL Server). The distinctions between them aren't always totally clear, so it's worth taking a moment to review the new and existing namespaces:

- System.Data: This is the root namespace for .NET data access. This namespace includes the classes and interfaces that make up the core ADO.NET architecture—in particular the DataSet, DataTable, and related classes.

- System.Data.Common: This namespace contains classes that are used by all .NET data providers.

- `System.Data.Design`: This new namespace contains classes used to generate strongly typed datasets.

- `System.Data.Sql`: This new namespace provides two classes that are used for SQL Server–specific functionality.

- `System.Data.SqlClient`: This is the .NET data provider for SQL Server (version 7.0 and above). It contains classes for accessing SQL Server data, both from an external .NET application and now also from within a SQL Server assembly using a new in-process provider.

- `System.Data.SqlTypes`: This namespace contains .NET types that map directly onto native SQL Server types, which allow you to avoid the overhead of implicit type conversions in SQL Server assemblies.

- `System.Transactions`: This new namespace provides a new transaction framework for .NET 2.0 that is integrated with both ADO.NET and the SQL CLR. We'll look at this namespace toward the end of the chapter.

- `Microsoft.SqlServer.Server`: This namespace provides classes that extend the .NET data provider for SQL Server to access data from within a SQL Server assembly, as well as miscellaneous classes, attributes, enumerations, and interfaces for creating SQL Server assemblies.

Four of these namespaces are new with SQL Server 2005/.NET 2.0: `System.Data.Design`, `System.Data.Sql`, `System.Transactions`, and `Microsoft.SqlServer.Server`. The last of these contains the classes we'll use for building SQL Server assemblies, so it's the classes in this namespace that we'll concentrate on in this chapter.

Accessing SQL Server Data

Most of the new classes that you use to build SQL assemblies reside in the `Microsoft.SqlServer.Server` namespace. These classes are used together with the ADO.NET provider for SQL Server (in the `System.Data.SqlClient` namespace) to access SQL Server data from within a SQL assembly. Together these are sometimes referred to as the *in-process provider*, although Microsoft seems largely to have abolished this term since the provider used for SQL assemblies was merged with the `SqlClient` provider. Apart from a couple of extensions to provide extra functionality, the chief difference between accessing SQL Server data from within a SQL assembly and from outside the database is in the way the connection is made.

Establishing the Context of a SQL Assembly

When you write the code inside a SQL assembly, you may need to know about the context under which it is running. For example, you might need to know what user account the code is executing under, and if the module that the assembly implements is a trigger, you will need to know the circumstances that caused the trigger to fire. This information is available through the `SqlContext` class, which provides an abstract representation of the context under which the assembly is running. The new extensions to the SQL Server .NET data provider include classes that give you access to this information, and the SqlContext class provides a number of static properties that you can use to get references to these objects, as shown in Table 3-1.

Table 3-1. *Properties of the SqlContext Class*

Property	Return Type	Description
IsAvailable	bool	Indicates whether you can access the context connection or not. This will return false if the code is running outside SQL Server and true if it's running in a SQL assembly. You can use this property if you write code that is run both in a SQL assembly and externally.
Pipe	Microsoft.SqlServer.Server.SqlPipe	Returns a SqlPipe object that you can use to send messages to the SQL Server output stream.
TriggerContext	Microsoft.SqlServer.Server. SqlTriggerContext	If the assembly is a trigger, the returned object contains information about the event that fired the trigger and the columns updated.
WindowsIdentity	System.Security.Principal. WindowsIdentity	Returns a WindowsIdentity object that you can use to impersonate the Windows user of the current Windows login. We'll look at role-based security in Chapter 10.

For example, to get a SqlPipe object that you can use to send messages back to SQL Server, you would use the following:

```
SqlPipe pipe = SqlContext.Pipe;
```

Creating the Context Connection

Just as when you access SQL Server from external .NET code, you start by creating a System.Data.SqlClient.SqlConnection object. To connect via the in-process provider, you use the connection string "context connection = true":

```
using (SqlConnection cn = new SqlConnection("context connection = true"))
{
    cn.Open();
    // Code that accesses SQL Server data
}
```

As in this example, it's good practice to enclose the code where you use the connection within a using statement to ensure that the connection is closed and disposed of once you're finished with it. You don't need to pass any user information into the connection because the connection exists in the current security context—the user must already be authenticated to call the object (CLR stored procedure, UDF, etc.) that the assembly implements.

One thing to note is that you can have only one context connection open within an assembly at a given time. In most circumstances this isn't a problem since, as you saw in Chapter 1, you shouldn't include threading code in a SQL assembly, so you'll be performing tasks sequentially. However, it can create problems if you're iterating through a data reader and want to perform some secondary data access for each row. You can't perform a second query while the data reader remains open. In most cases, of course, this is exactly the kind of thing T-SQL is designed to do with a single query, but you'll see an example of this when we examine Service Broker in Chapter 11. We get around it there by iterating through the data a second time, but if you really do need to open a second connection, it's possible to open one in the normal way, using the same connection string as you would use from external code. There's obviously a performance hit from this, as the SqlClient provider is designed for running outside the SQL Server process. You could potentially also use this technique if you need to open a second connection to SQL Server using a different security context from the current one, although in most cases impersonation using the new EXECUTE AS clause in the CREATE PROCEDURE statement would be a better option.

Making Requests Against SQL Server

Once you have a reference to the context connection, you'll need to instantiate and execute a SqlCommand object, exactly as you would in standard ADO.NET. This code is really just ADO.NET code, but since it's of paramount importance in creating SQL assemblies, we'll run through the basics very quickly.

Retrieving Data

The command needs to be initialized with the context connection and the SQL statement you want to execute. Once this is done, you can call one of the Execute methods to execute the command. For example, to execute a simple SELECT statement, getting the data into a SqlDataReader, you'd use code like this:

```
using (SqlConnection cn = new SqlConnection("context connection = true"))
{
    cn.Open();
    SqlCommand cmd = new SqlCommand("SELECT * FROM Person.Address", cn);
    SqlDataReader reader = cmd.ExecuteReader();
```

Once you have the reader, you can use it to iterate one row at a time through a resultset of data returned by a query. SqlDataReaders are always forward-only and read-only, so you can't go back to a row that you've already read, and you can't modify any of the data (we'll look at a way to get around these problems shortly).

When the reader is first opened, it points to the beginning of the data (BOF), so you need to move to the first row before any data can be accessed. You do this by calling the Read method, which moves the reader to the next row and returns false if there are no more rows or true if there is still more data to be read. To iterate through the whole of the data, you therefore need to call Read until it returns false:

```
while (rdr.Read())
{
    // Access current row here
```

```
    }
    rdr.Close();
}
```

Once you have the current row, there are a number of ways you can access the values in particular columns:

```
rdr.GetValue(int index);
rdr[int index];
rdr[string column_name];
rdr.Get<.NET type>(int index);
rdr.Get<SQL type>(int index);
```

Here, index is the number of the column from which you want to retrieve the data. The first three of these return a generic object, so the value needs to be cast to the specific type. The actual lines of code for an int would be as follows:

```
int i = (int)rdr.GetValue(0);
int i = (int)rdr[0];
int i = (int)rdr["AddressId"];
int i = rdr.GetInt32(0);
int i = rdr.GetSqlInt32(0);
```

Using an ordinal index rather than the column name is significantly faster; in a simple performance test repeated for string and integer columns, we found using the column names to be in the region of 20 percent slower than the other methods, as it needs to look up the column from its name. In some circumstances this may be a price worth paying, as using the column name guarantees you're accessing the right column, while using an ordinal index means you need to know the order in which the columns are retrieved, and if the SQL statement changes, this may break your code. This is, of course, particularly true if you use SELECT *, so it's worth stressing that this is usually a bad practice. In most circumstances, the best approach is to specify the column names in the SELECT statement and then use the ordinal indexer to access the column in a data reader, or (even better) use a constant or enumeration value to replace the ordinal. While this approach could also break if you change the T-SQL statement, it will be much easier to fix.

We found no significant difference between the other methods, although there was perhaps a very slight advantage to using the typed methods and a slight advantage to using GetSqlInt32 instead of GetInt32. However, these differences were within the margin of error and may not apply to the released product. Moreover, we found no corresponding advantage to calling GetSqlString over GetString. While our test simply dumped the data once it had retrieved it, your code will probably need to use the data after accessing it! Therefore, it makes sense to choose the method that returns the data type you need, rather than converting a SqlString to a System.String or vice versa.

Finally, you can also read all the data from the current row into an object array by calling the GetValues method. This takes as a parameter the object array you want to populate and returns the number of elements in the array:

```
object[] rowData = new object[rdr.FieldCount];
int i = rdr.GetValues(rowData);
```

Note that you need to initialize the array with the correct number of elements before passing it into the GetValues method; you can do this by calling the SqlDataReader's FieldCount property to ascertain how many columns are in the row. If the array is initialized with the wrong size, an exception will be thrown when GetValues is called. Default values (such as zero or an empty string) will be returned for any null columns, so these *will* be included in the array.

Handling Parameters

When you create a SqlCommand object, you'll very often need to execute the command it represents with different criteria. For example, you may need to retrieve multiple rows based on a selection of IDs. Therefore, you need a way to pass in parameters to your commands.

To allow this, the SqlCommand object has a Parameters collection, which contains a SqlParameter object for each parameter the command takes. You can indicate that a command requires parameters by using SQL-style variables in the command text, for example:

```
SqlCommand cmd = SqlContext.GetCommand();
cmd.CommandText = @"SELECT *
                    FROM HumanResources.EmployeePayHistory
                    WHERE EmployeeID = @id";
```

You can now create a parameter named @id, add it to the Parameters collection of the SqlCommand object, and set its value before executing the command, so that only the correct row will be returned from your query. To do this, you can use one of three methods of the SqlParametersCollection class: Add, AddRange, or AddWithValue. Add has several overloads that vary somewhat in how they're used. One overload lets you add a preconfigured SqlParameter object:

```
SqlParameter param = new SqlParameter("@id", SqlDbType.Int);
cmd.Parameters.Add(param);
```

Another overload takes the name of the parameter and its type (as one of the SqlDbType enumeration values):

```
SqlParameter param = cmd.Parameters.Add("@id", SqlDbType.Int);
```

The AddWithValue method provides a quick way of adding a parameter to the collection at the same time as the parameter itself:

```
SqlParameter param = cmd.Parameters.AddWithValue("@id", 17);
```

Finally, you can use the AddRange method to add an array of SqlParameter objects in a single method call:

```
SqlParameter param1 = new SqlParameter("@id", 23);
SqlParameter param2 = new SqlParameter("@name", "Bob");
cmd.Parameters.AddRange(new SqlParameter[] { param1, param2 });
```

Which of these methods you choose depends on whether the same command is going to be issued more than once. If it is, it makes sense to call Add to configure the parameters first, prepare the command, and then set the values for each call. If the command is going to be executed only once, it makes sense to add the parameter and value in one go. And, of course, it makes no sense to supply a value for an output parameter or return value.

Representing Row Metadata

In the next section, we'll look at how SQL Server allows us to work with individual rows of data to construct a resultset on the fly and return it to the user. To do this, we need a way of representing the metadata for each row, to which end we now have the SqlMetaData class. A SqlMetaData instance contains the metadata for a single column in a resultset, so we can represent the metadata for a row using an array of SqlMetaData objects. SqlMetaData objects can also be used to define parameters passed into stored procedures or UDFs.

The SqlMetaData class has 14 public properties, as shown in Table 3-2.

Table 3-2. *Public Properties of the SqlMetaData Class*

Property	Data Type	Description
CompareOptions	System.Data.SqlTypes. SqlCompareOptions	Indicates how data in the column/parameter is to be compared to other data (e.g., whether whitespace is to be ignored)
DbType	System.Data.DbType	Returns the type of the column/parameter as a DbType enum value
LocaleID	long	Returns the ID for the locale used for data in the column/parameter
Max	long	Static property that returns the maximum length for text, ntext, and image data
MaxLength	long	Returns the maximum length for the column/parameter represented by this SqlMetaData instance
Name	string	Returns the name of the column/parameter
Precision	byte	Returns the precision for the column/parameter
Scale	byte	Returns the scale for the column/parameter
SqlDbType	System.Data.SqlDbType	Returns the type of the column/parameter as a SqlDbType enum value
Type	System.Type	Returns the type of the column/parameter as a System.Type instance
TypeName	string	For a user-defined type column/parameter, returns the three-part name of the type
XmlSchemaCollectionDatabase	string	Returns the name of the database that contains the schema collection for an XML type

Continued

Table 3-2. *Continued*

Property	Data Type	Description
XmlSchemaCollectionName	string	Returns the name of the schema collection for an XML type
XmlSchemaCollectionOwningSchema	string	For an XML column/parameter, returns the name of the SQL Server relational schema to which the schema collection for the column belongs

The SqlMetaData class also has two public methods, which are listed in Table 3-3.

Table 3-3. *Public Methods of the SqlMetaData Class*

Method	Return Type	Parameter(s)	Description
Adjust	*<DataType>*	*<DataType>*	This method validates the value passed in as a parameter against the metadata represented by this instance and adjusts it if it isn't valid. There are many overloads for specific .NET and SQL data types, and the return type will be the same as the type of the parameter.
InferFromValue	SqlMetaData	object, string	This static method creates a new SqlMetaData instance based on the value of the object and the name passed in as parameters.

There are a number of ways to create a new SqlMetaData object, depending on the data type it represents. The easiest way is to call the InferFromValue method:

```
SqlMetaData md = SqlMetaData.InferFromValue(somevariable, "Column Name");
```

Alternatively, you can create a new instance using the constructor. The SqlMetaData constructor has seven overloads:

- The simplest takes the name as a string and the type as a SqlDbType enumeration value:

```
SqlMetaData md = new SqlMetaData("Column Name", SqlDbType.Int32);
```

- For string and binary types, you can also specify the maximum length:

```
SqlMetaData md = new SqlMetaData("Column Name", SqlDbType.NVarChar, 256);
```

- Additionally, you can include the locale ID and the compare options for string types:

```
SqlMetaData md = new SqlMetaData("Column Name",
                    SqlDbType.NVarChar, 256, 1033,
                    SqlCompareOptions.IgnoreCase);
```

- For Decimal types, you need to specify the precision and scale:

```
SqlMetaData md = new SqlMetaData("Column Name", SqlDbType.Decimal, 8, 4);
```

- If the type for this SqlMetaData instance is a user-defined type (UDT), you need to provide the type as a System.Type instance:

```
SqlMetaData md = new SqlMetaData("Column Name", SqlDbType.UDT,
                                 myUdt.GetType());
```

  where myUdt is an instance of the UDT. In this case, the second parameter must be set to SqlDbType.UDT.

- If the instance represents a strongly typed XML column or parameter, you need to supply the name of the database that contains the schema collection, the name of the owning schema, and the name of the schema collection:

```
SqlMetaData md = new SqlMetaData("Column Name", SqlDbType.Xml,
                                 "AdventureWorks", "HumanResources",
                                 "HRResumeSchemaCollection");
```

- The final constructor takes the name of the column, its type as a SqlType value, the maximum allowed length, its precision and scale, its locale ID, its compare options, and the type of a UDT as a System.Type. This constructor is presumably intended for cases where a UDT column requires string and/or floating-point options to be set.

You'll see the SqlMetaData class in action when we look at creating rows on the fly later in the chapter.

Working with Single Rows

As well as classes for communicating with SQL Server and for building specific types of CLR modules, the Microsoft.SqlServer.Server namespace also includes a new class for working with an individual row in a resultset. The SqlDataRecord class is basically very similar to a data reader that can only contain one row, but with one important difference: a SqlDataRecord can be updated as well as read.

Overview of SqlDataRecord

The public properties of the SqlDataRecord class are shown in Table 3-4.

Table 3-4. *Public Properties of the SqlDataRecord Class*

Property	Type	Description
FieldCount	int	Returns the number of columns in the row.
Item	object	Returns the value of the specified column in the row. This property takes an int or string parameter and is accessed as the indexer in C#.

The SqlDataRecord class also has a number of public methods, as shown in Table 3-5.

Table 3-5. *Public Methods of the SqlDataRecord Class*

Method	Return Type	Parameter(s)	Description
Get<*DataType*>	<*DataType*>	int	Returns the value of the specified column as the given data type
GetDataTypeName	string	int	Returns the name of the data type of the specified column
GetFieldType	System.Type	int	Returns the data type of the specified column as a System.Type
GetName	string	int	Returns the name of the specified column
Get<*SqlType*>	<*SqlType*>	int	Returns the value of the specified column as a SQL native type
GetSqlFieldType	System.Type	int	Returns the SQL type of the specified column as a System.Type
GetSqlMetaData	Microsoft.SqlServer. Server.SqlMetaData	int	Returns a SqlMetaData object describing the specified column
GetSqlValue	object	int	Returns the value of the specified column as a SQL native type cast as object
GetSqlValues	int	object[]	Populates the supplied object array with the values in the row (as native SQL types) and returns the number of elements in the array
GetValue	object	int	Returns the value of the specified column as a standard .NET type cast as object
GetValues	int	object[]	Populates the supplied object array with the values in the row (as standard .NET types) and returns the number of elements in the array
IsDbNull	bool	int	Indicates whether or not the value in the specified column is null
Set<*DataType*>	void	int, <*DataType*>	Sets the value of the column specified in the first parameter to the value of the second parameter, which must be castable to the same type as the type indicated by the method name
Set<*SqlType*>	void	int, <*SqlType*>	Same as the previous set of methods, but uses native SQL types instead of standard .NET types
SetValue	void	int, object	Sets the value of the column specified in the first parameter to the value of the second parameter, which is passed in as an object
SetValues	int	object[]	Sets the values of the row to those contained in the supplied object array and returns the number of column values set

As Table 3-5 implies, reading a field from a row works in exactly the same way as reading a value from a SqlDataReader: you can use an integer or string indexer, or you can call one of the Get methods. There are three ways to set a value for a column:

```
row.SetValue(int index, object value);
row.Set<.NET type>(int index, value);
row.Set<SQL type>(int index, value);
```

for example:

```
// Set string value using SetValue
row.SetValue(0, "10 Downing Street");

// Set string value using SetString
row.SetString(1, "Westminster");

// Set string value using SetSqlString
SqlString city = new SqlString("London");
row.SetSqlString(2, city);
```

Because all these methods take an integer index for the column rather than a string name, there's little difference in performance, although the typed methods performed slightly faster than SetValue. Again, your choice to use a method that takes a .NET type or one that takes a SQL type will depend on context: there's no point converting a value to a SqlString if you already have it as a System.String (our previous example where we created a new SqlString from a string literal was obviously contrived).

There's also a SetValues method that parallels GetValues:

```
string[] rowData = new string[] { "10 Downing Street",
                                  "Westminster",
                                  "London" };
// Set all three columns in one go
row.SetValues(rowData);
```

Of course, this relies on the elements in the array being in the same order as the columns in the SqlDataRecord, and on each being of the appropriate type. In this case, we've made it easy for ourselves, because all the columns are string columns, so we can define the array as of type string[]; normally we'd need the array to be of type object[], with elements of different types.

Creating Rows on the Fly

The SqlDataRecord class allows you to create new rows programmatically and send them as a resultset to SQL Server. This is where the SqlMetaData class comes in. The SqlDataRecord's constructor takes an array of SqlMetaData objects, each element of which represents a single column in the row.

The following code creates a SqlDataRow containing two columns, of type int and nvarchar, and sets their values to 0 and "SQL Server 2005 Assemblies", respectively:

```
SqlMetaData idMetadata = new SqlMetaData("id", SqlDbType.Int);
SqlMetaData titleMetadata = new SqlMetaData("title",
        SqlDbType.NVarChar, 255);
SqlMetaData[] rowMetadata = new SqlMetaData[] { idMetadata,
        titleMetadata };
SqlDataRecord record = new SqlDataRecord(rowMetadata);
record.SetInt32(0, 0);
record.SetString(1, "SQL Server 2005 Assemblies");
```

First you create two SqlMetaData objects to represent id and title columns of type int and nvarchar, respectively (notice that you need to specify a maximum length for columns of type nvarchar or varchar). You then create an array called rowMetadata consisting of these two objects. Once you have this, you can use it to create a new SqlDataRecord object. Finally, you set values for the row data.

Communicating with the Caller

Once you have the data from SQL Server and manipulated it, you need to return the results to the caller, or at least send the user a message saying that your work is done. You do this using a SqlPipe object, which provides a direct channel to SQL Server's output stream. Any messages or query results sent to the pipe will be displayed directly to the user in Query Analyzer or sent to the calling application.

Overview of SqlPipe

The SqlPipe class has just one property, as shown in Table 3-6.

Table 3-6. *Public Property of the SqlPipe Class*

Property	Type	Description
SendingResults	bool	Indicates whether the SqlPipe is currently being used to send rows back to the caller

The SqlPipe class also has five methods (excluding inherited methods), which are listed in Table 3-7.

Table 3-7. *Public Methods of the SqlPipe Class*

Method	Return Type	Parameters	Description
ExecuteAndSend	void	SqlCommand	Executes the specified SqlCommand and sends the results directly back to the caller
Send	void	System.Data.SqlClient. SqlDataReader Microsoft.SqlServer. Server.SqlDataRecord string	Sends the supplied string message, SqlDataReader, or SqlDataRecord back to the caller

Method	Return Type	Parameters	Description
SendResultsEnd	void		Signals that you've finished sending rows that form part of a resultset
SendResultsRow	void	Microsoft.SqlServer. Server.SqlDataRecord	Sends the specified row to the caller as part of a resultset
SendResultsStart	void	Microsoft.SqlServer. Server.SqlDataRecord	Signals that you want to send a number of SqlDataRecords to the caller as part of a resultset, and sends the first row

We won't spend too long covering the first two of these, as they're syntactically very simple. The Send method is overloaded and can take a plain string, a SqlDataReader, or a SqlDataRecord object as parameter. For example, to send all contact details back to the caller, you could use this code:

```
using (SqlConnection cn = new SqlConnection("context connection = true")
{
    cn.Open();
    string sql = "SELECT * FROM Person.Contact";
    SqlCommand cmd = new SqlCommand(sql, cn);
    SqlDataReader reader = cmd.ExecuteReader();
    SqlPipe pipe = SqlContext.Pipe;
    pipe.Send(reader);
}
```

Alternatively, you could call the SqlPipe.ExecuteAndSend method, which will send the results of a command straight back to the caller, bypassing your CLR module entirely (and thus saving you a line of code):

```
using (SqlConnection cn = new SqlConnection("context connection = true")
{
    cn.Open();
    string sql = "SELECT * FROM Person.Contact";
    SqlCommand cmd = new SqlCommand(sql, cn);
    SqlPipe pipe = SqlContext.Pipe;
    pipe.ExecuteAndSend(cmd);
}
```

Sending a Dynamic Rowset Back to the Caller

The last three methods of the SqlPipe class allow you to send a set of SqlDataRecord objects back to the caller, one row at a time. This means you can construct rows on the fly, as done a couple of pages back, and return them to the caller as a single resultset. You can't simply send the rows using the SqlPipe.Send method, as this will send a number of separate resultsets to SQL Server, each containing one row, rather than a single resultset containing multiple rows. To send individual rows as a single resultset, you need to tell SQL Server when you send the first row that there are more rows to come in the same resultset, and you also need to tell it when you're done and the resultset is finished. To do this, you call SendResultsStart to send the first row, SendResultsRow for all subsequent rows, and finally SendResultsEnd when you're finished.

Let's look at a simple example to see how this works. This example reads the details of employees who haven't had a pay rise for two years from the HumanResources.EmployeePayHistory table in the AdventureWorks database, including each employee's ID, the last date when that employee received a pay raise, and a computed column indicating when the employee's pay raise should be due (two years after the last one). For each row in the SqlDataReader, we create a new row for our dynamic resultset, checking the due date value for each row, and if it's over six months ago, we make a pay raise for that employee a priority and set it for a month's time; otherwise, we can defer it for a little, and add seven months to when it was due. There might not be a lot of logic behind this, but it does demonstrate the techniques involved!

```
using System;
using System.Data;
using System.Data.SqlClient;
using Microsoft.SqlServer.Server;

namespace Apress.SqlAssemblies.Chapter03
{
    public class SendResultsTest
    {
        // Define read-only fields to refer to the fields' ordinal indexes by
        readonly static int FIELD_ID = 0;
        readonly static int FIELD_LASTCHANGE = 1;
        readonly static int FIELD_DUECHANGE = 2;

        public static void GetPayRiseDates()
        {
            // Open the context connection
            using (SqlConnection cn = new SqlConnection("context connection=true"))
            {
                cn.Open();

                // Get a new SqlDataReader with the details of the
                // employees who are due a pay raise
                string sql = @"SELECT EmployeeID,
MAX(RateChangeDate) AS LastRateChange,
DATEADD(year, 2, MAX(RateChangeDate)) AS DueRateChange
FROM HumanResources.EmployeePayHistory
GROUP BY EmployeeID
HAVING MAX(RateChangeDate) < DATEADD(year, -2, GETDATE()))";
                SqlCommand cmd = new SqlCommand(sql, cn);
                SqlDataReader reader = cmd.ExecuteReader();
```

```csharp
// Get the SqlPipe
SqlPipe pipe = SqlContext.Pipe;

// Create the SqlMetaData objects for the rowset
SqlMetaData idMeta = new SqlMetaData("Id", SqlDbType.Int);
SqlMetaData lastRaiseMeta = new SqlMetaData("Last Rate Change",
                                        SqlDbType.DateTime);
SqlMetaData dueRaiseMeta = new SqlMetaData("Due Rate Change",
                                        SqlDbType.DateTime);
SqlMetaData[] rowMetaData = new SqlMetaData[] { idMeta, lastRaiseMeta,
                                        dueRaiseMeta };

// Keep track of whether or not it's the first row
bool firstRow = true;

// Iterate through the rows, update if necessary,
// and send them back to the caller
while (reader.Read())
{
    // Create a new SqlDataRecord for each row
    SqlDataRecord row = new SqlDataRecord(rowMetaData);

    // Add the ID and Last Rate Change values to the row
    row.SetInt32(FIELD_ID, (int)reader[FIELD_ID]);
    row.SetDateTime(FIELD_LASTCHANGE,
                (DateTime)reader[FIELD_LASTCHANGE]);

    // Store the change due date in a local variable
    DateTime dueDate = (DateTime)reader[FIELD_DUECHANGE];

    // If it's over six months overdue, set pay raise for
    // a month's time; otherwise, put it back seven months
    if (dueDate < DateTime.Now.AddMonths(-6))
        row.SetDateTime(FIELD_DUECHANGE, DateTime.Now.AddMonths(1));
    else
        row.SetDateTime(FIELD_DUECHANGE, dueDate.AddMonths(7));

    // If it's the first row, we need to call
    // SendResultsStart; otherwise, we call SendResultsRow
    if (firstRow == true)
    {
        pipe.SendResultsStart(row);
        firstRow = false;
    }
    else
```

```
            {
                pipe.SendResultsRow(row);
            }
        }

        // Close the SqlDataReader once we've finished iterating through it
        reader.Close();

        // Call SendResultsEnd after the loop has finished, to
        // say we're done
        pipe.SendResultsEnd();
    }
  }
 }
}
```

Let's run quickly through this code to clarify what's going on. First, we open the context connection and retrieve the details for all employees who haven't received a pay raise for two years into a SqlDataReader. Next, we get the SqlPipe object for the current context by calling SqlContext.Pipe. Then we create the SqlMetaData objects that define the name and data type for each column in our resultset, and add these to an array that contains all the metadata for each row. Because we need to call a different method for the first row we send back through the SqlPipe, we create a Boolean local variable with its value initialized to true to indicate that we're on the first row.

Now we're ready to iterate through each row in the data reader, creating a new SqlDataRecord object for each row and adding to it the employee ID and the date the employee last received a pay raise. Before adding the due date, we modify it as we think fit. Then we send the row back to the caller using the appropriate method of the SqlPipe object; if this is the first row, our firstRow Boolean variable will be true, so we know we have to call SendResultsStart, instead of SendResultsRow, which we'll use for all subsequent iterations. Once the loop has finished, we just need to close the data reader, call SendResultsEnd to indicate that our result-set is complete, and we're finished.

We compile this in the usual way:

```
csc /t:library SendResultsTest.cs
```

then register it as a stored procedure with SQL Server, and execute the procedure:

```
CREATE ASSEMBLY SendResultsTest
FROM 'C:\Apress\SqlAssemblies\Chapter03\SendResultsTest.dll'
WITH PERMISSION_SET = SAFE;
GO

CREATE PROCEDURE uspGetPayRiseDates
AS
EXTERNAL NAME SendResultsTest.[Apress.SqlAssemblies.Chapter03.SendResultsTest].
GetPayRiseDates;
```

```
GO
```

```
EXEC uspGetPayRiseDates
```

The results can be seen in Figure 3-1.

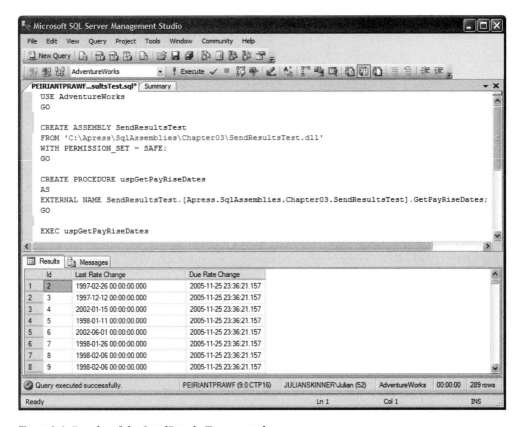

Figure 3-1. *Results of the SendResultsTest example*

CLR Triggers

The last class in the `Microsoft.SqlServer.Server` namespace is the `SqlTriggerContext` class, which provides information about the context in which a CLR trigger is running. We can gain access to this object from the `SqlContext`, similarly to the way we access the `SqlPipe` object:

```
SqlTriggerContext tc = SqlContext.TriggerContext;
```

We won't look at this in detail here, as we'll cover CLR triggers fully in Chapter 8, but for the sake of completeness, we will list its properties and methods. Table 3-8 lists its public properties.

Table 3-8. *Public Properties of the SqlTriggerContext Class*

Property	Data Type	Description
ColumnCount	int	Returns the number of columns in the table bound to the trigger.
EventData	System.Data.SqlTypes.SqlXml	A native SQL XML object that contains information about the event that caused the trigger to execute, including the time of the event, the system process ID of the connection that caused the event, and the type of event. Depending on the event type, it may also include additional information, such as the command that caused the event and the user who executed the command.
TriggerAction	Microsoft.SqlServer.Server.TriggerAction	A TriggerAction enumeration value that indicates the type of command that caused the trigger to fire. With the new ability to write DDL triggers, there are 76 of these values all told, so we won't list them all here. Please see Chapter 8 for more details.

Table 3-9 gives the details of the single public method of the SqlTriggerContext.

Table 3-9. *Public Method of the SqlTriggerContext Class*

Method	Return Type	Parameter	Description
IsUpdatedColumn	bool	int	Indicates whether the column with the supplied ordinal index was affected by an INSERT or UPDATE operation

Transactions

The latest version of the .NET Framework contains a whole new transaction framework in the shape of the System.Transactions namespace. This framework is integrated both with ADO.NET and with the SQL Server CLR. This isn't a topic specific to SQL assemblies, and the namespace is too large to cover in full, but one feature in particular needs to be highlighted: the ability to enroll a block of code implicitly in a distributed transaction using the TransactionScope class.

The transaction scope begins when the TransactionScope class is instantiated, and ends when the class is disposed of. If no errors occur, the transaction will be committed implicitly; otherwise, it will be rolled back when the scope ends. Because the scope ends when the Dispose method is called on the object, it's vital that this method is called in all cases. For that reason, Microsoft strongly recommends instantiating a TransactionScope object in a using statement so that Dispose will be called even if an exception occurs:

```
using (TransactionScope tx = new TransactionScope())
{
    // Code here is within the transaction scope
}
```

```
// Commit the transaction
tx.Complete();
```

The alternative is to place all code in the transaction scope within a `try` block, and then to call `Dispose` on it in the associated `finally` block.

The really neat trick, however, is that if you open a second connection within a transaction scope, the transaction will be promoted to a full distributed transaction, for example:

```
using (TransactionScope tx = new TransactionScope())
{
    using (SqlConnection cn1 = new SqlConnection("context connection = true"))
    {
        // This automatically enlists the connection in the transaction
        cn.Open();

        string connStr = "<connection string>"
        using (SqlConnection cn2 = new SqlConnection(connStr))
        {
            // This enlists cn2 in the transaction and thereby promotes it
            // to a distributed transaction
            cn2.Open();
        }
    }
}
// Commit the transaction
tx.Complete();
```

For this to work, Microsoft Distributed Transaction Coordinator (MSDTC) server must be running on the host machine.

Summary

Data access within a SQL assembly such as a CLR stored procedure or trigger is achieved by means of the .NET data provider for SQL Server (in the `System.Data.SqlClient` namespace), supplemented by several classes in the new `Microsoft.SqlServer.Server` namespace. In this chapter, we provided a very quick ADO.NET refresher and introduced the following new objects:

- `SqlContext`: Represents the current context and gives you access to the other objects in the provider

- `SqlMetaData`: Defines the metadata for a single column in a row of data

- `SqlDataRecord`: Provides you with access to a single row of data and allows you to create a resultset on the fly

- `SqlPipe`: Allows you to send data or messages directly to the SQL Server pipe

- `SqlTriggerContext`: Supplies information about the context in which a CLR trigger fired

We also looked very briefly at the new transaction framework in .NET 2.0 provided by the `System.Transactions` framework.

Now that we've introduced the main new classes, we can go on to present real examples of building SQL assemblies. This chapter has of necessity had more of a reference nature than the other chapters in the book, but from now on the emphasis will be firmly on practical examples. In the next chapter, you'll see the objects we presented in this chapter in action when we turn the focus to creating CLR stored procedures.

CHAPTER 4

■ ■ ■

CLR Stored Procedures

Having covered the finer details of data access within a SQL assembly, we'll now take a look at how to build CLR stored procedures. A word of caution: before you go ahead and create a CLR stored procedure to satisfy a particular requirement, carefully consider whether use of an assembly is truly justified. Often, set-based data processing lies at the heart of a stored procedure, and this is something that T-SQL already does very well. T-SQL is close to the data. Very strong links exist between data structures used in T-SQL and those used in the database—there is no conversion overhead. You will always require less code to process SQL with T-SQL than with any other language, so it's more efficient and easier to maintain. Also, bear in mind that when you call an assembly (basically a DLL) from T-SQL, a certain amount of work will be involved as the database engine loads the DLL into memory, JIT-compiles it to native code, and executes it. Subsequent calls will be cheaper, but overall this is still more expensive than calling a conventional T-SQL-based stored procedure.

In short, any proposal to migrate existing T-SQL stored procedures to CLR stored procedures will need to be convincingly justified and in many cases will simply not be practical or necessary. Of course, this isn't to say that CLR stored procedures don't bring additional useful capabilities—they do, and we will explore their potential uses in this chapter. Just remember the basic rule of *simplicity first*. Just as you shouldn't use a CLR-based user-defined function (UDF) if a built-in system stored function can do the job, you shouldn't use .NET to do the job of T-SQL. With this in mind, this chapter covers these topics:

- Discussing potential scenarios where CLR stored procedures can usefully extend the capabilities of T-SQL, and where you might consider migrating existing T-SQL stored procedures to an assembly

- Taking a detailed look at the syntax for creating CLR stored procedures

- Exploring three specific examples that demonstrate practical usage of CLR stored procedures, namely

  - Creating XML output

  - Storing and loading images

  - Executing operating system commands

Why Use a CLR Stored Procedure?

As we noted earlier, T-SQL has been created for optimal data processing, and there has to be a sound reason for moving away from it. Further, the ability to create a .NET stored procedure is not an excuse for ignoring potential existing or alternative solutions such as web services or SQL Server Integration Services (formerly Data Transformation Services). You should thoroughly consider each scenario and compare existing functionality and processes. There is no clear-cut right or wrong answer; it all depends on what your process is required to achieve. As always, the general rule is to avoid reinventing the wheel. If SQL Server already includes a tool specifically designed for the task you need to complete, such as Integration Services for bulk-loading data from another data source, then you should consider creating a .NET solution only if you need custom functionality that it can't deliver.

Having established a definite need to write some .NET code rather than use a traditional T-SQL stored procedure or some other solution, you also need to be sure that you are implementing the functionality in the right component. Should you be writing a stored procedure rather than a UDF or a user-defined aggregation?

A CLR stored procedure (as opposed to any other type of assembly) has to be used if you are performing any data modification that affects columns other than the one being directly updated. For example, a SQL UPDATE within your code that reduces the cost of a unit by, say, 10 percent due to a discount may well have an effect on shipping charges. If this is the case, then the code should be implemented as a stored procedure and cannot be a function. A function can only update the data in the column that invokes it. A CLR stored procedure should also explicitly be used if you need to send results (for example, tables of data) or a message (such as "Command has completed successfully") back to the calling process. These procedures can return an output value as well.

Let's now take a look at a few potential scenarios where you might consider using CLR stored procedures.

Migrating Complex T-SQL Procedures

Essentially, the prime candidates for migration are those procedures that perhaps "push T-SQL to the limit." A good place to start is to identify cases where you've developed a group of procedures to accomplish a single complex task. Will they benefit from converting to a single .NET assembly? If you have "forced" T-SQL to implement some complex mathematics or calculate a value based on a sophisticated formula, then you may well gain a performance advantage from switching to a .NET assembly. Furthermore, the computational capabilities of .NET far outstrip those of T-SQL, so you can perform calculations using assemblies that would simply not be possible in T-SQL.

A standard stored procedure is written in T-SQL code using functionality as defined by the ANSI SQL standard (SQL Server 2005 complies with SQL-99). Basically, T-SQL excels at set-based manipulation of basic character and numeric data types. If you need to extend this capability, when working in a .NET language, you can draw on any of the thousands of classes that the .NET Framework supports to achieve this. For example, you could use the String and StringBuilder classes in your CLR procedure to perform complex string manipulation, the DateTime class to deal with different time zones, or the CultureInfo class to handle multiple regional settings.

Not only can a CLR stored procedure provide more complex processing and extended functionality, but it can also aid in areas such as cross-database or even cross-server data retrieval. Unlike when using traditional T-SQL procedures, CLR procedures allow you to create new connections as a second connection to a database. These connections reside outside of SQL Server as an out-of-process connection and are separate to the connection that exists when the stored procedure is called. The ability to connect to web services, web sites, notification services, and so on is also something that is now available to these procedures.

Converting Extended Stored Procedures

Perhaps the most exciting aspect of CLR stored procedures for many developers is the prospect of implementing functionality that once had to be done using an extended stored procedure. Previously, if you needed functionality that was beyond T-SQL, then your only choice was to create an extended stored procedure, written in a language such as C++ and stored outside the database. So, if you needed, for example, to implement very complex math, expose operating system functionality, or get a directory listing, then you had to use an extended stored procedure.

Unfortunately, these extended stored procedures, no matter how well written, were potentially dangerous. They did not run under the control of SQL Server—they were unmanaged code—and it was not possible for SQL Server to verify that the code wasn't accessing memory locations that it shouldn't. The entire onus was on the programmer to avoid doing anything that would impact the performance or stability of the server, and poorly written code could cause memory leaks and other potentially fatal problems. As such, these extended procedures were unpopular with DBAs. CLR procedures, which can be managed and controlled by the database, are a very attractive alternative.

Creating a Stored Procedure

The CREATE PROCEDURE statement for a .NET assembly differs quite significantly from that used to create a standard T-SQL stored procedure. First of all, there is no T-SQL code, but only a declaration of the stored procedure name along with a few other details that link the stored procedure with accessing methods within the assembly. Basic usage of the CREATE PROCEDURE statement was covered in Chapter 2, where we created the uspGetEmployeesHiredAfter CLR-based procedure.

```
CREATE PROCEDURE uspGetEmployeesHiredAfter(@hireDate datetime)
AS
EXTERNAL NAME SimpleSprocTest.[Apress.SqlAssemblies.Chapter02.SimpleSprocTest].
GetEmployeesHiredAfter;
```

As you will recall, the EXTERNAL NAME clause represents the binding between the stored procedure and the loaded assembly. In this clause we provide the name of the assembly object in the SQL Server database (SimpleSprocTest), the namespace (Apress.SqlAssemblies.Chapter02), the name of the class in the assembly (SimpleSprocTest), and the name of the method in that class that will be invoked when the stored procedure is run (GetEmployeesHiredAfter). All three of these parameters are separated by periods (.). If in the second parameter of the EXTERNAL NAME you use a specific namespace (rather than the default global namespace), then you would surround all of the contents of the second parameter with square brackets.

Let's now look at the various command options in more depth. The following listing shows the full syntax of the command, used for both T-SQL and CLR procedures. This contains information about the stored procedure as an object within SQL Server, as well as indicating where SQL Server can find the .NET code that implements a CLR stored procedure. We will look quickly at the various components of this command, concentrating on the new options that are relevant for .NET assembly stored procedures.

```
CREATE PROC [ EDURE ] [schema_name.] procedure_name
    [ { @parameter [ type_schema_name ]data_type }
   [ VARYING ] [ = default ] [ [ OUT [ PUT ]
    ] [,...n ]
[ WITH < procedure_option > [,...n ]
[ FOR REPLICATION ]
AS { < sql_statement > [ ...n ] | <method_specifier> }

< procedure_option > ::=
    [ ENCRYPTION ]
    [ RECOMPILE ]
    [ EXECUTE_AS_Clause ]

< sql_statement > ::=
{ [ BEGIN ] statements [ END ] }

<method_specifier > ::=
EXTERNAL NAME assembly_name.class_name[.method_name]
```

As with other database objects in SQL Server 2005, you can specify the schema that the stored procedure will belong to. Schemas represent a new level in the SQL Server security hierarchy, below the server and database levels; by granting users access to a schema, you allow them to access the objects within that schema in the database, but not the other objects in the database. Also, because DDL events are scoped at the database level, even ownership of a schema doesn't give a user permission to create objects within it.

Parameters are specified for a CLR stored procedure in exactly the same way as for a T-SQL stored procedure in SQL Server 2000. It's worth reiterating, though, that stored procedures are designed to be called from within SQL Server, and therefore any parameters passed in will be native SQL types, not .NET types. These types can be automatically converted to .NET types, or they can be referenced in .NET code using the classes in the System.Data.SqlTypes namespace.

Finally, there are three possible procedure options: ENCRYPTION, RECOMPILE, and EXECUTE AS. Encryption cannot be applied to CLR stored procedures. There is no T-SQL to encrypt, as the contents of our assembly are loaded into SQL Server using the CREATE ASSEMBLY statement. All we are doing is providing a link between the assembly and our stored procedure declaration.

The RECOMPILE option is also restricted to T-SQL sprocs. It stipulates that SQL Server shouldn't cache an execution plan for the stored procedure, but that it should be compiled at runtime.

More interesting is the EXECUTE AS option. This allows you to specify the database user that the procedure will execute as. This can be a username, CALLER (the default), SELF, or OWNER. These options cause the procedure to execute under the context of a named user, the calling module, the user who is creating or modifying the procedure, or the owner of the procedure, respectively. The advantage of setting the EXECUTE AS option is that it provides a way to force users to access database resources through a particular stored procedure, because they can be granted access to the procedure without requiring access to the database objects themselves.

Now that we've explored the syntax of the CREATE PROCEDURE statement, let's look at a couple of examples to see how to use CLR sprocs in real life.

Creating XML Output

The first example will demonstrate how to call a stored procedure that's installed in SQL Server, retrieve the results, and produce an XML document as the output. This might be useful if you have a set of data that you want to publish to an external application that consumes XML data.

Our example involves a supplier of goods who wants its customers to know about the latest discounts available for a particular order, along with details of how to get those discounts. This example shows how to present the output as either an XML document or as an RSS feed, thus allowing syndicating clients to obtain the information directly from the supplier's web site. Both of these examples could be created as client programs that run on demand, but by creating them as .NET assemblies and linking them to a stored procedure, you get the flexibility of using SQL Server job scheduling to run them at defined intervals. It also removes the cross-network traffic that would occur if the data were accessed by a traditional external client.

This example demonstrates several aspects of using .NET stored procedure assemblies, including the following:

- Using the SqlPipe class to send data and/or messages back to the calling application.

- Building a .NET assembly that accesses another assembly from the Framework Class Library (FCL). However, calling some of the methods it exposes means that we need to give our procedure a security setting of EXTERNAL_ACCESS instead of SAFE.

The example consists of three stored procedures:

- A CLR stored procedure that extracts a set of data from the AdventureWorks database and generates from that an XML document

- A second CLR stored procedure that similarly extracts data from AdventureWorks, but this time formats it as an RSS feed

- A T-SQL stored procedure that this CLR sproc calls to retrieve the data from the database

The CLR stored procedure at the heart of our example takes as parameters the **path** and **filename** for the output file and a **Boolean flag** that indicates whether or not the returned document should be formatted as an RSS feed. We will construct the XML document by using the first column as the parent element and all the other columns as child elements of that node. The T-SQL stored procedure that retrieves the data returns a description of each discount available, together with the details of that discount, such as the minimum purchase necessary to qualify for it.

The XML for the XML file that we will be outputting would start something like this:

```
<?xml version="1.0" ?>
<Offers>
    <NoDiscount>
        <item>
            <Name>HL Road Frame - Black, 58</Name>
            <DiscountPct>0.00</DiscountPct>
            <MinQty>0</MinQty>
            <MaxQty>No max</MaxQty>
        </item>
        <item>
            <Name>HL Road Frame - Red, 58</Name>
            <DiscountPct>0.00</DiscountPct>
            <MinQty>0</MinQty>
            <MaxQty>No max</MaxQty>
        </item>
        <item>
            <Name>Sport-100 Helmet, Red</Name>
            <DiscountPct>0.00</DiscountPct>
            ...
```

Here, Offers is the root element of the XML document (passed into the stored procedure when it's called). This contains child elements for each discount available; the name of the element representing each discount (NoDiscount in the previous snippet) is taken from the value in the first column of the query. Each of these child elements contains an <item> element for each row in the resultset that has that value in its first column. This element in turn has a child element for each of the subsequent columns; the element's name is taken from the column's name, and the text content of the element is taken from the column's value for that row.

The XML output for an RSS feed would start something like this:

```
<?xml version="1.0" ?>
<rss version="2.0">
  <channel>
    <title>AdventureWorks Special Offers</title>
    <link>http://www.AdventureWorks.com/specialoffers/</link>
    <description>
      Special offers on Mountain Bike gear from AdventureWorks
    </description>
    <item>
      <title>No Discount</title>
      <description>&lt;table border='1'&gt;&lt;thead&gt;&lt;th&gt;Name&lt;/th&gt;
&lt;th&gt;DiscountPct&lt;/th&gt;&lt;th&gt;MinQty&lt;/th&gt;&lt;th&gt;MaxQty
&lt;/th&gt;&lt;/thead&gt;...
```

To comply with the RSS standard, all the data is contained within a child element named <channel> of a root <rss> element. The <channel> element has three required child elements: <title> (the title of the RSS feed), <link> (the URL of the web site that the RSS feed corresponds to), and <description> (a description of the RSS feed). The text content for these elements is

passed into the stored procedure as parameters. Each available discount is contained in an
`<item>` element directly below the `<channel>` element. This element has two children: a `<title>`
element that contains the name of the discount, and a `<description>` element that contains an
HTML-formatted table detailing the products available with this discount.

The T-SQL Stored Procedure

Now we're ready to write some code. Before we get started on the .NET code for our CLR
procedures, though, we first have to create the T-SQL procedure that will perform the actual
data access. The `SpecialOffers` T-SQL stored procedure simply returns some data from the
AdventureWorks database that details the discounts available for various products and the
minimum order quantity required to qualify for that discount:

```
USE AdventureWorks
GO
CREATE PROCEDURE SpecialOffers @OfferID int = NULL
AS
BEGIN
SELECT so.Description, p.Name, so.DiscountPct, so.MinQty,
    ISNULL(CONVERT(varchar(10),so.MaxQty),'No max') AS MaxQty
  FROM Sales.SpecialOfferProduct sop
  JOIN Sales.SpecialOffer so ON so.SpecialOfferID = sop.SpecialOfferID
  JOIN Production.Product p ON p.ProductID = sop.ProductID
  WHERE sop.SpecialOfferID >= ISNULL(@OfferID,0)
  AND sop.SpecialOfferID <= ISNULL(@OfferID,999)
END
GO
```

Once you've created the procedure by running this SQL statement in Management Studio,
it's time to get to the real point of this example—the .NET assembly that contains the code for
the CLR procedures.

Writing the Assembly

Start by opening Visual Studio 2005 and creating a SQL Server project called `XMLOutput`. As this
example contains two CLR stored procedures, this project will contain two source code files,
although if you're using Notepad or another text editor, it's easier to include the two methods
for our procedures in a single file.

The OutputXML Procedure

The first procedure we'll write outputs the data as standard XML, so add a new stored procedure class to the project and call it `OutputXml`. Once the stored procedure item is open, add
`System.Xml` to the namespaces imported so we can work with XML documents and contents
without fully qualifying the classes we use. The `System.Xml` namespace contains classes that
implement both SAX- and DOM-style parsers; for this example, we'll use the DOM classes to
create the XML document. We also, of course, import the standard namespaces for working
with data in a SQL assembly: `System.Data`, `System.Data.SqlClient`, `System.Data.SqlTypes`,

and `Microsoft.SqlServer.Server`. These namespaces are all added automatically by Visual Studio 2005.

```
using System;
using System.Data;
using System.Data.SqlClient;
using System.Data.SqlTypes;
using System.Xml;
using Microsoft.SqlServer.Server;
```

It is good coding practice to organize the classes in your assemblies into namespaces. This allows you to group related classes together. Try to use meaningful namespace names for each grouping. It is common to start with the name of the corporation and then either the general functionality area of the code or the name of the application. Our SQL assembly will contain one partial class, named `StoredProcedures`. Partial classes are a new feature of C# in .NET 2.0 that allow a class definition to be split over multiple source code files; they were added primarily for the convenience of applications that generate source code. When the project is compiled, a single class will be assembled from all the partial classes with the same fully qualified name in the separate source code files. This allows us to add both our stored procedures to the same `StoredProcedures` class, even though the code for them is saved in different source files.

We place this class in the `Apress.Xml` namespace to declare it to be one of a group that provides functionality for working with XML.

This class will have one public member in this file—the `OutputXml` method that implements the CLR stored procedure for outputting standard XML, and that will be called by SQL Server whenever the sproc is executed. It will also have a second method in the second source code file for the RSS stored procedure.

```
namespace Apress.Xml
{
  public partial class StoredProcedures
  {
    [SqlProcedure]
    public static void OutputXML(string sprocName, string rootName,
                                 string fileName)
    {
```

The `OutputXML` method accepts three parameters:

- The name of the procedure that we will call to get the set of results (in this case, it will be the `SpecialOffers` procedure)

- The root element of the target XML document (if we don't wish to output as RSS)

- The name of the output file that the method will create

Also, notice that the method is defined as `static` and `void`. SQL Server executes SQL assemblies by calling a static method on a class. In some cases, such as table-valued UDFs, this method will return an instance of a .NET class that SQL Server will call further methods on, but for stored procedures, this is the only method that SQL Server will call. Stored procedure methods can either be void (as here) or return an integer. In the latter case, the integer returned from the method will be treated by SQL Server exactly like the return value of a T-SQL stored procedure. If you want to return any data from the method, rather than merely an error code, you need to include output parameters, just like in a T-SQL sproc.

Within the method body, we start by initializing a string that will hold the name of the XML element representing a special offer. This will be populated from the data returned from the T-SQL stored procedure, and we'll use it when we're building the XML document to check when we reach a different special offer and need to start a new "special offer" node. Apart from that, the first thing we need to do is to create an XmlDocument object that will hold our XML document:

```
string parentNodeValue = "";
XmlDocument xmlDoc = new XmlDocument();
```

After this we define and save our XML version declaration:

```
XmlDeclaration decl = xmlDoc.CreateXmlDeclaration("1.0", "", "");
xmlDoc.AppendChild(decl);
```

The XmlDocument class represents an XML DOM document—a hierarchical view of the XML document that we can navigate at will. Every child node in this document is represented by an XmlNode instance. The XmlNode class itself is abstract, and there are subclasses to represent every possible type of node, such as XmlElement and XmlText.

Once we've added the XML declaration, we need to add the root element (using the name passed into the method). Our "special offer" nodes will go directly underneath this element:

```
XmlElement rootElem = xmlDoc.CreateElement("", rootName, "");
xmlDoc.AppendChild(rootElem);
```

We can now retrieve the resultset from the SpecialOffers stored procedure and process each returned row. We get and open the context connection, and then create a new SqlCommand object, passing in the connection and the name of the stored procedure that was passed into the method as the sprocName parameter, and set its CommandType property to CommandType. StoredProcedure. Next, we call the ExecuteReader method of the SqlCommand object. This invokes a call to SQL Server to execute the stored procedure and returns the rows of information to our method in the form of a SqlDataReader object.

```
using (SqlConnection cn = new SqlConnection("context connection=true"))
{
  cn.Open();
  SqlCommand sqlComm = new SqlCommand(sprocName, cn);
  sqlComm.CommandType = CommandType.StoredProcedure;
  SqlDataReader rdr = sqlComm.ExecuteReader();
```

As we iterate through the reader, we'll need to keep track of which element to add new items to (the products available with a particular discount), and of the element to which we will add any new parent elements (our "special offer" elements). The latter of these is represented by the parentElement variable, the former by itemNode:

```
XmlElement parentElement = null;
XmlElement itemNode = null;
```

Now we need to iterate through each row in the SqlDataReader one at a time by calling its Read method until it returns a value of false, indicating that there are no more rows to read. For each row in the resultset, we store the value of the first column into a string variable (the SqlDataReader columns are zero-based, so the first column has an index of zero rather than one). If the value of the first column (our SpecialOffer.Description column) for this row is different from the previous row, we need to create a new parent node. Elements within an XML document cannot have spaces in their name, so before we actually create the element we must also remove any spaces. We can do this by calling the Replace method, which returns a new string with every instance of the first parameter replaced with the value of the second one. Here we are replacing a space with nothing; the double quotation marks in the second parameter have no character between them. We then store the name of the new "special offer" node so that we can tell when it changes again.

```
while (rdr.Read())
{
  string name = (string)rdr.GetSqlString(0);
  if (parentNodeValue != name)
  {
    parentElement = xmlDoc.CreateElement("", name.Replace(" ", ""), "");
    rootElem.AppendChild(parentElement);
    parentNodeValue = name;
  }
```

For each row we then create a child element called <item> underneath the "special offer" element, and add to this another child element for every subsequent column in the SqlDataReader. We don't need to know beforehand how many columns there are within the resultset returned from the stored procedure: the SqlDataReader exposes a property called FieldCount, so we loop through the columns of the SqlDataReader as many times as there are fields minus one (because the first field is used as the name of the parent node). Notice that we retrieve the data from the column using the GetSqlValue method, because this avoids the need to know in advance the data type of the column value; all data will be returned in the appropriate data type. For each column we add a new element below the <item> element, again removing any spaces from the name. Because we'll be adding the data as text nodes in the XML document by setting the element's InnerText property, we need to convert the value to a string. We can do this very simply just by calling its ToString method.

```
  itemNode = xmlDoc.CreateElement("", "item", "");
  parentElement.AppendChild(itemNode);

  for (int i = 1; i < rdr.FieldCount; i++)
  {
    XmlElement xmlElem = xmlDoc.CreateElement("",
                          rdr.GetName(i).Replace(" ", ""), "");
    xmlElem.InnerText = rdr.GetSqlValue(i).ToString();
    itemNode.AppendChild(xmlElem);
  }
}
```

The last actions we need to take are to save the XML document and clean up our code. It is not always necessary to close the reader and dispose of the connection, as .NET will clean up after itself, but it is better to code for this yourself because you are then in control of when this happens. Also, by explicitly coding for it, you know for sure it will be taking place.

```
xmlDoc.Save(fileName);
rdr.Close();
sqlComm.Dispose();
      }
    }
  }
};
```

The OutputRSS Procedure

The second stored procedure for this example outputs the data formatted as an RSS feed. The structure of the code is similar to the previous example, but because the structure of the XML document is very different, and the information passed into the method is different, it needs to be written as a separate method.

So, add a new stored procedure called OutputRSS to the VS project, and VS will auto-generate the same skeleton code as before. And as before, we'll start by modifying the using statements. As well as adding System.Xml, as in the previous example, we need to import System.Text. This namespace contains the StringBuilder class that is useful for concate-nating large numbers of strings.

```
using System;
using System.Data;
using System.Data.SqlClient;
using System.Data.SqlTypes;
using System.Text;
using System.Xml;
using Microsoft.SqlServer.Server;
```

As we noted earlier, although VS generates a separate source code file for this procedure, our code will be placed in the same partial class as the previous example, namely Apress.Xml. StoredProcedures.

```
namespace Apress.Xml
{
  public partial class StoredProcedures
  {
```

The method that implements the stored procedure takes five parameters, all of type string. These specify the name of the stored procedure through which the data will be extracted, the name of the file where the RSS output will be saved, the title of the RSS feed, the URL of the web page that the feed corresponds to, and the description of the feed.

```
[SqlProcedure]
public static void OutputRSS(string sprocName, string fileName, string title,
                             string link, string description)
{
```

Now we come to the method body. As before, we start by declaring a string to hold the name of the current "special offer" node, and then creating a new XmlDocument and adding the XML declaration to it:

```
string parentNodeValue = "";
XmlDocument xmlDoc = new XmlDocument();

XmlDeclaration decl = xmlDoc.CreateXmlDeclaration("1.0", "", "");
xmlDoc.AppendChild(decl);
```

The root element of all RSS feeds is the <rss> element. It has a version attribute that indicates which version of RSS the feed uses; we'll use the latest one, 2.0. This <rss> element contains a child <channel> element for the channel that the feed represents. This *must* contain child <title>, <link>, and <description> elements, which we'll populate with the information passed into our stored procedure.

```
XmlElement root = xmlDoc.CreateElement("rss");
XmlAttribute attr = xmlDoc.CreateAttribute("version");
attr.Value = "2.0";
root.Attributes.Append(attr);
xmlDoc.AppendChild(root);

XmlElement channel = xmlDoc.CreateElement("channel");
root.AppendChild(channel);

XmlElement titleElem = xmlDoc.CreateElement("", "title", "");
titleElem.InnerText = title;
channel.AppendChild(titleElem);

XmlElement linkElem = xmlDoc.CreateElement("", "link", "");
linkElem.InnerText = link;
channel.AppendChild(linkElem);

XmlElement descElem = xmlDoc.CreateElement("", "description", "");
descElem.InnerText = description;
channel.AppendChild(descElem);
```

The <channel> element also contains one <item> element for each item or headline in the channel. In our case, we'll use this element for the top-level items in our data (our special offers). Before we create these, though, we need to retrieve the data from the T-SQL stored procedure; this code is exactly the same as in the previous example:

```
using (SqlConnection cn = new SqlConnection("context connection=true"))
{
    cn.Open();
    SqlCommand sqlComm = new SqlCommand(sprocName, cn);
    sqlComm.CommandType = CommandType.StoredProcedure;
    SqlDataReader rdr = sqlComm.ExecuteReader();
```

Again, as we iterate through the data reader, we'll need to keep track of the elements that we need to add our data to. The top-level <item> nodes representing the special offers aren't a problem, as they'll be added directly to the <channel> element, but the data for each product with a specific discount requires more work; it will be stored within an HTML table within a <description> child element below the <item> element. We'll build up the HTML table using a StringBuilder, as this is much faster than a normal string for concatenating many substrings, so we need to declare this; we also need to declare the XmlElement object that will represent the item's <description> element, as this is the node that we'll add the HTML to.

```
XmlElement descNode = null;
StringBuilder sb = null;
```

Now we're ready to iterate through the SqlDataReader. As before, if the first column in the current row has a different value from the one stored in our parentNodeValue variable, we'll need to create a new parent element, this time called <item>.

```
while (rdr.Read())
{
  string name = (string)rdr.GetSqlString(0);
  if (parentNodeValue != name)
  {
    XmlElement parentElement = xmlDoc.CreateElement("", "item", "");
    channel.AppendChild(parentElement);
    parentNodeValue = name;
```

At this point, if we're not on the first iteration, we'll also have to finish off the HTML table that we're building by adding closing <tbody> and <table> tags, and also set the InnerText property of the descNode variable to the string that we've been building up in our StringBuilder. Because we can only do this if we've already got a reference to the current item's <description> element, we check whether or not descNode is equal to null before finishing off the table—if descNode is equal to null, we must be on the first iteration.

```
if (descNode != null)
{
  sb.Append("</tbody></table>");
  descNode.InnerText = sb.ToString();
}
```

Now we can create the children for the new <item> node. First we create the <title> element, and set its text to the value of the first column. Then we create the <description> element, and also create a new StringBuilder to hold the HTML table that it will contain. We also start off the table by adding the initial <table> tag, generating the table headings from the names of the columns in the data reader, and then adding the opening <tbody> tag. The angled brackets of the HTML tags in the description must be replaced by the entity references < (for <) and > (for >); however, this isn't a problem, as these characters are automatically replaced by the appropriate entity references when we set the XmlElement's InnerText property.

```
XmlElement titleNode = xmlDoc.CreateElement("", "title", "");
titleNode.InnerText = name;
```

```
        parentElement.AppendChild(titleNode);
        descNode = xmlDoc.CreateElement("", "description", "");
        parentElement.AppendChild(descNode);
        sb = new StringBuilder();
        sb.Append("<table border='1'><thead>");
        for (int i=1; i<rdr.FieldCount; i++)
          sb.AppendFormat("<th>{0}</th>", rdr.GetName(i));
        sb.Append("</thead><tbody>");
      }
```

Once we've created the new <item> element as necessary, we can iterate through each subsequent column in the current row of the data reader, and add an HTML table cell for each value to our StringBuilder. Each row is enclosed in opening and closing <tr>...</tr> tags.

```
      sb.Append("<tr>");
      for (int i = 1; i < rdr.FieldCount; i++)
      {
        sb.AppendFormat("<td>{0}</td>", rdr.GetSqlValue(i).ToString());
      }
      sb.Append("</tr>");
    }
```

Now that we've finished processing all the rows in the data reader, we finish off the HTML table and set the text of the final <description> element, and then save the XML document and clean up the SqlDataReader and SqlCommand objects.

```
      sb.Append("</tbody></table>");
      descNode.InnerText = sb.ToString();

      xmlDoc.Save(fileName);
      rdr.Close();
      sqlComm.Dispose();
    }
   }
  }
};
```

That completes the .NET code for this example. Build the two stored procedures into a DLL by selecting Build ➤ Build XMLOutput from the main menu in VS.

Deploying the Procedures to SQL Server

Now that we have the CLR procedures created and compiled within Visual Studio 2005, we can either deploy them using Visual Studio 2005 or copy our DLL to a prespecified location and manually deploy. Manual deployment does require more work; however, you may prefer this method from a source control view, as all of the deployment commands can be saved within your query, and you will know exactly what occurred.

As we discussed earlier, our assembly references another .NET assembly, which means that when we install our assembly into SQL Server through the CREATE ASSEMBLY statement, we need to define it as EXTERNAL_ACCESS.

When you build a SQL Server project within Visual Studio 2005, the assemblies that are available to you are assumed to have the SAFE permission set. Of course, this is the ideal scenario, as it means you will be secure in the knowledge that safe assemblies should not bring down your server. However, there will be times, such as this, where you need to do more.

System.Xml sits between SAFE and EXTERNAL_ACCESS. In general the namespace is SAFE; it is only when you wish to save or load any XML output to/from a physical hard drive that it requires the EXTERNAL_ACCESS permission set. System.Xml does not write out any output itself, but internally the assembly does call classes in the System.IO namespace to write out the information or to load a file. When you write to the CREATE ASSEMBLY statement, whether you need to use SAFE or EXTERNAL_ACCESS is determined by whether System.IO is called. In our case, of course, we've saved the XML document to disk, so we need to install the assembly in SQL Server with external access.

One consequence of this is that the assembly can't be deployed to SQL Server without a modification of the database. Non-safe assemblies can only be deployed if two conditions are met: either the database must be marked as TRUSTWORTHY and the user installing the assembly must have the UNSAFE ASSEMBLY or EXTERNAL_ACCESS ASSEMBLY permission as appropriate; or the assembly must be signed with a certificate or asymmetric key associated with a login with the appropriate permission. We'll look at installing non-safe assemblies in Chapter 10, but for now the simplest option is to run the CREATE ASSEMBLY statement in the sysadmin fixed server role and to set the TRUSTWORTHY property of the AdventureWorks database to ON:

```
ALTER DATABASE AdventureWorks
SET TRUSTWORTHY ON;
```

We can now deploy the assembly to SQL Server:

```
SET QUOTED_IDENTIFIER OFF
GO
CREATE ASSEMBLY XMLOutput
AUTHORIZATION [dbo]
FROM "C:\Program Files\SQL Server Assemblies\XMLOutput.dll"
WITH PERMISSION_SET = EXTERNAL_ACCESS
GO
```

Now that the assembly is loaded into SQL Server, we can define the procedures. The parameters defined as strings within our assembly must be defined as nvarchar. If you try to define them as varchar, there is no direct correlation between the native SQL type and the .NET type, and an error occurs.

The format of the EXTERNAL NAME clause is that of a three-part name. The first part is the assembly name used in the CREATE ASSEMBLY statement, followed by the class name prefixed by any namespace used, and the final part is the name of the method that is called when the procedure is invoked.

```
CREATE PROCEDURE XMLDoc (@SprocName nvarchar(255), @RootName nvarchar(255),
@FileName nvarchar(255))
```

```
AS EXTERNAL NAME XMLOutput.[Apress.Xml.StoredProcedures].OutputXML
GO
```

```
CREATE PROCEDURE RSSDoc (@SprocName nvarchar(255), @FileName nvarchar(255),
                        @Title nvarchar(255), @Link nvarchar(255),
                        @Description nvarchar(255))
AS EXTERNAL NAME XMLOutput.[Apress.Xml.StoredProcedures].OutputRSS
GO
```

The final part of our example is to test our procedures and ensure we get the correct results into our XML file. This code will execute the two procedures, both times calling the SpecialOffers T-SQL stored procedure, and creating a standard XML file called C:\Apress\ SqlAssemblies\Chapter04\Discounts.XML and an RSS feed in a file called C:\Apress\SqlAssemblies\ Chapter04\DiscountsRSS.XML.

```
XMLDoc 'SpecialOffers', 'ROOT', 'C:\Apress\SqlAssemblies\Chapter04\Discounts.XML'
GO
```

```
RSSDoc 'SpecialOffers', 'C:\Apress\SqlAssemblies\Chapter04\DiscountsRSS.XML',
  'AdventureWorks Special Offers', 'http://www.AdventureWorks.com/specialoffers/',
  'Special offers on Mountain Bike gear from AdventureWorks'
GO
```

Figure 4-1 shows the RSS feed displayed in a freeware .NET 1.1-based RSS reader called, appropriately enough, RssReader. You can download this reader from http://www.rssreader.com.

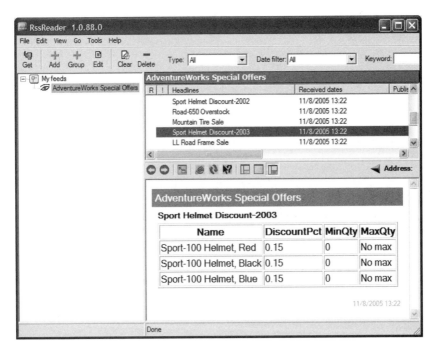

Figure 4-1. *The RSS feed displayed in the freeware RssReader utility*

Now that we have our first example up and running, we can move on to take a look at how we can also use CLR stored procedures to work with image files.

Working with Images

One topic that has proven to be a constant source of irritation to web site developers is the loading of images into a SQL Server database. Prior to SQL Server 2005, it was possible to do it, but only if the data was in bit format, and even then using the WRITETEXT functions was very cumbersome. It meant that you always had to have an external program written in C++ or VB that loaded and retrieved the image. A secondary effect was that if you were retrieving an image and some information about the picture for display on a web page, it was a two-stage process: loading the information first, followed by the image. Furthermore, this process was out of the control of SQL Server. The alternative was to use DTS and TEXTCOPY, but this provided limited functionality.

The fact was that SQL Server 2000 just wasn't a great place to store image files, and this was a pity because it is a common requirement. For example, we often encounter a company that stores images from web cams on its web cam server. The images are backed up, but the company would like to store them in a SQL Server database for further security and other processing. Storing them in the database would also provide a faster and more convenient way of retrieving an image, if required, rather than having to fetch it from the backup tapes (often stored at an offsite location).

With the advent of SQL Server 2005 and CLR stored procedures, the situation has improved dramatically. It is possible to complete this action in one transaction. This reduces the possibility of orphan information on the loading of the image into a table. It also greatly simplifies the processing required to get the image in a format that allows you to manipulate it easily.

■**Caution** Image storage and retrieval in SQL Server 2005 is much improved by use of CLR stored procedures and has security and accessibility advantages. However, if speed is of the essence, or you have a large numbers of files or have to store very large files, then you still may want to consider alternative storage techniques.

Furthermore, once you have the functionality in the database assembly, you can directly take advantage of other database functionality. For example, you could set it up to run as part of a scheduled job to load images at specified times of the day. Also, of course, you will have access to much more sophisticated image manipulation capability, through the .NET framework classes to which you now have access. For example, the System.Drawing namespace provides access to GDI+ graphics functionality, which allows the conversion and manipulation of images.

However, there is a potential drawback here. Because the images are loaded from and saved to the file system, you will need to assign the procedure a security setting of EXTERNAL_ACCESS instead of SAFE (as for the XML example). The DBA isn't in control of what data is saved to or loaded from the physical server (although this can be managed with code access security, which we'll look at in Chapter 10). You'll need to take into account any effect this could have on other SQL Server instances on the server, as well as other processes that might be running. Also, some corporations may not allow this assembly to be loaded into your SQL Server.

Furthermore, if you make use of classes such as System.Drawing, then the assembly will need to be defined as UNSAFE.

Storing and Retrieving Images

The example here demonstrates how a stored procedure could store and retrieve images from SQL Server 2005.

In our example scenario, the images (such as from a web cam) are stored in the database for security reasons. The images are stored there for further analysis or retrieval for printing onto security cards. Many corporations have visitors (and employees) who are required to visit a security point where their photograph is taken and then printed onto an access card. The image could also then be placed into SQL Server for future use.

In this example, the SQL Server database that will be loading and retrieving the web cam images will reside on the same server as the web cam itself, though ideally the SQL Server would be offsite for extra security. Also, if at any time there was an emergency, photographs of those in the building could be retrieved for emergency services almost instantly.

These are relatively specialist examples, but scenarios such as these do justify the ability to work with external access to SQL Server. This example demonstrates

- How to work with binary data in a SQL assembly

- How to access external resources from a SQL assembly

We will be building procedures to load a single image, or multiple images, into a table, and to allow images to be retrieved from the table back onto a hard drive. We'll create all these procedures within a single class in our assembly.

For this example, we'll use the AssembliesTesting database so there's no risk of corruption to the example databases. We need to create three objects before we start writing the .NET code for this: a table to hold our images, together with an identifier and the name of the image; a T-SQL procedure for inserting an image into the table as a SQL image type; and finally a T-SQL stored procedure for retrieving an image from the table, again as a SQL Server image. These T-SQL stored procedures will do the actual work of inserting the binary data into or selecting the binary data from the table, and they'll be called from our CLR stored procedures, which will load or write images from or to a file.

```
USE AssembliesTesting
GO

CREATE TABLE ImageLoadTest (
ImageId int NOT NULL IDENTITY(1,1 ),
ImageName nvarchar(255)  NOT NULL,
LoadedImage image NOT NULL)
GO

CREATE PROCEDURE InsertImage @ImageName as nvarchar(255),  @ImageToLoad image
AS
```

```
BEGIN
  INSERT INTO ImageLoadTest (ImageName,  LoadedImage)
  VALUES(@ImageName,  @ImageToLoad)
END
GO

CREATE PROCEDURE RetrieveImage @Id int
AS
BEGIN
  SELECT ImageName,LoadedImage
  FROM ImageLoadTest
  WHERE ImageId = @Id
END
GO
```

Time to have a look at our example. Create a Visual Studio 2005 C# Class Library project (found under the Windows node), call it ImageManipulation, and rename the class within the project to ImageManipulation. We also include the partial keyword in the class definition in case we want to add further methods to the class in different source files.

```
using System;
using System.Data;
using System.Data.SqlClient;
using System.Data.SqlTypes;
using System.IO;
using Microsoft.SqlServer.Server;

namespace FatBelly.Images
{
  public partial class StoredProcedures
  {
```

The first of our three stored procedures will load a single image into a SQL Server table. There is only one parameter—the path and filename of the image.

```
    [SqlProcedure]
    public static void LoadAnyImage(string imageLocation)
    {
```

Here we start to use our EXTERNAL_ACCESS functionality as we need to access the file to load it into a byte array. To do this, we create a FileInfo object that contains information about the image file we want to open. To read the file into the byte array, we call the OpenRead method of this FileInfo object. This opens the file for reading and returns a FileStream instance into which the data from the file is streamed. FileStream is a specialist streaming class designed for outputting data to a file, and exposes methods for creating files and so on. It is not until the OpenRead method is called that the EXTERNAL_ACCESS permission set is required. Once we have the FileStream object, we can use its Length property to determine how big our byte array needs to be to hold all the data from the file and initialize the array. We can then read the entire file into this array with one call to the `FileStream.Read` method. Finally, we close the `FileStream` to release resources.

```
FileInfo imgFile = new FileInfo(imageLocation);
Stream fileStream = imgFile.OpenRead();
Byte[]byteImage = new Byte [fileStream.Length];
fileStream.Read(byteImage,0 ,(int)  imgFile.Length);
fileStream.Close();
```

The `FileStream.Read` method takes three parameters: the byte array we want to store the data in, the position in the stream we want to start reading at, and the number of bytes we want to read. Notice that the last parameter is an int, whereas the `FileStream.Length` property is a long. There's a risk of data loss in this conversion, so it can't be performed implicitly—we need an explicit cast. If there's a danger that the file size will be longer than the maximum value for an int, you'll need to read the file in chunks. However, since the C# int type contains four bytes, your image would have to be unfeasibly large for this to cause a problem (4GB, in fact).

Once we have the byte array, we can call our `InsertImage` T-SQL stored procedure to load the image. The code to do this is similar to the code in the previous example that called the `SpecialOffers` stored procedure. We open the context connection and create a new `SqlCommand` object on this connection, passing in the name of the procedure we want to call, and then set its `CommandType` to `CommandType.StoredProcedure`.

```
using (SqlConnection cn = new SqlConnection("context connection=true"))
{
  cn.Open();
  SqlCommand sqlCmd = new SqlCommand("InsertImage", cn);
  sqlCmd.CommandType = CommandType.StoredProcedure;
```

There are two advantages to using stored procedures instead of building up a SQL query on the fly. The first is security. Although not a major threat at this moment to the .NET function, it is possible to place code into image files; you may have seen the security threat and Windows patch from Microsoft that will clamp down on this security hole. Similarly with SQL Server, by reading in the data in bytes, it may be possible to place key code that could drop tables, create new users, and so on, if the byte information were placed directly as T-SQL inline code. By having the image as a parameter, the data is handled as a separate unit to the code to execute. The second reason is as you would expect: it does mean that your stored procedure will sit on SQL Server and gain the same performance benefits as standard stored procedures with query plans. In a similar vein, it also will mean less information being passed through to SQL Server from this stored procedure, and therefore for both of these reasons performance will be better than T-SQL.

Unlike the `SpecialOffers` procedure, `InsertImage` takes parameters that we have to populate before executing the command. Adding parameters to a `SqlCommand` is as simple as calling the `Add` method on the `Parameters` property. It is not necessary to get the parameters in the same order as the stored procedure; all of this is taken care of for you. For input parameters, we obviously also need to set the value of the parameter before calling the sproc. Because the `Add` method returns the `SqlParameter` object that's been added to the `Parameters` collection, we can set its value without storing the `SqlParameter` in a variable, keeping the code to add each parameter down to a single line.

```
sqlCmd.Parameters.Add("@ImageName", SqlDbType.NVarChar,255).Value =
                                                        imgFile.Name;
sqlCmd.Parameters.Add("@ImageToLoad", SqlDbType.Image).Value = byteImage;
```

Once the command is configured and the parameters added, you can call the
ExecuteAndSend method of the SqlPipe class to take you back to SQL Server and execute the
command.

```
SqlContext.Pipe.ExecuteAndSend(sqlCmd);
    }
}
```

The second CLR stored procedure will load all images found in a specified directory that
have a specific file extension. It will load each image one at a time from the directory into SQL
Server by calling the LoadAnyImage method we have just walked through.

■**Note** This example does not then delete the images, so subsequent calls to the same directory location
will cause multiple loads of the same image. This is a safety feature for you so that if anything does go
wrong, you won't lose any precious family pictures!

To search a directory for files with a particular extension, we create a DirectoryInfo
object to represent the directory passed in as the first parameter to the method. This has a
GetFiles method that returns an array of FileInfo objects representing all the files in that
directory that match the given name. We call this method, using an asterisk wildcard to
retrieve any files that end in a period followed by the file extension that was passed into the
method as the second parameter. Once we have this array, we simply iterate through each
FileInfo object in it, and call the LoadAnyImage method, passing in the full name of the file.

```
public static void LoadAllImages(string imagesLocation,  string fileSuffix)
{
  DirectoryInfo dirFiles = new DirectoryInfo(imagesLocation);
  FileInfo[]listOfFiles = dirFiles.GetFiles("*."+fileSuffix);

  foreach (FileInfo aFile in listOfFiles)
  {
    LoadAnyImage(aFile.FullName);
  }
}
```

Our third and final method retrieves a single image from the table. It takes two parameters: a unique identifier for the image, generated when images are added to the ImageLoadTest
table; and the directory where we should save the file. Again we call a T-SQL stored procedure
(the RetrieveImage procedure in this case), passing in the image's ID; this returns a row of data
for the image in the form of a SqlDataReader, and we retrieve from this the filename. Then we
check that the directory where we are to save the file exists, and if it doesn't, we create it. When

we've found the directory, we check whether there's already a file with the same name as our image in that directory, and if there is, we delete it to make way for the image we've retrieved from the database. If you feel, however, that the action of overwriting the image could overwrite an image you want to keep, then it would also be possible to throw an exception and an error code back from the stored procedure saying an error occurred.

```
public static void ExtractImage(Int32 photoID, string location)
{
  SqlDataReader sqlReader = null;
  using (SqlConnection cn = new SqlConnection("context connection=true"))
  {
    cn.Open();
    SqlCommand sqlCmd = new SqlCommand("RetrieveImage", cn);
    sqlCmd.CommandType = CommandType.StoredProcedure;
    sqlCmd.Parameters.Add("@Id", SqlDbType.Int);
    sqlCmd.Parameters[0].Value = photoID;
    sqlReader = sqlCmd.ExecuteReader();
    sqlReader.Read();
    string fileName = (string) sqlReader.GetSqlString(0);

    // Create a file to hold the output.
    if (!Directory.Exists(location))
    {
      Directory.CreateDirectory(location);
    }

    string fileNameWithPath = location + "\\" + fileName;
    if (File.Exists(fileNameWithPath))
    {
      File.Delete(fileNameWithPath);
    }
```

Just as we used a FileStream to read the bytes into a byte array when loading the image, we use a FileStream to put the image back onto a hard drive. We'll write to this object using a BinaryWriter object; BinaryWriter is a class designed specifically for writing binary data to a stream.

Both of these objects are declared and instantiated within using statements. This type of statement provides us with a way to create and initialize a new object, but more importantly it ensures that the object is disposed of at the end of the code block. No matter what happens, even if you exit your code with an exception, your object will be disposed of and cleaned up, releasing memory resources. This is ideal with complex code and also avoids missing any cleanup code that you want to put in other areas such as exception handling. We take a look at exception handling in Chapter 9.

```
using (FileStream outputStream =
    new FileStream(fileNameWithPath,  FileMode.Create,  FileAccess.Write))
  {
```

```
using (BinaryWriter binOutput = new BinaryWriter(outputStream))
{
```

Now that we have our file stream and our binary writer to write to the stream, we can read the data returned from our stored procedure. We don't know in advance how large the image will be, so we need to read the binary data from the SqlDataReader in chunks. We set a variable to hold the number of bytes read from the SqlDataReader at a time. Because we'll loop through the data reading this many bytes until we've read the whole image, the larger the value, the better. This will reduce the number of calls to the data reader to get the data back. We've used 4096 here, but we could increase this value from 4KB to 100KB or even greater. However, by returning 4KB, the example is guaranteeing that we will go through the loop processing. We create a byte array of this length to hold the data as it's read from the SqlDataReader by calling its GetBytes method. This takes no fewer than five parameters:

- The index of the column in the reader (one in this case, because the image is the second column).

- The position in the data we want to start reading from; because we're reading in chunks of 4096 bytes, this will be zero for the first read, 4096 for the second, 8192 for the third, and so on.

- The byte array that we want to store the data in.

- The position in the byte array buffer where we want to write the data to; we'll always write to the beginning of the array, so this will always be zero.

- The number of bytes we want to read. This is the value stored in our length variable, or 4096.

This method returns the actual number of bytes read. While there's still more data to be read, this will be 4096, but on the last loop there will be fewer than 4096 bytes left to read, so we need to carry on reading more chunks of data until the return value is less than our length variable.

As we retrieve each block of byte data, we use our binary writer to write it out to our file stream. Finally, when we've finished writing the data, we flush and close the BinaryWriter. By completing a flush at the end of our processing, we are ensuring that all the data is written and there is nothing left in any buffers.

```
int length = 4096;
byte[]pictBlob = new byte[length];
int startPoint = 0;
long retval = sqlReader.GetBytes(1, startPoint, pictBlob, 0,
                                                      length);
binOutput.Write(pictBlob,0 ,(int) retval);
while (retval == length)
{
  startPoint += length;

  retval = sqlReader.GetBytes(1, startPoint,pictBlob, 0,length);
```

```
            binOutput.Write(pictBlob,0 ,(int) retval);
          }

          binOutput.Flush();
          binOutput.Close();
        }
      }
      sqlReader.Close();
    }
  }
}
}
```

Compile this file into a DLL and you're almost ready to install the procedures into SQL Server. However, as we mentioned earlier, this example uses a "nonstandard" CLR stored procedure assembly, so let's first discuss what this means.

Using Nonstandard Assemblies

The version of the System.IO assembly that is normally called by .NET clients is the one installed in the global assembly cache (GAC). However, all assemblies installed into the GAC must be strong named, and strong named assemblies may not be called from partially trusted code unless they are marked with a special assembly-level attribute. We'll discuss partially trusted code in Chapter 10, but the key point for our purposes is that *all* SQL Server assemblies are partially trusted. While the most frequently used assemblies (including System.Xml) are marked with the AllowPartiallyTrustedCallers attribute, System.IO isn't, so by default it isn't available to SQL assemblies.

There are two ways that the System.IO DLL can be placed into SQL Server 2005. The first is to copy the assembly to the same directory as the DLL that requires it. Then when you register the XML assembly example we are about to build, it will find the System.XML DLL and retrieve the necessary manifest information.

The preferred method, though, is to load the System.IO DLL into SQL Server using the CREATE ASSEMBLY statement, defining the location as the Microsoft .NET Framework location, declaring it as UNSAFE or EXTERNAL_ACCESS, and setting the visibility to off. This avoids having different versions of the System.IO DLL in different locations on your computer, as you would have your CREATE ASSEMBLY point to the version of .NET Framework installed.

Testing the Example

With that diversion out of the way, we can now come to testing our example.

Ensure that you've created the table and the T-SQL procedures for the example in the AssembliesTesting database, and you're now ready to load the assembly and the stored procedure. As we have said, our assembly contains three methods that implement CLR stored procedures, and hence we have three CREATE PROCEDURE statements. Each procedure has different parameters and calls the specific method within our .NET assembly. Run the following script in Management Studio to create the assembly and the three procedures in the

AssembliesTesting database, and to test the code by inserting some images into the database and then extracting them to file:

```
SET QUOTED_IDENTIFIER OFF
GO
USE AssembliesTesting

CREATE ASSEMBLY LoadUnloadImages
AUTHORIZATION [dbo]
FROM "C:\ Program Files\SQL Server Assemblies\ImageManipulation.dll"
WITH PERMISSION_SET = EXTERNAL_ACCESS
GO
CREATE PROCEDURE LoadASingleImage (@Loc nvarchar(255))
AS EXTERNAL NAME LoadUnloadImages.[FatBelly.Images.StoredProcedures].LoadAnyImage
GO
CREATE PROCEDURE LoadingAllImages (@Loc nvarchar(255),  @Type nvarchar(255))
AS EXTERNAL NAME LoadUnloadImages.[FatBelly.Images.StoredProcedures].LoadAllImages
GO
CREATE PROCEDURE ExtractAnImage (@ImageId int,  @Loc nvarchar(255))
AS EXTERNAL NAME LoadUnloadImages.[FatBelly.Images.StoredProcedures].ExtractImage
GO
LoadASingleImage "C:\Pics\Cameron.jpg"
GO
LoadingAllImages "c:\Pics","jpg"
go
SELECT * FROM ImageLoadTest
go
ExtractAnImage 1," c:\temp"
GO
ExtractAnImage 2," c:\temp"
GO
ExtractAnImage 11," c:\temp"
GO
```

Executing Operating System Commands

For our final example of this chapter, we'll write a CLR stored procedure that allows a DBA to execute operating system commands from within SQL Server. It is true that this can already be done using the xp_cmdshell system stored procedure, but this is potentially a major security risk, so the extra security options that .NET provides make this worth rewriting as a CLR stored procedure. In addition to SQL Server's security features, we can use .NET's code access security mechanism to ensure that the procedure can only be used with certain named files, and we can use role-based security to restrict the Windows user accounts that are permitted to execute the assembly. We won't cover these here, as we look in detail at both code access security and role-based security in Chapter 10.

The procedure will be implemented as a CLR stored procedure that takes a single parameter containing the name of the command to execute. In the procedure, we execute the command and return any output from it to SQL Server by sending it to the context pipe. The .NET code behind this example is very simple, so we'll run through it very quickly.

As in all .NET code, we start with the using directives to import some namespaces so we don't need to refer to all classes by their fully qualified names:

```
using System;
using System.Diagnostics;
using System.IO;
using Microsoft.SqlServer.Server;
```

As well as the usual System namespace, we have Microsoft.SqlServer.Server for the SqlPipe class. We also need System.IO for the stream manipulation classes that we'll use to redirect output back to SQL Server, and System.Diagnostics, which contains the classes we need to start an external process.

The procedure is implemented in a class called OSCmdExample. This class has one method, ExecuteOSCmd, which contains the C# code that implements our stored procedure. ExecuteOSCmd has one parameter—a string containing the name of the command to be executed. We indicate that this method is a stored procedure method by decorating it with the SqlProcedure attribute.

```
namespace Apress.SqlAssemblies.Chapter04
{
    public class OSCmdExample
    {
        [SqlProcedure]
        public static void ExecuteOSCmd(string filename)
        {
```

Within the method body, all the code is contained with try ... catch blocks to ensure that any exceptions will be dealt with (relatively) gracefully. To execute an external process from within a CLR assembly, we need to use the Process class. This can be used in two ways: it has a static Start method that can be called with the name of an executable to run or a document to open in an external application. For example, we can run Internet Explorer using this command:

```
Process.Start("IExplore.exe");
```

Alternatively, we can create an instance of the Process class to represent the external process, set properties of its StartInfo object, and then call its parameterless nonstatic Start method. This is the approach we'll be taking in this case. We need to set three properties on the StartInfo object: the FileName (the name of the executable we want to run); UseShellExecute, which we want to set to false so that Windows won't create a new command shell to execute the program; and RedirectStandardOutput, which we need to set to true, so that any output from the program will be redirected from its standard channel (the console window). Once we've set these, we can start the process:

```
try
{
    Process p = new Process();
    p.StartInfo.FileName = filename;
```

```
p.StartInfo.UseShellExecute = false;
p.StartInfo.RedirectStandardOutput = true;
p.Start();
```

Now that the process has started, we need to redirect any output back to SQL Server. We can access the program's output through the `Process` class's `StandardOutput` property. This provides us with a `StreamReader` object, and we can read the characters in this object into a string and send it to the `SqlPipe.Send` method. Unfortunately, however, the `Send` method can only take strings of 4,000 characters or fewer, so we need to read the data from the `StreamReader` in blocks of 4,000. To do this, we set up a new 4,000-element `char` array to act as a buffer, and call the `StreamReader`'s `ReadBlock` method, passing in this array, a starting position of zero (to indicate we want to store the data at the start of the array), and a value of 4,000 to say that we don't want to read more than 4,000 characters in one go. This returns an `int` value containing the number of characters actually read. This will return 4,000 if 4,000 or more characters are left in the string, or a value less than 4,000 if there are fewer characters left.

Once we've got the character data into the buffer array, we can convert it into a string by calling one of the many overloads of the `string` constructor. This particular overload takes a `char` array, the position in the array to start the string from, and the number of characters to include in the string. By using the `length` value returned from `ReadBlock` as the last parameter, we ensure that if fewer than 4,000 characters were read, any characters remaining in the array from a previous read won't be written to the string. We then pass this string to the `Send` method. We carry on reading from the `StreamReader` for as long as the `length` variable has a value of 4,000, as the `ReadBlock` method will always read exactly 4,000 characters if there are that many characters left. Finally, once all the data has been read and sent back to SQL Server, we close the `StreamReader`.

```
        StreamReader sr = p.StandardOutput;
        SqlPipe pipe = SqlContext.Pipe;
        char[] buffer = new char[4000];
        int length = 0;
        do
        {
            length = sr.ReadBlock(buffer, 0, 4000);
            string msg = new string(buffer, 0, length);
            pipe.Send(msg);
        } while (length == 4000);
        sr.Close();
    }
```

All that remains is to catch any exceptions that were thrown and send the message back to SQL Server:

```
    catch (Exception e)
    {
        SqlContext.Pipe.Send(e.Message);
    }
  }
 }
}
```

Compile this file into a DLL, and open Management Studio to install the assembly and the procedure into SQL Server. Naturally enough, the assembly will need to be created with the UNSAFE permission set:

```
CREATE ASSEMBLY OSCmdExample
FROM 'C:\Apress\SqlAssemblies\Chapter04\OSCmdExample.dll'
WITH PERMISSION_SET = UNSAFE;
GO

CREATE PROCEDURE uspExecuteOSCmd(@filename nvarchar(256))
AS
EXTERNAL NAME
OSCmdExample.[Apress.SqlAssemblies.Chapter04.OSCmdExample].ExecuteOSCmd;
GO
```

To test the procedure, execute the `tasklist` command, which displays details of the currently executing processes:

```
EXEC uspExecuteOSCmd 'tasklist.exe';
```

You should see something similar to what appears in Figure 4-2.

```
  Messages

  Image Name                    PID Session Name      Session#   Mem Usage
  ========================= ====== ================ ======== =============
  System Idle Process            0 Console                 0         16 K
  System                         4 Console                 0         24 K
  smss.exe                     888 Console                 0         28 K
  csrss.exe                    960 Console                 0      2,196 K
  winlogon.exe                 984 Console                 0      2,396 K
  services.exe                1028 Console                 0      1,880 K
  lsass.exe                   1040 Console                 0      2,936 K
  svchost.exe                 1196 Console                 0      1,504 K
  svchost.exe                 1276 Console                 0      1,580 K
  svchost.exe                 1316 Console                 0      9,920 K
  svchost.exe                 1436 Console                 0        888 K
  svchost.exe                 1516 Console                 0        788 K
  spoolsv.exe                 1828 Console                 0        896 K
  explorer.exe                 276 Console                 0     17,848 K
  Apoint.exe                   392 Console                 0        540 K
  stacmon.exe                  408 Console                 0        132 K
  ezSP_Px.exe                  416 Console                 0        256 K
  ico.exe                      424 Console                 0        132 K
  HKServ.exe                   432 Console                 0        688 K
```

Figure 4-2. *Executing the Tasklist command*

Summary

This chapter has not looked at returning results sets or data in a "normal" fashion. This was covered in Chapter 3. The aim of this chapter was to demonstrate how to extend functionality of stored procedures beyond that to currently client-based areas that can gain a great deal by being rewritten as stored procedures. The first example of producing XML or an RSS feed could be linked with the job scheduling to produce monthly files. The second example similarly could also be linked in with job scheduling to load images from a web cam on a regular basis, either hourly or even as an overnight process.

The image example could also be used to load AVIs, MPEGs, or even MP3 files if you wanted to create a file-sharing database solution as part of the back end of something like the popular Napster or iTunes.

Finally, we also demonstrated how you can use CLR procedures to execute external processes such as operating system commands. This demonstrates the power of SQL assemblies, but also illustrates something of its potential danger.

CHAPTER 5

■■■

User-Defined Functions

Just as we can create stored procedures using .NET code, we can also create functions that we can call from within SQL statements just like in-built functions or user-defined functions (UDFs) written in T-SQL. As with T-SQL UDFs, there's a marked difference between creating CLR functions that return a single value (scalar-valued UDFs) and those that return a whole resultset of data (table-valued UDFs). In fact, while we use the same CREATE FUNCTION T-SQL command to create the database object representing either type of function, the .NET code behind each of the two function types really has little in common. However, both scalar- and table-valued functions have certain restrictions on the functionality that they can contain (e.g., functions are not allowed to modify the data in the database).

In this chapter we'll cover the following topics:

- Looking at restrictions on code in CLR UDFs

- Examining the SqlFunction attribute

- Writing a scalar-valued UDF in .NET that returns a value extracted from Active Directory

- Writing a table-valued UDF that creates a resultset derived from SQL Server and Active Directory data

- Writing a table-valued UDF that lists details of the files and subfolders in a file system folder

Creating CLR UDFs

One thing we need to stress at the outset is that the distinction between a CLR stored procedure and a function does *not* correspond to the distinction between subroutines and functions in Visual Basic (VB) and VB .NET. In VB, procedures that return a value are called *functions* and those that don't are called *subroutines*. While the .NET methods that implement SQL Server functions *must* return a value (after all, they'd be pretty useless if they didn't), it's not the case that CLR procedure methods are necessarily void; they may return an integer value. Fortunately, we're writing our code in C# in this book, so there's less chance of confusion—in fact, C# makes no significant distinction between methods that return a value and methods that return void.

There are significant differences between the way we write scalar-valued functions and table-valued functions, so we'll look at these separately. The similarity lies in the way the functions are created within SQL Server. In both cases, we need to install the containing assembly in SQL Server using the CREATE ASSEMBLY statement, and then create the function as a database object using the CREATE FUNCTION statement. The CREATE ASSEMBLY statement is, of course, exactly the same as for CLR stored procedures, which we looked at in the last chapter. The way you refer to a CLR method in place of the function body is also similar to the way you create CLR stored procedures:

```
CREATE FUNCTION function_name(parameter_list)
RETURNS return_type
WITH options
AS
EXTERNAL NAME clr_assembly.[full_typename].method_name
```

If the function is table-valued rather than a scalar function, the return type will be TABLE (column_list), just as if you were defining a T-SQL multiline table-valued function. You'll see examples of both types of CREATE FUNCTION statement in the course of the chapter.

There are two options that you can specify. First, you can say what you want to happen when the function is called with parameters that are null. There are two alternatives here:

- CALLED ON NULL INPUT (the default) specifies that even if the function is called with a null parameter, the function will be called and will execute as normal.

- RETURNS NULL ON NULL INPUT specifies that the method won't be called if any of the supplied input parameters are null, but the null value will be returned instead. This option can't be specified for table-valued functions.

The second option you can include is the EXECUTE AS clause. This indicates the security context that the function will run under and is the same as the EXECUTE AS clause of the CREATE PROCEDURE statement, which we looked at in Chapter 4.

Restrictions on UDF Code

We said previously that the code for table- and scalar-valued UDFs has little in common. There are, however, certain restrictions on what functionality your functions can perform, and these apply to both types of function, so we'll look at these first, before we go on to look at code examples.

Certain database restrictions on function code apply equally to T-SQL and CLR UDFs. UDFs may not alter the state of the database, so they are not permitted to

- Modify the data in the database. In the case of CLR functions, this means that you can't use the in-process provider to execute INSERT, UPDATE, or DELETE commands against any of the nontemporary tables in the database. However, it is possible to create temporary tables within the function and to modify the data in those tables.

- Create new database objects (except for temporary objects).

- Perform Data Control Language (DCL) queries such as granting permissions to a user.

- Return data directly to the client.

- Participate in a Service Broker conversation (unless called as part of another participant).

- Begin a new transaction, or commit or roll back the context transaction.

Because CLR UDFs cannot send data directly to the client, they may not access the `SqlPipe` object. This means that you can't use it to send error messages or debugging information directly to the user. Instead, you need to throw a new exception containing the appropriate information. So instead of writing code like this:

```
try
{
    // Do something that could throw an exception...
}
catch (Exception e)
{
    SqlContext.Pipe.Send("<error/debugging info>");
}
```

you need to do something like this:

```
try
{
    // Do something that could throw an exception...
}
catch (Exception e)
{
    throw new Exception("<error/debugging info>");
}
```

The SqlFunction Attribute

A second feature that both scalar- and table-valued functions have in common is that both can take a special .NET attribute, the `SqlFunction` attribute. The `SqlFunctionAttribute` class lives in the `Microsoft.SqlServer.Server` namespace and contains information about the function, which SQL Server can use to optimize the execution of that function. The attribute is placed on the method that contains the code for the function, and it has a number of properties that provide information about the code in the function. Most of these are optional, but two of them, `DataAccess` and `SystemDataAccess`, are mandatory if your function accesses user or system tables, respectively, using the in-process provider.

The full list of properties is shown in Table 5-1.

Table 5-1. *SqlFunction Properties*

Property	Type	Description
DataAccess	Microsoft.SqlServer.Server. DataAccessKind	Indicates whether the function uses the in-process provider to access SQL Server data. If it does, DataAccess should be set to DataAccessKind.Read; otherwise, it should be set to DataAccessKind.None.
FillRowMethodName	string	For a table-valued UDF, indicates the name of the method that will be called by SQL Server to populate a row in the returned resultset.

continued

Table 5-1. *Continued*

Property	Type	Description
IsDeterministic	bool	Specifies whether the function is deterministic or not. *Deterministic* functions always return the same value for a given set of input parameters and can be used within computed columns that are indexed.
IsPrecise	bool	Indicates whether the function returns an exact value, or whether there is a degree of imprecision (e.g., because the function performs floating-point operations).
Name	string	Used by Visual Studio to set the name of the UDF when it is deployed to SQL Server. This property is ignored by SQL Server itself.
SystemDataAccess	Microsoft.SqlServer.Server. SystemDataAccessKind	Indicates whether the function reads data from the system tables using the in-process provider (SystemDataAccessKind.Read) or not (SystemDataAccessKind.None).
TableDefinition	string	Used by Visual Studio to set the return type of a table-valued UDF when it is deployed to SQL Server. This property is ignored by SQL Server itself.

If the function attempts to access user or system tables but doesn't have the appropriate DataAccess or SystemDataAccess properties configured to allow this, the function will still compile and can be installed in SQL Server, but a runtime exception will be thrown when the function is executed.

Scalar-Valued UDFs

Because scalar-valued UDFs return a single value, they work in a very similar way to standard .NET methods. In fact, if the function doesn't perform any data access using the in-process provider, the body of the method won't be any different from a method in any normal .NET assembly running outside SQL Server. The only thing you need to do to use a .NET method as a UDF is add the SqlFunction attribute to it if it will be accessing any SQL Server data.

To see how this works in practice, let's look at a fairly simple scalar-valued UDF in the next section.

Scalar-Valued UDF Example

This example uses an e-mail address from a table in SQL Server to look up a user held in an Active Directory installation and return a list of all the proxy e-mail addresses for that object. This is something that can't be done using T-SQL—although we can use sp_addlinkedserver to link to the ADsDSOObject OLE DB provider, that provider can't retrieve the values from multi-valued properties, which are very common in LDAP-compliant directories. Moreover, the ADsDSOObject provider can't be used to modify data in a directory, so if we want to write a stored procedure that updates Active Directory, we have to either use this technique or write an extended stored procedure in unmanaged code.

Because we're going to use our function in SELECT statements that act on columns in the database, this example is also something that would be hard to accomplish using standard data access code outside the database. We'd have to construct a DataTable programmatically, look up the e-mail address in each row, use that to query the Active Directory, and then manually insert that value into the DataTable. In contrast, by writing a SQL assembly UDF, we can perform a single query that returns a single resultset, which we can use within other queries as necessary.

This example uses a simple table that contains the name and e-mail address of employees (this table could be created in any database):

```
CREATE TABLE employees
(
    id int IDENTITY PRIMARY KEY,
    name nvarchar(255),
    email nvarchar(255)
);
```

To test the function, you'll also need to add a couple of rows:

```
INSERT INTO employees
VALUES ('Julian Skinner', 'Julian@JulianSkinner.com');
INSERT INTO employees
VALUES ('Administrator', 'Administrator@JulianSkinner.com');
```

The e-mail addresses should be addresses of actual users in your Active Directory.

Now let's look at the .NET code for the UDF. This is included in a file called SimpleUdf.cs. We start by importing the namespaces we'll be using. As well as the standard System namespace, we need Microsoft.SqlServer.Server, where the SqlFunctionAttribute class resides; System.DirectoryServices, which contains the classes we need to access Active Directory from .NET code; and System.Text, for the StringBuilder class that's used to build up strings from smaller strings.

```
using System;
using System.DirectoryServices;
using System.Text;
using Microsoft.SqlServer.Server;
```

Next we need to define the type that will contain our UDF method. We'll call this SimpleUdf:

```
namespace Apress.SqlAssemblies.Chapter05
{
    public class SimpleUdf
    {
```

Now we come to the method itself. First, we'll define the SqlFunction attribute for the method. Our function won't access any SQL Server data, and it isn't deterministic because it accesses an external data source, so we set its DataAccess property to DataAccessKind.None and `IsDeterministic` to `false`. The method itself takes one string parameter (the e-mail address to look up) and returns a string value (the ADsPath of the user object):

```
[SqlFunction(DataAccess=DataAccessKind.None,
             IsDeterministic=false)]
public static string GetProxyAddresses(string email)
{
```

The code within the method is fairly straightforward. Don't worry if you're not familiar with accessing Active Directory from .NET code, as we'll explain what's going on in each step. First, we create a reference to the `Users` object in Active Directory, which contains all the user accounts stored in the directory. We use this as the root for a search for any object with the `mail` property set to the value passed in as the parameter of our function:

```
DirectoryEntry root = new
    DirectoryEntry("LDAP://daufiltri.julianskinner.local" +
                   "/CN=Users,DC=JulianSkinner,DC=local");
```

The path of this object will need to be changed for your Active Directory. It takes the following form:

`LDAP://<server_name>.<domain>/CN=Users,DC=<domain_name>,`
`DC=<domain_extension>`

So, for example, if your Active Directory server is called `ADServer`, and your domain is `mycompany.com`, the path will be

`LDAP://ADServer.mycompany.com/CN=Users,DC=mycompany,DC=com`

If this object can't be found, we can't perform the search, so we'll throw a `NullReferenceException`:

```
if (root == null)
    throw new NullReferenceException(
        "The directory service cannot be referenced.");
```

Next, we perform the search. To do this, we create a new `DirectorySearcher` instance (as its name suggests, this object is designed for searching a directory for objects that meet specific criteria), passing in the root of the search and the LDAP filter string that defines the objects we're looking for:

```
DirectorySearcher searcher = new DirectorySearcher(root,
        "(&(objectClass=user)(mail=" + email + "))");
```

LDAP filters are somewhat idiosyncratic in format. Each condition is contained within parentheses, and if you want to join conditions using a logical operator, the operator is placed before all the conditions, and then the whole lot is placed within parentheses. We're looking for user objects with a specific e-mail address, so we want to find objects that have an `objectClass` property with the value `user` and a `mail` property with the appropriate value. So, if we were looking for a user with the e-mail address `jdoe@johndoe.com`, our filter would be

`(&(objectClass=user)(mail=jdoe@johndoe.com))`

Note that LDAP property values aren't contained within quote marks in the filter. We only want to find objects that are directly below the Users object in the directory hierarchy. To do this, we set the DirectorySearcher object's SearchScope property to SearchScope.OneLevel; alternative values are SearchScope.Base (to search just the root object itself) or SearchScope.Subtree (to search all the objects below the root). As our function is scalar, we want to find only one matching result, so we call its FindOne method:

```
searcher.SearchScope = SearchScope.OneLevel;
SearchResult result = searcher.FindOne();
```

This method returns an object of type SearchResult. If an object with the specified e-mail address wasn't found, the SearchResult object will be null, and we'll return null from our function:

```
if (result == null)
    return null;
```

Otherwise, we'll need to access the proxyAddresses property of the SearchResult to get the list of proxy e-mail addresses. The Properties collection of the SearchResult has an indexer that takes the name of the property. Each property of an Active Directory object can have multiple values, so when we access an item in the Properties collection of a SearchResult object, we get not a single value, but a ResultPropertyValueCollection. We iterate through all the property values in this collection and add each one to a StringBuilder. We add a comma as a separator after every value except the last one (we use a comma rather than a semicolon because Exchange e-mail address contain semicolons). When we've finished iterating through the property values, we return the contents of our StringBuilder as a string:

```
else
{
    ResultPropertyValueCollection propvals =
                                    result.Properties["proxyAddresses"];
    StringBuilder sb = new StringBuilder();
    for (int i = 0; i < propvals.Count; i++)
    {
        sb.Append(propvals[i]);
        if (i < propvals.Count - 1)
            sb.Append(",");
    }
    return sb.ToString();
}
        }
    }
}
```

Then we compile this file into a DLL. On our system the command is

```
csc /t:library SimpleUdf.cs
```

So far, so good. Unfortunately, however, we hit a slight snag when we want to use this function as a CLR UDF. As we'll see in Chapter 10, CLR assemblies run in a partially trusted context, and the System.DirectoryServices assembly in the GAC doesn't allow partially trusted callers. To get around this, we need to install System.DirectoryServices into the database. This means that SQL Server will create a private copy of this assembly, instead of attempting to use the version in the GAC. However, this assembly requires the UNSAFE permission set, so we'll need to install this with a user that has UNSAFE ASSEMBLY permission, and we'll also need to alter the database so that it has the TRUSTWORTHY property set to ON (we'll look at the reason for this in Chapter 10):

```
ALTER DATABASE AdventureWorks
SET TRUSTWORTHY ON;
```

Once this is done, we can deploy the System.DirectoryServices assembly to the AdventureWorks database:

```
CREATE ASSEMBLY [System.DirectoryServices]
FROM 'C:\WINDOWS\Microsoft.NET\Framework\v2.0.50727\System.DirectoryServices.dll'
WITH PERMISSION_SET = UNSAFE;
```

The assembly needs to be given the unsafe permission set because System.DirectoryServices is essentially a wrapper over unmanaged APIs, and so it isn't verifiably type-safe (no code that directly calls unmanaged code is verifiable).

Now we install the assembly into SQL Server:

```
CREATE ASSEMBLY SimpleUdf
FROM 'C:\Apress\SqlAssemblies\Chapter05\SimpleUdf\SimpleUdf.dll'
WITH PERMISSION_SET = UNSAFE;
GO
```

SQL Server will check for dependencies and also install the System.DirectoryServices assembly when this statement is executed. Again, we need to specify the PERMISSION_SET as UNSAFE, because this permission set is required to access the System.DirectoryServices assembly. This does mean that we can't access directory services in this way if we're not prepared to give the assembly the unsafe permission set. However, this is still safer than an unmanaged stored procedure written in C++, as .NET's memory management mechanism makes memory leaks far less likely in .NET code.

The CREATE FUNCTION statement for our example UDF looks like this:

```
CREATE FUNCTION GetProxyAddresses(@email nvarchar(255))
RETURNS nvarchar(1000)
AS
EXTERNAL NAME
    SimpleUdf.[Apress.SqlAssemblies.Chapter05.SimpleUdf].GetProxyAddresses;
GO
```

The list of proxy e-mail addresses could be quite long, so we've allowed up to 1,000 characters in the return value.

To test the function, execute the following statement from Query Analyzer:

```
SELECT id, name, email, dbo.GetProxyAddresses(email) AS [Proxy Addresses]
FROM employees;
```

All being well, you should see a resultset similar to that shown in Figure 5-1.

	id	name	email	Proxy Addresses
1	1	Julian Skinner	Julian@JulianSkinner.com	smtp:webmaster@julianskinner.com,smtp:contact@julianskinner.com,smtp:Julian...
2	2	Administrator	Administrator@JulianSkinner.com	smtp:Administrator@JulianSkinner.local,SMTP:Administrator@julianskinner.com,s...
3	3	Webmaster	webmaster@JulianSkinner.com	NULL

Figure 5-1. *Results of the GetProxyAddresses function*

Note that the Proxy Addresses column for the last row is NULL, because that e-mail address doesn't exist in this machine's Active Directory.

Table-Valued UDFs

Table-valued CLR UDFs are used in a similar fashion to T-SQL table-valued functions. They are powerful alternatives to views, allowing you to read from a resultset of data that you can create with complex processing. One difference from T-SQL table-valued UDFs is that the table returned from CLR functions can't contain PRIMARY KEY, UNIQUE, or CHECK constraints. In general, we don't think these restrictions will be too burdensome. If you need to ensure that values for a column in the returned table fall within a certain range, that can easily be achieved by checks in your .NET code. You can simply compare the value to the permitted range when you load the value from the data source, and if it doesn't match, throw an exception. Unique constraints would take only slightly more work: you'd need to keep an ArrayList of the values already loaded into the column and call its Contains method every time you load a new value. You could then throw an exception if the value already exists in the ArrayList.

Writing a table-valued UDF in .NET is slightly more complicated than writing a scalar-valued one (but much less complicated now than it was in the earlier betas). The .NET method that implements the UDF needs to return an implementation of the IEnumerable interface, and its SqlFunction attribute needs to have a FillRowMethodName property that indicates which method should be called to populate each individual row in the returned resultset. When the UDF method is called, you create a new instance of an IEnumerable implementation, such as an ArrayList or a Collection object, and populate this with one object for every row in the returned table. The most obvious way to do this is to define a struct with one field for each column in the resultset.

You also need to implement the method that is referred to in the FillRowMethodName property. This method will take one input parameter of type object, which SQL Server will use to pass in the object representing the row, and one output parameter (of the appropriate SQL native type) for each column in the returned resultset. The method needs to extract the individual columns from the input object and populate the output parameters with this data.

Table-Valued UDF Example

To see how this works in practice, let's look at an example. We'll use a similar example to the scalar-valued UDF, but this time, instead of returning a single value, we'll return a resultset containing all the fields from our employees table, as well as the list of proxy e-mail addresses, the ADsPath (LDAP address), and the globally unique identifier (GUID) of the Active Directory user object, and the value (if any) of its userPrincipalName property. This last property may not have a value for some users, in which case we'll need to return null.

The C# code is in a file called TableUdfExample.cs, and as usual it starts with the using directives:

```
using System;
using System.Collections;
using System.Data;
using System.Data.SqlClient;
using System.Data.SqlTypes;
using System.DirectoryServices;
using System.Text;
using Microsoft.SqlServer.Server;
```

As well as the standard System namespace and the Microsoft.SqlServer.Server namespace where many of the classes and interfaces involved with writing CLR assemblies live, we also have System.Data.SqlClient, because our function accesses SQL Server data using the in-process provider, and System.Data.SqlTypes, because we will return the data to SQL Server in the appropriate native SQL type. The ArrayList class that we use to store the data and the IEnumerable interface it implements reside in the System.Collections namespace, so we need to import this, too. Finally, we also need System.DirectoryServices for Active Directory access and System.Text for the StringBuilder, as in the previous example.

All the code for this example is contained within a class called TableUdfExample. Within this class, we start by defining the TableRow nested struct that will hold the data for a single row of our resultset. This struct has one public field for each column in the resultset and one public constructor that simply populates these fields with the data passed in as input parameters:

```
namespace Apress.SqlAssemblies.Chapter05
{
    public class TableUdfExample
    {
        public struct TableRow
        {
            public int Id;
            public string Name;
            public string Email;
            public string ProxyAddresses;
            public string ADsPath;
            public string UserName;
            public SqlGuid Guid;

            public TableRow(int id, string name, string email, string proxyAddresses,
                        string adsPath, string userName, SqlGuid guid)
```

```
        {
            Id = id;
            Name = name;
            Email = email;
            ProxyAddresses = proxyAddresses;
            ADsPath = adsPath;
            UserName = userName;
            Guid = guid;
        }
    }
```

Notice that we use the native SQL type for the GUID. This is because System.Guid is a value type and therefore can't be null; however, this value could be unknown for a particular row in the resultset, in which case we'll need the value to be null in a database rather than a .NET sense. The SqlGuid type has a special field to allow this, so we'll convert all the GUIDs to this type immediately, rather than waiting until we return the data to SQL Server.

Next comes the method that actually implements the UDF. Here we'll query the employees table and iterate through the returned SqlDataReader. For each row, we'll query Active Directory to find a user object with the e-mail address of the current row and add a new row to the DataTable to store both the SQL Server and Active Directory data. This method has a SqlFunction attribute with the DataAccess property set to DataAccessKind.Read, as we need to query the AdventureWorks database and its FillRowMethodName property set to point to the GetRowData method, which will extract the individual column data from a TableRow object.

First, though, we initialize the ArrayList and get a reference to the Users container object that will be the root for our Active Directory search:

```
[SqlFunction(DataAccess=DataAccessKind.Read, FillRowMethodName="GetRowData")]
public static IEnumerable ReadDirectoryData()
{
    ArrayList entries = new ArrayList();

    DirectoryEntry root = new DirectoryEntry(
            "LDAP://daufiltri.julianskinner.local/" +
            "CN=Users,DC=JulianSkinner,DC=local");
    if (root == null)
        throw new NullReferenceException(
                "The directory service cannot be referenced.");
```

Now we can retrieve the data from the employees table into a SqlDataReader:

```
    using (SqlConnection cn = new SqlConnection("context connection=true"))
    {
        string sql = "SELECT id, name, email FROM employees";
        cn.Open();
        SqlCommand cmd = new SqlCommand(sql, cn);
        SqlDataReader reader = cmd.ExecuteReader();
```

For each row, we need to look up the e-mail address in Active Directory. The code for performing the search is identical to that in the scalar example:

```
while (reader.Read())
{
    string email = (string)reader[2];
    DirectorySearcher searcher = new DirectorySearcher(
        root, "(&(objectClass=user)(mail=" + email + "))");
    searcher.SearchScope = SearchScope.OneLevel;
    SearchResult result = searcher.FindOne();
```

If no match was found, we create a new TableRow object containing the data we got from the employees table, but with null values for the Active Directory columns:

```
TableRow row;
if (result == null)
{
    row = new TableRow((int)reader[0], (string)reader[1], email, null,
                       null, null, SqlGuid.Null);
}
```

Notice that we use the static SqlGuid.Null field to get a SqlGuid object that has a null value. Because it's a value type, we can't just pass null in here. The SqlGuid.Null static field returns a new instance of SqlGuid that allows us to insert a null value into a uniqueidentifier column in SQL Server.

If a match was found, we get the data we want from Active Directory. Each object in a directory service is represented in .NET code by a DirectoryEntry object, and we can get the DirectoryEntry object that represents our user from the SearchResult by calling its GetDirectoryEntry method. From this, we can build up the list of proxy e-mail addresses in almost exactly the same way as in the previous example. The only difference is that, because we're accessing the properties through the DirectoryEntry object rather than through the SearchResult, we get a PropertyValueCollection instead of a ResultPropertyValueCollection. However, we can iterate through the two objects in exactly the same way, so the code is otherwise identical:

```
else
{
    DirectoryEntry de = result.GetDirectoryEntry();
    PropertyValueCollection proxyAddresses =
                                de.Properties["proxyAddresses"];
    StringBuilder sb = new StringBuilder();
    for (int i = 0; i < proxyAddresses.Count; i++)
    {
        sb.Append(proxyAddresses[i]);
        if (i < proxyAddresses.Count - 1)
            sb.Append(",");
    }
}
```

Next, we check whether the userPrincipalName property of this object has any values. As with the proxyAddresses property, when we access the userPrincipalName property, we get not a single value, but a `PropertyValueCollection`. If the `Count` property of this is one or more, we can get the first value by calling the collection's `Value` property. This returns an object, so we need to call its `ToString` method before adding it to the `DataTable`. If it has no values, we'll add null to the `TableRow` object instead, so we use the ternary operator to store either the correct value or `null` in the `userName` local variable. Finally, we can get the ADsPath directly from the `SearchResult` through its `Path` property, and we can get the object's GUID from the `DirectoryEntry.Guid` property and use this to create a new `SqlGuid` instance. Once we've gathered all these values, we can create a new `TableRow` object:

```
PropertyValueCollection userNameVals = de.Properties
                                     ["userPrincipalName"];
string userName = userNameVals.Count > 0 ?
                      userNameVals.Value.ToString() : null;
row = new TableRow((int)reader[0], (string)reader[1], email,
        sb.ToString(), result.Path, userName, new SqlGuid(de.Guid));
}
```

Now we can add the new `TableRow` object to the entries `ArrayList`:

```
entries.Add(row);
}
```

When we've finished iterating through the `SqlDataReader`, we just need to close it and the connection, and return the entries `ArrayList` from the method. That completes the code for the `ReadDirectoryData` method.

```
    reader.Close();
    cn.Close();
}
return entries;
}
```

Next comes the `GetRowData` method that we pointed to in the `SqlFunction` attribute's `FillRowMethodName` property. SQL Server calls this method to extract the individual fields from one of the objects in the `IEnumerable` implementation that was returned from the method that implements the UDF (in our case, this is the entries `ArrayList`). It takes as an input parameter one entry from this `IEnumerable` implementation, and we need to extract from this the individual column data and return it as output parameters. To do this, we simply cast the input object to our `TableRow` type, and then read the public fields of this object into the output parameters, converting to the appropriate SQL types (of course, we don't need to convert the GUID to a SQL type, as we did this earlier):

```
public static void GetRowData(object o, out SqlInt32 id, out SqlChars name,
    out SqlChars email, out SqlChars proxyAddresses, out SqlChars adsPath,
    out SqlChars userName, out SqlGuid guid)
{
    TableRow row = (TableRow)o;
    id = new SqlInt32(row.Id);
    name = new SqlChars(row.Name);
    email = new SqlChars(row.Email);
```

```
            proxyAddresses = new SqlChars(row.ProxyAddresses);
            adsPath = new SqlChars(row.ADsPath);
            userName = new SqlChars(row.UserName);
            guid = row.Guid;
        }
    }
}
```

We compile the `TableUdfExample.cs` file as usual into a DLL:

```
csc /t:library TableUdfExample.cs
```

To install the function into SQL Server, you'll again need to make sure that the database contains a private copy of the `System.DirectoryServices` assembly. Assuming that you've already run the previous example, and you're installing both functions into the same database, there won't be a problem. Otherwise, you'll need to install the `System.DirectoryServices` assembly into the same database as the `TableUdfExample` assembly, in the same way that you did for the scalar example.

The SQL command to create the assembly should be familiar to you by now:

```
CREATE ASSEMBLY TableUdfExample
FROM 'C:\Apress\SqlAssemblies\Chapter05\TableUdfExample\TableUdfExample.dll'
WITH PERMISSION_SET = UNSAFE;
GO
```

Again, the assembly has to be declared with `PERMISSION_SET = UNSAFE`, because the classes in the `System.DirectoryServices` namespace perform unsafe operations.

The `CREATE FUNCTION` statement is similar to the previous example, but because this is a table-valued function, we need to include the table definition in the `RETURNS` clause:

```
CREATE FUNCTION ReadDirectoryData()
RETURNS TABLE (
    id int,
    name nvarchar(255),
    email nvarchar(255),
    [proxy addresses] nvarchar(1000),
    adspath nvarchar(1000),
    principalName nvarchar(255),
    guid uniqueidentifier)
AS EXTERNAL NAME
 TableUdfExample.[Apress.SqlAssemblies.Chapter05.TableUdfExample].ReadDirectoryData;
GO
```

Once this statement has executed, we can use the function as we would a view, for example:

```
SELECT id, name, [proxy addresses], adspath, guid FROM ReadDirectoryData()
WHERE guid IS NOT NULL;
```

This returns the sample results shown in Figure 5-2.

	id	name	proxy addresses	adspath	guid
1	1	Julian Skinner	smtp:webmaster@julianskin...	LDAP://daufiltri.julianskinner.local/CN=Julian Ski...	0203FE45-1BCD-4028-A53A-2D12E3C09D16
2	2	Administrator	smtp:Administrator@JulianS...	LDAP://daufiltri.julianskinner.local/CN=Administr...	F64505F9-60D8-4F78-A897-E863C808B803

Figure 5-2. *Results of the ReadDirectoryData function*

Listing the Contents of a Folder

In the previous example, we demonstrated the typical approach that you'll take to creating table-valued CLR UDFs: defining a struct to hold each row of data in the returned table. However, in some cases it's even easier—sometimes each row will be represented by a type that already exists within the Framework Class Library (FCL).

To demonstrate this, we'll write a table-valued UDF that returns a listing of the contents of a folder in the file system. The function returns a table containing a row for each file or subfolder in the specified folder, with columns for the name of the entry, the type (whether it's a file or folder), the file extension (if appropriate), and the time the entry was created and last accessed. Each file or folder is represented by a FileSystemInfo object, so we don't need to define a struct of our own to represent a row of data. This function can be useful when you need to process all the files of a particular type in a certain directory—for example, if you need to load a number of images into a database.

The C# source code for this example is contained in a file called DirectoryReader.cs. As ever, we begin with the using directives:

```
using System;
using System.Collections;
using System.IO;
using System.Data.SqlTypes;
using Microsoft.SqlServer.Server;
```

Notice that we import the System.IO namespace, which is where the classes that we need to browse the file system live. We also need to import System.Collections for the IEnumerable interface.

The method that implements the function is in a class named DirectoryBrowserExample. This method, called BrowseDirectory, takes a single string parameter—the path of the directory to examine—and has the SqlFunction attribute set to tell SQL Server that the method that extracts the data for the individual columns is called GetFolderInfo. Within the BrowseDirectory method, we simply get a reference to the DirectoryInfo object.

.NET provides two classes, DirectoryInfo and FileInfo, which encapsulate information respectively about folders and files in the file system. These classes supply the information that we'll be returning from the function, such as the time the item was created and when it was last accessed. Both of these classes derive from the FileSystemInfo abstract class, which provides most of the functionality we need, so each row in our returned resultset will be represented by an instance of this class. Therefore, within the BrowseDirectory method, we start by instantiating a DirectoryInfo object for the folder, and then call its GetFileSystemInfos method. This returns an array of FileSystemInfo objects representing each file and subfolder within the directory. As the standard `Array` class implements `IEnumerable`, we can just return this from the method:

```
namespace Apress.SqlAssemblies.Chapter05
{
    public class DirectoryBrowserExample
    {
        [SqlFunction(FillRowMethodName="GetFolderInfo")]
        public static IEnumerable BrowseDirectory(string directoryName)
        {
            DirectoryInfo dir = new DirectoryInfo(directoryName);
            return dir.GetFileSystemInfos();
        }
```

The `GetFolderInfo` method that we point to in the `SqlFunction` attribute just needs to extract the relevant data from the `FileSystemInfo` object and return it as output parameters. To do this, we cast the `object` input parameter that SQL Server passes into the method to the `FileSystemInfo` type, and then get the data from its properties, converting it to the appropriate SQL native types. The only bits of logic we have to perform are for the `Type` and `Extension` columns, where the values will depend on whether the item is a file or a folder. In the case of the `Type` column, we use the ternary operator to check whether this particular `FileSystemInfo` object is a `DirectoryInfo` object or not. If it is, we set the column to the literal value `"FOLDER"`; if not, we set it to the value `"FILE"`.

We can get the extension of a file from the `Extension` property of the `FileSystemInfo` class (without even having to cast to `FileInfo`), but if it's a folder, we want to set the value to null. To do this, we again use the ternary operator, this time checking whether or not the `FileSystemInfo` is of type `FileInfo`. If it is, we access its `Extension` property; if it isn't, we set the extension output parameter to `SqlChars.Null`, because, even though `string` is a reference type, its behavior isn't typical and we can't set a string variable to null.

```
        public static void GetFolderInfo(object o, out SqlChars name,
            out SqlChars type, out SqlChars extension, out SqlDateTime timeCreated,
            out SqlDateTime timeAccessed)
        {
            FileSystemInfo fileInfo = (FileSystemInfo)o;
            name = new SqlChars(fileInfo.Name);
            type = fileInfo is DirectoryInfo ? new SqlChars("FOLDER") :
                                               new SqlChars("FILE");
            extension = fileInfo is FileInfo ? new SqlChars(fileInfo.Extension) :
                                               SqlChars.Null;
            timeCreated = new SqlDateTime(fileInfo.CreationTime);
            timeAccessed = new SqlDateTime(fileInfo.LastWriteTime);
        }
    }
}
```

And that's it! The whole example runs to barely a couple of dozen lines of code. Compile the code as usual into a DLL:

```
csc /t:library DirectoryReader.cs
```

The CREATE ASSEMBLY statement should be very familiar by now. The only point to note is that we need to give the assembly EXTERNAL_ACCESS permissions, because it accesses external file system resources:

```
CREATE ASSEMBLY DirectoryReader
FROM 'C:\Apress\SqlAssemblies\Chapter05\DirectoryReader\DirectoryReader.dll'
WITH PERMISSION_SET = EXTERNAL_ACCESS;
GO
```

Finally, create the function in SQL Server:

```
CREATE FUNCTION BrowseDirectory(@dirpath nvarchar(1000))
RETURNS TABLE (
    Name nvarchar(256),
    Type nvarchar(6),
    Extension nvarchar(10),
    [Time Created] datetime,
    [Time Accessed] datetime
)
AS EXTERNAL NAME DirectoryReader.[Apress.SqlAssemblies.Chapter05.
DirectoryBrowserExample].BrowseDirectory;
GO
```

To test the function, execute the following SELECT statement, which retrieves all the subfolders from the code directory for this chapter:

```
SELECT * FROM BrowseDirectory('C:\Apress\SqlAssemblies\Chapter05')
WHERE Type = 'FOLDER';
```

You should see something similar to Figure 5-3.

	Name	Type	Extension	Time Created	Time Accessed
1	DirectoryReader	FOLDER	NULL	2005-09-26 12:33:17.500	2005-09-26 13:00:12.253
2	images	FOLDER	NULL	2004-10-24 22:40:20.980	2005-03-13 17:36:57.840
3	SimpleUdf	FOLDER	NULL	2005-09-23 14:09:15.090	2005-09-23 19:52:49.280
4	TableUdfExample	FOLDER	NULL	2005-09-23 20:08:40.820	2005-09-26 11:18:41.597

Figure 5-3. *Results of the BrowseDirectory function*

Summary

The ability to write user-defined functions in .NET is a very powerful addition to the database developer's armory. Even more so than stored procedures, CLR functions allow us to take data from outside SQL Server and integrate it completely with SQL data—for example, incorporating the function as a subquery into a larger query.

UDFs come in two distinct flavors, scalar-valued and table-valued functions, and in this chapter we looked at examples of both types. Our first two examples demonstrated how we can merge data from an Active Directory installation with data from inside SQL Server. While there could sometimes be performance issues with this approach, as accessing Active Directory is a relatively resource-expensive operation, it does guard against the danger of replicating data, with all the risks of loss of data integrity entailed in that. While it is theoretically possible to access a directory service without writing a CLR assembly, by creating a linked server using the ADsDSOObject OLE DB provider, this has a very serious limitation in that it can't retrieve the values from multivalued properties. You would also need to use .NET instead of ADsDSOObject if you wanted to write a stored procedure or trigger that updated Active Directory.

Our final example illustrated how you can use a CLR assembly to access details of the file system from within SQL Server. This is clearly something that you'd want to restrict access to very carefully, but it could prove useful for DBAs who have to work with files such as images that are linked to a database.

In the next chapter, we'll examine how to use SQL assemblies to create entirely new types that we can use to store data in SQL Server.

CHAPTER 6

■ ■ ■

User-Defined Types

User-defined types (UDTs) have existed in SQL Server for several years, albeit in a "restricted" state. UDTs prior to SQL Server 2005 had always to be a derivative of a base SQL Server data type. So, for example, if you wanted a UDT to cover for every columnar instance of an alphanumeric order identifier, you would define the UDT as a derivative of varchar. This would allow you to use the same data type in many different tables that required order identifiers, thereby helping to ensure data consistency. Unfortunately, these UDTs have their limitations. It is impossible to modify the type once it has been used in a table, so if the order identifier needs to be lengthened, it could be quite an ordeal to fix it.

Now with SQL Server 2005, you can create UDTs based on .NET assemblies. This means that you are no longer restricted to the base (single, scalar) SQL Server data types such as varchar, int, and so on. In fact, it is now possible to create complex types that can expose their own properties, methods, and operators. This is known as an *extensible type system*.

This chapter will demonstrate how to create and use CLR-based UDTs and investigate the specific interfaces that must be implemented. Specifically, this chapter covers the following topics:

- Understanding the differences between traditional UDTs and CLR-based UDTs

- Creating CLR UDTs

- Using CLR UDTs

Traditional vs. CLR UDTs

SQL Server supports many scalar data types, such as varchar, integer, and datetime, but it's often useful to create a set of custom types to enforce a degree of consistency and standardization in your code. The classic examples include custom types for such applications as addresses, tax codes, or ZIP codes. Once defined, these user data types can be used in multiples tables and procedures in your database. By using these types for development, you'll know that, for instance, every address in the system will use the same data types for its street, city, and postal code attributes. You won't have to worry that the definition for the column differs in various areas. For example, you can create a UDT called zipcode as follows:

```
CREATE TYPE [dbo].[zipcode] FROM [char](5) NULL
```

Then, wherever you need to use a ZIP code, you can use the `zipcode` UDT in place of the base data type definition (`char(5) NOT NULL`), and you don't have to worry about making it consistent with other columns in other tables that also store ZIP codes. For example, one developer may use `char(5)`, but a different developer may have used `char(7)` or `varchar(7)`. This sort of type mismatch can create consistency problems. However, you're restricted in this case to SQL Server data types as the basis of your UDT.

In SQL Server 2005, you can create CLR-based UDTs in addition to these T-SQL–based UDTs. This gives you greater flexibility in two different areas. First, you can write a .NET class or structure that can then be registered to act as a scalar type within the SQL Server type system. Like other types in .NET, your SQL Server UDTs can expose properties and methods. These methods will be available from your database code.

Second, your data types no longer have to be consistent with a base SQL Server data type; instead, they can be based on a mixture of data types. For example, a CLR UDT could be built for a grid that holds the definition of a chessboard. One property exposed by this type would be the position on the grid and another would be the character occupying that position. Furthermore, logic can be embedded in the type, since it is programmed in a .NET language. For instance, a rook can move either vertically or horizontally, but it can't move in both directions simultaneously. We could program this data type to obey the rules of chess when updates are made to the positions of the grid. This type of logic can't be embedded in T-SQL user-defined data types.

So now that you understand the basic differences between a traditional UDT and a CLR UDT, let's take a look at how to create a CLR-based UDT.

■**Caution** CLR UDTs are limited to 8KB in size. They should not be used for storing large sets of data.

Creating CLR-Based UDTs

As with all the CLR-based objects we've discussed thus far, creating a UDT follows the same basic pattern:

1. Write the .NET code for the assembly.

2. Compile the .NET code.

3. Create and register the assembly as a database object within SQL Server.

4. Create the UDT based on your assembly.

Once you've created your assembly in step 3, creating a UDT based on that assembly is very straightforward. The syntax is simply as follows:

```
CREATE TYPE [ schema_name. ] type_name
EXTERNAL NAME assembly_name [ .class_name ]
```

After building CLR stored procedures, you should already feel comfortable with the syntax for defining a CLR data type to SQL Server, so we'll just cover a few areas.

When creating a CLR type, you can prefix the type name with a schema name such as dbo. You then define the assembly name that matches the name used in the CREATE ASSEMBLY statement followed by an optional class_name parameter. UDTs are implemented as classes rather than methods. Therefore, unlike CLR stored procedures, which have a third parameter for the name of the method to execute, data types require only a class name.

Before you get to step 3 of creating UDTs, you need to write your .NET assembly, and this is actually a little more complex than anything you've seen so far. This is because, in order for a CLR-based UDT to be used as if it is a base data type in the SQL type system, it must implement a defined set of interfaces and methods. There are also some optional methods that your CLR UDT can implement. We'll cover the required and optional implementations in turn.

Required Implementations

A CLR UDT is really nothing more than a .NET type that's been registered for use in SQL Server. However, that doesn't mean that you can use any .NET type as a UDT; there are significant restrictions and requirements that UDTs must conform to.

UDTs must implement the INullable interface and must expose a number of public methods that aren't defined in any formal .NET interface. We'll go through these in a moment, but there are also a couple of class attributes that you must apply when defining your UDT. These attributes define the behavior of your type with regard to how data is held and passed to and from SQL Server.

Attributes

There are two required attributes for a CLR UDT: Serializable and SqlUserDefinedType.

Serializable

This is a class attribute that defines that the class data can be stored in a serial storage format. When SQL Server reads and writes instances of a UDT, it does so in a binary serialized format. The type, therefore, must be able to produce a serialized version of itself. Serialization can be done automatically (this is called *native* serialization), or it can be user-defined (this is called, not surprisingly, *user-defined* serialization).

SqlUserDefinedType

The SqlUserDefinedType attribute of the UDT allows you to define several properties of the CLR UDT that govern, for example, how it is serialized, its maximum size, and how it should be sorted when used in comparisons and ORDER BY clauses. The following sections examine each of these properties in turn.

Format
The Format property determines the types of serialization that is used.

- `Native`: This method of serialization is used when all the data types can be serialized automatically by SQL Server. This is possible if your type only makes use of .NET value types. If your UDT makes use of any reference types, such as arrays or other classes, it can't be natively serialized and you'll receive a compilation error. If you're creating a UDT that is number-based only, for example, then you can set `Format=Native` and let the serialization be taken care of for you. This is a less complex method to implement, as there is no extra serialization code to write, but it's also quite limiting.

- `UserDefined`: When the UDT requires the use of reference types such as strings, then you have to take care of the serialization yourself. If this is the serialization method you have to use, then you must implement the `IBinarySerialize` interface on your class, which adds two functions: `Read` and `Write`. These two functions are where you write out the values for your UDT and read them back in. The order you read in the values will be the same order that they were written out to the stream. For example, if you have a UDT that has a string and a numeric value, then both of these properties of the UDT will have to be written out to the stream and read back in the same order when you deserialize the UDT. This method of serialization can be just as fast as `Native`, providing that code for the streaming of the values is all that is contained within the `Read` and `Write` functions and there is no other processing involved.

■**Note** In other CLR objects, you will also write out values in variables using `Native` or `UserDefined` serialization.

IsByteOrdered
SQL Server often needs to compare two values from a perspective of greater-than or less-than. For instance, this kind of comparison is done internally when indexing a column or ordering a resultset by a column. To allow these kinds of comparisons for CLR UDTs, you need to set `IsByteOrdered = true`. This tells SQL Server that it can order instances of the UDT based on their binary serialized values. If this type is not set to `true`, it can't be used in indexes or for ordering. However, keep in mind that this type should be set to `true` only if the serialized binary can be sorted. If it does not make sense to sort instances of this type based on the binary representation, set this type to `false`.

IsFixedLength
This is a Boolean value where a value of `true` indicates that every serialized instance of the UDT is of the same fixed length.

MaxByteSize
This type sets the maximum size of the UDT in a similar fashion to the way you define the maximum size of a `varchar` and column. The UDT size limit is 8,000 bytes. This option is not required if the serialization is `Native`, but the limit does still apply.

Name

This property allows the Visual Studio 2005 deployment task to use a different name for the type than the name of the class or structure that defines it.

INullable Interface

When defining CLR UDTs, you must implement the INullable interface. The INullable interface only has one member property: IsNull. This property is defined as a boolean return setting informing the caller as to whether or not the UDT's value is NULL. Within your code, you need to store a local variable that defines whether or not the current value of the UDT is NULL. You can then pass this variable via the IsNull property interface. When you call IS NULL from T-SQL, IsNull is called on the instance of the type.

It's important to remember that a SQL Server NULL isn't the same as a .NET null. If an instance of a type is NULL in SQL Server, it may or may not be null from a .NET point of view; that is, a valid instance of the type may or may not exist. SQL Server handles this automatically via the IS NULL property, so developers should remember that a direct call to the IsNull method from T-SQL won't necessarily deliver accurate results. If an instance of the type doesn't exist, the method will not be available and will cause an exception.

Methods

The three methods discussed in the sections that follow must be implemented by a CLR UDT.

ToString

All .NET types inherit from the base type, System.Object, which includes a virtual method called ToString. .NET types may or may not override this method, but it's vital to properly override it when defining CLR UDTs. A UDT needs to have the ability to convert its value to and from a string. To facilitate this action, types must have two publicly defined methods: ToString and Parse. Within the ToString method, you need to implement code to convert the value of the UDT into a string. This might mean concatenating strings, but likely it will also require changing any nonstring data type, such as integer, long, datetime, to a string and concatenating the results after that. You may also have to include formatting of the string so that the data is displayed in the correct format.

■**Note** ToString is an output method. In other words, it can be used when retrieving information from the UDT type into a query.

When implementing ToString and Parse in order to pass strings to and from the UDT, the formatting passed out should exactly match the incoming format. That is, any value output by the ToString method should be able to be reused by Parse to create an instance of the UDT.

■**Note** You also have to take into account whether a value is null when returning a string value. Therefore, if your UDT value is NULL, then return a string that defines it as such.

Parse

The second requirement for string conversion is the Parse method. This is a static method that is invoked when values are assigned to an instance of the type.

When a string value is assigned to the UDT, Parse is called behind the scenes. This method should populate each property of the UDT as necessary from the input string and return the instance of the populated UDT. See the section "Understanding the UDT Life Cycle" for more information on when Parse and related methods get called.

Null

The final required property is Null. This property does nothing more than return a NULL instance of the UDT; in this case, that means an instance of the UDT where IsNull returns true. The default implementation of this property, as shown in the previous template, will generally suffice. The property creates a new instance of the UDT and sets the m_IsNull variable to true, and then it returns the instance.

This property is used extensively by SQL Server when dealing with UDTs. For instance, the NULL value returned by this type will be used as a default value when creating nullable columns of the type. For this reason, it's important to make sure that Null always returns a consistent value. Every NULL instance of your type should be equivalent such that it can be efficiently used in comparisons.

Optional Method Attributes

In addition to public properties, UDTs can also expose methods. These methods can be thought of in the same way as UDFs—an optional attribute can be used for controlling the method's behavior. The syntax for this attribute is

```
[SqlMethodAttribute(attribute = value)]
```

Here are the method attributes that can be attached:

- IsDeterministic: A setting of true defines the method as deterministic; false indicates that it isn't deterministic. This is useful when building an index on a UDT, as you will find out later in the book.

- OnNullCall: A setting of true (the default) means that the value out of the method will be evaluated even if the input is Null. However, a setting of false indicates the method will return a value of NULL if one of the input values is NULL.

- DataAccess: The method includes SQL SELECT statements (note that a UDT shouldn't modify data).

Understanding the UDT Life Cycle

When you work with UDTs, it's very important that you understand what methods are called at what point during the life cycle of the type. If you're familiar with the life cycle of a normal .NET type, you may be surprised to find out that there are some differences in the way SQL Server UDTs are handled.

The first thing to realize is that the constructor for a type will never be called directly from SQL Server. For instance, when a variable of a CLR UDT is declared, SQL Server internally sets a NULL reference to an instance of the type, but no actual object creation occurs.

To make the instance non-NULL, it's necessary to assign a string value to the type. *This is the only way to make a type non-NULL in SQL Server!* When a string value is assigned to the instance (e.g., a variable or a column), the Parse method is called internally. This method is what calls the constructor, creates the new object, and returns a valid instance of the type.

At this point, the instance of the type is immediately serialized and returned to SQL Server. Whenever SQL Server needs to access properties or methods of the type, the type is deserialized. If the internal state of the type has changed ("mutated"), the instance will be reserialized. You should keep this in mind when working with UDTs, in order to create the most efficient types possible. Serialization and deserialization of large types can become very expensive.

Building and Using Example UDTs

Once the UDT is built and has been loaded into SQL Server, it's available to be used within table definitions or variable declarations just as if it was a standard type with no length value attached, such as image, text, or datetime. UDTs differ from standard types, though, in that they expose more flexibility from a programmatic point of view, as they can have properties and methods that extend their functionality.

In this section, we'll build and use two example UDTs: one for duration and the other for e-mail addresses.

Creating a Duration UDT

In this section's first example, we're going to build a UDT called Duration. When working with SQL Server, you have two options for storing temporal data: DATETIME and SMALLDATETIME. Both of these types represent both dates and times, but what should you use when working only with times? In the .NET world, the answer to this is the TimeSpan class. By wrapping the TimeSpan class in a simple CLR UDT, you can bring its functionality into SQL Server.

This first example shows how wrapping .NET types in a CLR UDT can broaden your available options when working with SQL Server. Although this example is fairly simple, you can extend it with as many properties or methods as you need to gain the required functionality for a project. In addition, you can use it as a model for wrapping other functionality from the .NET Base Class Library (BCL).

Building the UDT

The first step when creating a UDT in Visual Studio 2005 is to start a project and add a new type to it. Doing so produces the following template code:

```
using System;
using System.Data;
using System.Data.SqlClient;
using System.Data.SqlTypes;
using Microsoft.SqlServer.Server;
```

```csharp
[Serializable]
[Microsoft.SqlServer.Server.SqlUserDefinedType(Format.Native)]
public struct Duration : INullable
{
    public override string ToString()
    {
        // Replace the following code with your code
        return "";
    }

    public bool IsNull
    {
        get
        {
            // Put your code here
            return m_Null;
        }
    }

    public static Duration Null
    {
        get
        {
            Duration h = new Duration();
            h.m_Null = true;
            return h;
        }
    }

    public static Duration Parse(SqlString s)
    {
        if (s.IsNull)
            return Null;
        Duration u = new Duration();
        // Put your code here
        return u;
    }

    // This is a place-holder method
    public string Method1()
    {
        //Insert method code here
        return "Hello";
    }

    // This is a place-holder static method
```

```
public static SqlString Method2()
{
    //Insert method code here
    return new SqlString("Hello");
}

// This is a place-holder field member
public int var1;
// Private member
private bool m_Null;
}
```

Notice that this type is implemented by default as a structure rather than a class. This is the recommended way to implement a UDT, as using a class requires that we also include an attribute called StructLayout, which influences the order of native serialization. This really does not buy us any functionality, so it's recommended to always implement UDTs as structures. Should you need to convert a pre-existing class into a UDT, keep in mind that you'll have to set the LayoutKind.Sequential option of the StructLayout attribute.

The structure is decorated with two attributes that control the behavior of the UDT. The first, Serializable, indicates that instances of the type can be serialized, or converted into a stream of binary or character data that can later be deserialized to reconstitute the object (e.g., in another application domain). For a class to be serializable, all its public data members must also be serializable.

■**Note** Not all data types are serializable; we cover how to work with nonserializable types in the second example (presented in the section "Creating an E-mail Address UDT").

The second attribute, SqlUserDefinedType, defines what type of serialization we will be performing. This is the only one of these attributes that is new and directly related to SQL Server. In this case, we'll have to change the attribute slightly, so that our type can be indexed:

```
[Microsoft.SqlServer.Server.SqlUserDefinedType(
    Format.Native,
    IsByteOrdered=true)]
```

The structure implements one .NET interface, INullable, which exposes the IsNull method. This template code implements nullability using the m_Null private member, which is tested in the IsNull method and set in the Null method. This is a robust default implementation that won't have to be changed in most cases.

The Duration type requires only a single private member variable aside from m_Null. This member variable will hold the number of milliseconds represented by the duration:

```
// number of milliseconds
private int milliseconds;
```

Now we need to start implementing the required public methods that all UDT types must implement. The first we'll look at is the Parse method. This method is called by SQL Server when we create a new Duration object by setting an instance of the UDT to a string value. This method will take its input string and call System.TimeSpan.Parse to create an instance of System.TimeSpan. From there, we can determine how many milliseconds are represented and populate the milliseconds member variable:

```
public static Duration Parse(SqlString s)
{
    if (s.IsNull)
        return Null;
    Duration u = new Duration();

    TimeSpan ts = TimeSpan.Parse((string)s);
    u.milliseconds = (int)ts.TotalMilliseconds;

    return u;
}
```

Notice that the default code to check for NULL input values hasn't been removed. Whenever you design UDTs, try to think of how to properly address the issue of NULL values. It's important to not forget about them; NULL is always an issue when working with databases, and UDTs are no exception.

As well as being able to parse a string to get a new Duration object, we have to be able to convert an instance of Duration into a string for output purposes. This is done in the ToString method. The default System.Object implementation of the ToString method simply returns the full name of the type, so we have to override this return value to provide a more meaningful value.

```
public override string ToString()
{
    //Convert to ts and return ToString()
    return TimeSpan.FromMilliseconds(this.milliseconds).ToString();
}
```

This method simply converts the milliseconds private member variable into a TimeSpan, and then returns the string representation. Keep in mind that we don't handle NULL-valued instances of the UDT in this method, for two reasons. First, ToString must return an instance of System.string and that type isn't nullable. Second, if our UDT has been declared but not initialized, the ToString method won't be called at all. It's extremely important when working with UDTs to always check IS NULL before attempting to call an instance-scoped method or property.

The Null property and IsNull method require no modifications. Their default implementation is fine for the purposes of this UDT.

The two placeholder methods can be removed. In their place, to demonstrate the extensibility potential of UDTs, we will create our own method that lets us add the duration from another instance to the duration of the instance on which the method is called (think of it as duration addition):

```
public Duration AddDuration(Duration other)
{
    if (other.IsNull)
        return Null;
    else
    {
        this.milliseconds += other.milliseconds;
        return this;
    }
}
```

This method simply adds the milliseconds value from the other instance of the type to that of the current instance.

Although this is a very simple example, it shows that types can be extended in virtually any way. The potential for this UDT alone is quite extensive. For instance, the TimeSpan class has many properties, each of which could be turned into properties of the Duration UDT if necessary for a project. For instance, if we wanted to be able to query based on hours, we could add the following property:

```
public SqlDouble TotalHours
{
    get
    {
        return TimeSpan.FromMilliseconds(this.milliseconds).TotalHours;
    }
}
```

Deploying the UDT

Once the code is created and the assembly is compiled in Visual Studio 2005, we'll switch to Query Analyzer so we can create and test out our UDT. First, we need to create the assembly that contains the UDT implementation, as usual. You can use any database; we're using the AssembliesTesting database here:

```
USE AssembliesTesting
go
CREATE ASSEMBLY TestUDT
FROM 'C:\Program Files\Microsoft SQL Server\Assemblies\TestUDT.dll'
WITH PERMISSION_SET = SAFE
GO
```

Next, we register the type for use within SQL Server using a CREATE TYPE statement. Here we specify the name of the type as it will be used in SQL Server and the EXTERNAL NAME (i.e., the name of the type that implements the UDT). This takes the following form:

```
AssemblyName.[FullyQualifiedTypeName]
```

The AssemblyName is the name of the SQL Server assembly where the UDT is defined, and the FullyQualifiedTypeName is the name of the .NET type that implements the UDT, including the namespace that it belongs to. In our case, since we have no namespace, the CREATE TYPE statement will look like this:

```
CREATE TYPE Duration
EXTERNAL NAME [TestUDT].[Duration]
GO
```

The next action is to create a table with one column containing values of our new UDT type, defined to allow NULL values:

```
CREATE TABLE Durations
(
  DurationId int,
  theDuration Duration NULL
)
GO
```

The theDuration column is defined as the Duration type using the name we supplied in the CREATE TYPE statement, just as we would define a column of a built-in type.

Now let's test our UDT. To start, we perform a quick, simple test for an empty table to ensure that there are no problems:

```
SELECT * FROM Durations
GO
```

If everything has been loaded properly, we get back an empty rowset. But that's not especially interesting, so let's create some test data:

```
--20 seconds
INSERT Durations VALUES (1, '00:00:20')

--15 hours, 30 minutes
INSERT Durations VALUES (2, '15:30')
```

Notice that the values inserted into the column of type Duration are just strings. Of course, they're properly formatted strings; an improperly formatted string passed into the Parse method will result in an exception. For information on the allowable input formats for this type, see the Visual Studio 2005 documentation on the .NET TimeSpan class.

Next, we'll perform a SELECT statement to display the rows in the table, the results of which are shown in Figure 6-1:

```
SELECT * FROM Durations
GO
```

	DurationId	theDuration
1	1	0x80124F8000
2	2	0x835370C000

Figure 6-1. *Results of the SELECT*

You may notice that those results don't look quite the same as what was inserted; as a matter of fact, the data is not quite human readable at all. What you're seeing is the binary serialized form of the UDT, which is what is returned when you select an instance of it. To get a string representation of the data that's human readable—and therefore what we want to see—we need to use the `ToString` method (see Figure 6-2 for the output):

```
SELECT DurationId, theDuration.ToString() AS theDuration
FROM Durations
GO
```

	durationid	theDuration
1	1	00:00:20
2	2	15:30:00

Figure 6-2. *Use ToString for human readability.*

As you can see, the syntax for calling a method on a column is the same as for calling a method on an object in C#: the column name, followed by a dot or period, and then the method name. After the method name, enclose in parentheses any parameter values to pass in, or empty parentheses if there are no parameters as in the preceding example.

Of course, we are also free to use this type in a variable. For instance, we might want to create two instances and use the `AddDuration` method:

```
DECLARE @Twenty_Hours Duration
SET @Twenty_Hours = '20:00'

DECLARE @Forty_Seconds Duration
SET @Forty_Seconds = '00:00:40'

SET @Twenty_Hours =
    @Twenty_Hours.AddDuration(@Forty_Seconds)
```

This code results in the @Twenty_Hours variable having a value equal to 20 hours and 40 minutes.

UDTs can be used in virtually all of the same places that built-in data types can be used, including in stored procedures, UDFs, views, tables, and dynamic SQL batches. In this way, they are a true extensibility mechanism for the database's type system.

Indexing the UDT

UDTs, like base data types, can be indexed. Indexing can occur at two levels for a UDT. It is possible to index the whole column or any individual property exposed by the UDT, if it is created as a computed column.

In the `Duration` example just created, we defined the UDT with the `IsByteOrdered` attribute set to `true`. This allows us to index the entire column. To create an index, we could use the following syntax:

```
CREATE CLUSTERED INDEX ix_Durations ON Durations (theDuration)
GO
```

An index of this type will be used only when we're referencing the whole column rather than an attribute for the column. Keep in mind that if we reference a property in a WHERE clause, this index can't be used to help efficiently satisfy the query. For instance, if we wanted to query for all durations greater than three hours, we might try the following query:

```
SELECT *
FROM Durations
WHERE theDuration.TotalHours > 3
```

Unfortunately, the index can't be used to help satisfy this query, because that property isn't known to the index. Instead, the query engine must deserialize the type for every row of the table and interrogate the property for that row. That's not especially efficient! To remedy this situation, the first step is to add this property as a computed column of the table:

```
ALTER TABLE Durations
ADD TotalHours AS (theDuration.TotalHours) PERSISTED
```

We can now use the following query, treating the property as a column:

```
SELECT *
FROM Durations
WHERE TotalHours > 3
```

However, we still need to create an index. Doing so will require a bit of code modification; we can index computed columns only if they're the result of deterministic functions. And although our property is deterministic, we haven't told the query optimizer as much. In order to inform the optimizer that our property is deterministic, we'll have to use the SqlMethod attribute mentioned earlier:

```
public SqlDouble TotalHours
{
    [SqlMethod(IsDeterministic=true)]
    get
    {
        return TimeSpan.FromMilliseconds(this.milliseconds).TotalHours;
    }
}
```

Once the attribute has been added, the assembly can be recompiled and redeployed. Since the UDT is in use in the database (it's a column of the Durations table), you'll need to drop the table before you can re-create the UDT. Keep this in mind, as it's one of the hurdles when working with UDTs.

When the type and table have both been re-created, we can finally create the index that can be used to help satisfy the query:

```
CREATE INDEX ix_hours ON Durations (TotalHours)
```

Now that we've covered building, using, and indexing a UDT, let's look at another UDT example to see some other possible applications.

Creating an E-mail Address UDT

One area where CLR UDTs really shine compared with T-SQL UDTs is in their ability to encapsulate logic. T-SQL UDTs in previous versions of SQL Server could be bound to rules for validation, but that feature is now deprecated. Luckily, we have the power of the .NET BCL at our disposal, and we can create a CLR UDT that includes any validation logic we need, in addition to adding our own methods and properties—all of which would be impossible with T-SQL UDTs.

When designing a system that collects e-mail addresses, a good first step is to ensure that those addresses are valid. While actually validating the address (via a return e-mail system) is beyond the scope of a UDT, validating the *format* of the address is certainly a good idea. Whenever we insert data into a database, we should make sure that the data is of the highest quality, and malformed e-mail addresses are not quality e-mail addresses.

The easiest and most efficient way to validate an e-mail address is to use a regular expression. *Regular expressions* (*regex*) are powerful and complex string matching tools that are common in many programming languages. Unfortunately, T-SQL doesn't include regular expression capabilities. However, the .NET BCL certainly does, and we can use these capabilities to form an e-mail address type that can automatically validate itself. So without further ado, let's jump into the code for the type!

Building the Type

As usual, the code starts with the `using` declarations:

```
using System;
using System.Data;
using System.Data.SqlClient;
using System.Data.SqlTypes;
using Microsoft.SqlServer.Server;
using System.Text.RegularExpressions;
```

To the default declarations, we've added `System.Text.RegularExpressions`. This namespace contains the regular expression classes that we need to perform the e-mail address validation.

Next, we need to define the structure for our type and work with the required attributes. In the case of this type, since we're dealing with strings—which are reference types—we will not be able to use native serialization. Instead, we set the user-defined option. That option requires that we also implement the `IBinarySerialize` interface:

```
[Serializable]
[Microsoft.SqlServer.Server.SqlUserDefinedType(
    Format.UserDefined,
    IsByteOrdered=true,
    MaxByteSize=256)]
public struct EMail : INullable, IBinarySerialize
{
```

We also might want to be able to index this type, so `IsByteOrdered` is set to `true`. A `MaxByteSize` is also set, since it is required for user-defined serialization.

This UDT will have three private member variables: one to determine nullability, one for the username portion of the e-mail address (the part before the @ symbol), and one for the domain address part of the e-mail address (the part after the @ symbol).

```
private string userName;
private string domainAddress;
private bool m_Null;
```

As before, the default Null method and IsNull properties will not need to be modified:

```
public bool IsNull
{
    get
    {
        // Put your code here
        return m_Null;
    }
}

public static EMail Null
{
    get
    {
        EMail h = new EMail();
        h.m_Null = true;
        return h;
    }
}
```

We can now move on to the most complex part of this UDT: the Parse method. This method must do a few different things. First, it must determine whether or not the input is NULL. If the input is NULL, the Parse method should do nothing more than return a NULL instance of the UDT. Once that has been taken care of, the method will invoke a regular expression in order to validate the input e-mail address. Should validation fail, an exception will be thrown and the type will not be returned. If everything checks out, another regular expression will be used to find the @ symbol, and the e-mail address will be split into its component parts—the username and domain address—in order to populate the private member variables. The code for the Parse method follows:

```
public static EMail Parse(SqlString s)
{
    if (s.IsNull)
        return Null;
    EMail u = new EMail();

    //Validate the e-mail address
    Regex r =
        new Regex(@"\w+([-+.]\w+)*@\w+([-.]\w+)*\.\w+([-.]\w+)*");
```

```
    if (!r.IsMatch((string)s, 0))
        throw new ApplicationException("Not a valid address.");

    //Find the @ symbol
    Regex r_at = new Regex("@");
    Match atSymb = r_at.Match((string)s);

    //Populate the username and address
    u.userName = ((string)s).Substring(0, atSymb.Index);
    u.domainAddress = ((string)s).Substring(atSymb.Index + 1);

    return u;
}
```

■Note Regular expressions are a complex but very worthwhile topic. If you find the expressions used in this code difficult to understand, consult a book on regular expressions, such as *Regular Expression Recipes for Windows Developers: A Problem-Solution Approach* by Nathan Good (Apress, 2005).

The ToString method, as opposed to the Parse method, is extremely simple. Since we already have the component parts for the address, all the method needs to do is concatenate them, adding back the @ symbol:

```
public override string ToString()
{
    return userName + "@" + domainAddress;
}
```

Next, we can add a couple of public properties to our type: one property for the user name and one for the domain address. Both of these properties will be accessors and mutators (also known as *getters* and *setters*). The important thing to notice about the code is that the set blocks include validation logic. We do not want anyone to mutate an instance of the type such that its format becomes invalid. Whenever working with code that does any kind of data modification, try to be wary of holes that might lead to inconsistencies. The code for the properties follows:

```
public SqlString UserName
{
    get
    {
        return ((SqlString)userName);
    }

    set
    {
```

```
                //Validate the username
                Regex r =
                    new Regex(@"\w+([-+.]\w+)*");

                if (!r.IsMatch((string)value, 0))
                    throw new ApplicationException("Not a valid username.");

                this.userName = (string)value;
        }
    }

    public SqlString DomainAddress
    {
        get
        {
            return ((SqlString)domainAddress);
        }

        set
        {
            //Validate the domain address
            Regex r =
                new Regex(@"\w+([-.]\w+)*\.\w+([-.]\w+)*");

            if (!r.IsMatch((string)value, 0))
                throw new ApplicationException("Not a valid address.");

            this.domainAddress = (string)value;
        }
    }
```

To finish coding the type, we need to implement the methods for the IBinarySerialize
interface. This interface exposes two methods: Read and Write. The Read method takes as input
a binary serialized instance of the type and deserializes it, populating the private member
variables for the type in the process. The Write method does the opposite of this; it serializes
the private member data and returns the binary form.

Both methods are fairly easy to use. The BinaryReader and BinaryWriter objects that they
make use of for serialization are overloaded to read and write virtually all .NET scalar types.
The important thing to remember is that the Read and Write methods should always mirror
each other. That is, Read should retrieve the serialized data in the exact order in which it was
serialized by Write.

The code for the Read method is as follows:

```
public void Read(System.IO.BinaryReader r)
{
    m_Null = r.ReadBoolean();
```

```
    if (!m_Null)
    {
        userName = r.ReadString();
        domainAddress = r.ReadString();
    }
}
```

As you can see, this method is quite simple. The first piece of data expected from the binary serialized instance is the m_Null member variable. If the instance is NULL, there is no reason to continue processing. If it is non-NULL, the userName and domainAddress variables are deserialized.

The code for the Write method is nearly identical:

```
public void Write(System.IO.BinaryWriter w)
{
    w.Write(m_Null);

    if (!m_Null)
    {
        w.Write(userName);
        w.Write(domainAddress);
    }
}
}
```

This method writes the data in the exact same order that it is read later. Keep in mind that these two methods are tightly coupled. Any change to one must be accompanied by a change to the other. Failure to keep these methods in sync will result in exceptions and possibly corrupt instances of the type. Test these methods carefully!

Using the Type

Once the assembly has been compiled in Visual Studio 2005, it can be deployed using the CREATE TYPE statement, as described earlier in the section "Deploying the UDT."

Just like the Duration UDT, the EMail type can be used anywhere a built-in type can be used. For instance, it can be used as a local variable, or it can be used to define a column of a table. However, unlike T-SQL UDTs, the validation logic for this type is bound within the type. Using it in any context will result in verification of the input e-mail address. The following code illustrates this:

```
DECLARE @address EMail
SET @address = 'this_is_not_valid'
```

Running this code results in an exception that includes the following message: "Not a valid address." This is as expected; the regular expression defined in the Parse method will only match strings that are formatted such that they include one @ symbol between two sets of period-delimited characters.

The following code results in no exceptions, since the address is of a valid format (and yes, that address is real):

```
--Set the address for requesting SQL Server features
DECLARE @address EMail
SET @address = 'sqlwish@microsoft.com'
```

In addition to being able to set addresses, we can use the properties of the type to alter them, for instance:

```
--Set the address for requesting SQL Server features
DECLARE @address EMail
SET @address = 'sqlwish@microsoft.com'

--I doubt that this address exists!
SET @address.DomainAddress = 'oracle.com'
```

In this case, the resultant value of the UDT is sqlwish@oracle.com. Of course, the value oracle.com was validated by the mutator, so the value of the type stays consistently formatted.

UDTs such as this one are invaluable in defining database solutions with data consistency in mind. The real benefit comes with reuse; once you've coded this UDT, you'll never have a need to define e-mail address validation in the database again.

Summary

No longer are database developers and administrators limited to using SQL Server's base data types when defining database objects. Through the power of UDTs, we can now create types of limitless complexity. Furthermore, we can encapsulate data validation logic within these types, thereby helping to improve our systems' overall data quality. By using CLR UDTs, we will be able to define databases that are simpler, yet more flexible and functional.

CHAPTER 7

■■■

User-Defined Aggregates

T-SQL aggregate functions are very powerful tools that have been available with all versions of SQL Server. Rather than act on individual rows, aggregate functions such as SUM, MAX, and COUNT iterate over a set (or group) of rows and provide a single-row, aggregated answer for each set of rows.

Prior to SQL Server 2005, a limited number of built-in aggregate functions were available, such as SUM, MIN, MAX, and COUNT. If a function did not exist to support your desired aggregation, then you were forced to resort to use of cursors, temp tables, or extremely complex queries to build the aggregate functionality.

With SQL Server 2005 comes the ability to create user-defined aggregates (UDAs). UDAs allow developers and database administrators to have more control over data within the database. You should often find that a UDA provides a solution that not only is easier to manage than current options, but is also more flexible and provides better performance.

In this chapter, we'll cover the following topics:

- The benefits and limitations of UDAs

- Using UDAs to perform complex aggregations on sets of data

- Using UDAs in conjunction with UDTs to create very flexible aggregations

- Understanding UDA serialization issues when working with reference types

UDA Benefits

The potential benefits of UDAs in terms of flexibility, reusability, maintenance, and performance are enormous, for example:

- Since all of the .NET Framework classes are available to you while authoring these UDAs, they do not need to be solely based on mathematical functions. You can perform aggregations on strings, or even on date and time fields.

- If no built-in T-SQL aggregate function suits your needs, then instead of implementing row-by-row iteration using cursors, it may be possible to implement the required aggregation using a UDA.

- A UDA can be shared between as many stored procedures as you wish in a single database, with one central point for any code changes.

- UDAs can be used in conjunction with CLR-based, user-defined data types to achieve even more flexibility.

Let's look at a simple example to highlight the benefits UDAs can offer. SQL Server's built-in aggregate functions allow for simple aggregations over sets of data. For instance, say you need to query to determine the average sales price of all of the products that have sold in the last month. You could write a simple query such as the following:

```
SELECT AVG(Price)
FROM Sales
WHERE SalesDate >= DATEADD(mm, -1, GETDATE())
```

Simplicity is the key in this scenario. SQL Server's built-in set of aggregates includes average, sum, count, minimum, maximum, and standard deviation. But what about more complex situations? Users might require median calculations or more sophisticated summation logic. And although it's possible to achieve a higher level of functionality by using complex T-SQL expressions, the level of difficulty in creating and maintaining these queries is often not worth the effort.

CLR UDAs allow developers to express this complex logic in a much simpler way, by harnessing the power of the .NET Base Class Library (BCL) and the power of languages such as C#, which are much easier for most developers to grasp than T-SQL. UDAs can be used just like built-in aggregates and are called with the same syntax. They require no building of loops or other procedural logic, as do cursor-based solutions. Finally, UDAs promote encapsulation and reuse. Once created in a database, a UDA can be reused by as many queries as needed. The same cannot be said for most T-SQL–based solutions.

UDA Limitations

Although UDAs are much easier to work with in many cases than pure T-SQL solutions, they do have certain limitations that can make them less than desirable in some cases.

First and foremost is that UDAs, like UDTs, have an 8,000-byte limit. This can be greatly limiting for applications such as a "list" (string concatenation) aggregate. Should an instance of the aggregate exceed 8,000 bytes, an exception will occur and the query will stop processing.

Another issue present in the current implementation of UDAs is that of ordering. UDAs should not be used for aggregation algorithms that are sensitive to the order of input data. There is currently no mechanism by which a developer can ensure that data will be passed to the UDA in a consistent order. This feature will be provided in a future version of SQL Server, but until then, these types of calculations should not be done using CLR UDAs.

Finally, it's important to keep performance in mind when working with UDAs. As a UDA is processed, it is serialized and deserialized for every row in the input resultset. Should the UDA's internal data store grow large (e.g., in the case of a "list" UDA), the serialization and deserialization processes can become quite expensive, especially if many users are using the UDA concurrently. Try to avoid using UDAs for situations that require a lot of internal storage; in such cases, it will often be much more efficient to do the work in the application tier.

Building a UDA

Like UDTs, UDAs can be implemented as classes or structures, and they must expose a predefined set of methods. The core methods that make up a UDT are `Init`, `Accumulate`, `Merge`, and `Terminate`.

The life cycle of a UDA is as follows:

1. When a user runs a query including an aggregation, the SQL Server engine creates one or more instances of the UDA, depending on whether multiple threads (parallelism) can be used.

2. For each instance of the UDA, the `Init` method is called to initialize the internal state of the aggregate as the first row is returned from the query.

3. As rows are processed in each group, the `Accumulate` method is called on a row-by-row basis. This method should contain the logic for adding a new row's worth of data to the aggregation.

4. During aggregation, the query engine may use multiple instances of the aggregate on different threads. Before returning the answer, the intermediate aggregates will all be combined using the `Merge` method.

5. When the last row of a group is detected by the SQL Server engine, the `Terminate` method is called. This method returns the final result of the aggregation. At this point, the instance of the UDA may be dereferenced, or it may be reused for another group, in which case `Init` will be called to clean up the internal state of the aggregate.

The four methods in a bit more detail are as follows:

- `Init`: This method is called when the query engine prepares to begin aggregation. Any initialization code specific for the aggregation should be performed here. This method should reset the aggregate to a base state, as the same aggregate can be reused for multiple groups. Therefore, the initialization logic should not include any processing specific to building up the aggregation.

- `Accumulate`: As each row is processed, including the first and last rows, this method is called to add that row's value into the running aggregation. For example, if you were writing an aggregate to count the number of rows, this method would simply increment an internal counter. But if instead the aggregate was an average, this method would both increment the counter and add the current row's value to a running tally. Note that this method does not finalize the result of the aggregation; its only job is to keep track of new data as it comes into the aggregate.

- `Merge`: The SQL Server query optimizer can decide, if multiple processors are present in the server, to use more than one in parallel to satisfy a query. If this occurs for an aggregate operation, the `Merge` method may be automatically used. Two or more partial aggregations may be created in parallel; before calling the `Terminate` method, any partial aggregations will be joined using this method.

- `Terminate`: Once all the rows have been processed and any parallel aggregates merged, the `Terminate` method is invoked. This method returns the final result to the SQL Server engine for the group being aggregated.

The class used to define a UDA must be decorated with an attribute called
`SqlUserDefinedAggregate`. This attribute is used by SQL Server to show that the .NET assembly is an aggregation and it meets the contract of having the four methods just defined as its
interface. As part of this aggregation, you also define the serialization format that you will be
using. Similar to UDTs, UDAs can use either native or user-defined serialization.

The `SqlUserDefinedAggregate` attribute has various options that should be configured by
developers to control how the aggregate will be processed:

- `IsInvariantToDuplicates` *(optional)*: Setting this option to `true` tells the query optimizer that the aggregate will return the same result whether or not duplicates are
  passed in. Some query plans may produce duplicate intermediate rowsets; if the aggregate does not depend on uniqueness of input data, setting this option will allow for
  more flexibility when the optimizer determines a query plan.

- `IsInvariantToNulls` *(optional)*: Similar to the `IsInvariantToDuplicates` option, this
  option allows the query optimizer greater flexibility when creating a query plan. Some
  query plans may result in intermediate `NULL` values. If the result of the aggregation will
  not be affected by `NULL`s, this can be set to `true`.

- `IsInvariantToOrder` *(optional; default = `false`)*: This option is a placeholder for use in
  future versions of SQL Server.

- `IsNullIfEmpty` *(optional)*: This option is set to `true` if the aggregation should return a
  `NULL` if no rows have been aggregated. This is another optimization—the query engine
  will not have to call the `Terminate` method if it detects an empty group. Instead, it can
  infer that the correct return value is `NULL`.

* `MaxByteSize` *(optional; required only if using user-defined serialization)*: Similar to the
  same option used for UDTs, this option should be set to the maximum size that the
  serialized state of the aggregate should reach during processing.

Aggregations are relatively straightforward to build, so let's take a look at one now.

Building a Simple UDA

An uncomplicated first example for a UDA is one that counts the number of `NULL` values
passed in. The class for this UDA requires each of the four necessary methods, but only one
private member variable, which will be used to maintain the count.

To begin, we'll create a new database project in Visual Studio 2005 and add an aggregate
called `CountNulls`. This will populate the following empty template from which the UDA can
be created:

```
using System;
using System.Data;
using System.Data.SqlClient;
using System.Data.SqlTypes;
using Microsoft.SqlServer.Server;
```

```
[Serializable]
[Microsoft.SqlServer.Server.SqlUserDefinedAggregate(Format.Native)]
public struct CountNulls
{
    public void Init()
    {
        // Put your code here
    }

    public void Accumulate(SqlString Value)
    {
        // Put your code here
    }

    public void Merge(CountNulls Group)
    {
        // Put your code here
    }

    public SqlString Terminate()
    {
        // Put your code here
        return new SqlString("");
    }

    // This is a place-holder member field
    private int var1;

}
```

Building UDAs based on this template is quite simple. For this aggregate, the template is nearly complete as is. We simply need to populate a few bits and pieces to get it up and running.

First, the private member variable should have a new name to indicate what it will be used for:

```
// The current count of NULLs
private int theCount;
```

This variable will have to be initialized in the Init method (set to 0) as well as incremented in the Accumulate method if the input value is NULL. The following code shows how we do this:

```
public void Init()
{
    this.theCount = 0;
}

public void Accumulate(SqlString Value)
```

```
{
    if (Value.IsNull)
        this.theCount++;
}
```

Next, let's consider the Merge method. This method is used for joining partial aggregates (i.e., groups that are calculated in parallel) before returning the final value. As such, it can be thought of as a set-based version of Accumulate. In this case, each partial group will have an intermediate count, so all Merge has to do is add the counts together:

```
public void Merge(CountNulls Group)
{
    this.theCount += Group.theCount;
}
```

The final method required is Terminate. In the case of this aggregate, no additional work will be done, and the method can simply return the count:

```
public SqlInt32 Terminate()
{
    return ((SqlInt32)this.theCount);
}
```

Once this aggregate is compiled, we can deploy it to our SQL Server database by using Visual Studio's deployment task, or we can create the assembly in SQL Server using the CREATE ASSEMBLY statement and expose the aggregate using CREATE AGGREGATE. The syntax for CREATE AGGREGATE is similar to that of CREATE FUNCTION; the developer must specify a return data type and an input data type. If the aggregate just listed has been exposed in an assembly called MyUDAs, the following syntax can be used to create the aggregate:

```
CREATE AGGREGATE dbo.CountNulls(@Value VARCHAR(8000))
RETURNS INT
EXTERNAL NAME MyUDAs.CountNulls
```

Once created, the aggregate can be used just like a built-in aggregate—for example, in a query like the following:

```
SELECT dbo.CountNulls(StringColumn)
FROM myTable
```

This query returns the number of NULLs in the StringColumn column of the myTable table.

Using UDTs with a UDA

The example UDA presented in the previous section shows how easy it is to build a simple aggregate function, but even when you have to control the serialization yourself, the process isn't much more difficult. To help develop a deeper understanding of aggregations and .NET assemblies, the next example shows how to build an aggregate using a .NET UDT, and we'll work with this type within the aggregate.

The Duration type shown as an example in the last chapter is a UDT that can be used to record time spans. The example UDA in this section allows us to calculate the average duration over columns of this type. The SQL Server AVG aggregate doesn't work on the user-defined Duration data type; therefore, if we wish to calculate averages we must build our own. This functionality is useful for getting averages for scientific experiments, time trials, or time over distance.

This UDA will take advantage of the fact that the Duration UDT is a simple wrapper over the .NET TimeSpan data type. The UDA will get the ToString() value of the UDT for each input row, and it will use TimeSpan.Parse() to get the value as a TimeSpan. From there, the number of milliseconds can be determined using the TotalMilliseconds property and added to the UDA's internal counter.

A performance optimization might be to add a TotalMilliseconds property to the UDT, using that instead of ToString() to get the value. That would eliminate some object creation, thereby yielding a faster UDA.

Creating the .NET Assembly

Open the SQL Server project from the previous chapter in Visual Studio 2005 and add an aggregate called AvgDuration. Alternatively, you can simply enter the following code into a text editor such as Notepad and use the command-line compiler.

As usual, the code commences with the using statements:

```
using System;
using System.Data;
using System.Data.SqlClient;
using System.Data.SqlTypes;
using Microsoft.SqlServer.Server;
```

The aggregate is implemented in a structure named AvgDuration. This class is decorated with attributes very similar to the ones we applied to the UDT in the previous chapter:

- Serializable: This attribute indicates that the class can be serialized into a stream of binary or character data by the .NET Framework.

- SqlUserDefinedAggregate: Like the SqlUserDefinedType attribute we encountered in Chapter 6, we use this attribute to specify what format the serialized class will be stored in, in this instance using the native format:

```
[Serializable]
[Microsoft.SqlServer.Server.SqlUserDefinedAggregate(Format.Native)]
public struct AvgDuration
{
```

We need two private int fields within the class, to hold the accumulation of the times in milliseconds and to hold the number of values passed in. We will initialize both of these to zero in the Init method such that they will be reset when aggregation starts for a new group:

```
    private int totalTime;
    private int totalCount;
```

```
public void Init()
{
    this.totalTime = 0;
    this.totalCount = 0;
}
```

As each row is processed, the Accumulate method will be called. The data will be passed in as an instance of the Duration UDT that is used for the column within the table that the aggregate function will operate on. We need to reflect this within our input parameter.

Within the Accumulate method, we simply increment the count of rows that we've processed and add the number of milliseconds represented by the Duration object to the totalTime class variable that's keeping track of the total number of milliseconds in the aggregation. The Duration exposes the time via its ToString() method in a format that we can process using TimeSpan.Parse() to get the number of milliseconds represented. We also check for NULLs, which will be ignored as they are for the built-in aggregates.

```
public void Accumulate(Duration Value)
{
    if (!Value.IsNull)
    {
        TimeSpan ts = TimeSpan.Parse(Value.ToString());
        this.totalTime += (int)ts.TotalMilliseconds;

        this.totalCount++;
    }
}
```

The Merge method is quite simple; it simply adds the counts from the partial aggregation into the total for the current group.

```
public void Merge(AvgDuration Group)
{
    this.totalTime += Group.totalTime;
    this.totalCount += Group.totalCount;
}
```

As we reach the end of each of the GROUP BY groupings, the Terminate method is called. Here we find the average time and return the value back as an instance of the Duration UDT. The sum value of the times from the Accumulate method is divided by the number of rows processed to get the average time in milliseconds. Once we have that, we can create a new instance of Duration to return:

```
public Duration Terminate()
{
    double avg = this.totalTime / this.totalCount;
    TimeSpan ts = TimeSpan.FromMilliseconds(avg);

    return(Duration.Parse(ts.ToString()));
}
}
```

This project is now ready to be compiled and deployed to SQL Server 2005 for testing. If you're compiling using the command-line compiler, you can use the following syntax:

```
csc /t:library /r:"C:\Program Files\Microsoft SQL Server\MSSQL.1\
MSSQL\Binn\sqlaccess.dll" TimeAggregation.cs
```

Next, we create a simple table that will hold a set of duration values that can be grouped. For our example, the number of groups is kept to two to reduce the amount of data to work through.

```
CREATE TABLE AvgTime
(TimeId int NOT NULL,
TimeTaken Duration null)
GO
INSERT INTO AvgTime VALUES (1,'11:30:00')
INSERT INTO AvgTime VALUES (1,'11:32:00')
INSERT INTO AvgTime VALUES (1,'11:34:00') -- Avg 11:32:00
INSERT INTO AvgTime VALUES (2,'00:30:00')
INSERT INTO AvgTime VALUES (2,'00:32:20')
INSERT INTO AvgTime VALUES (2,'00:32:44')
INSERT INTO AvgTime VALUES (2,'00:39:21') -- Avg 2016.25 =00:33:36.25
GO
```

Now that we have the data set up, we can load the aggregate assembly into the database. If you used the project from the last chapter, it will have both the Duration UDT and AvgDuration UDA, so be sure to load both. We can then create the UDA within SQL Server 2005 and test it out.

```
CREATE ASSEMBLY DurationObjects
FROM 'C:\Program Files\SQL Server Assemblies\Duration.dll'
WITH PERMISSION_SET = SAFE
GO
CREATE AGGREGATE AvgDuration(@TimeValue Duration)
RETURNS Duration
EXTERNAL NAME DurationObjects.AvgDuration
GO
SELECT dbo.AvgDuration(TimeTaken) As AvgDuration
  FROM AvgTime
 GROUP BY TimeId
```

Serialization

We have been able, so far, to let SQL Server manage the serialization of our data between calls. The Duration UDT was serialized with Format.Native. This was possible because we were using value types internally within its structure. The CLR runtime is able to automatically serialize value types into a binary stream. However, not all data types are like this; when reference types are used, we need to manage the serialization ourselves. One good example of this is an array. Arrays are held by the CLR in heap memory rather than on the call stack. Holding data in this way is referred to as a *reference* because the CLR maintains a reference (a pointer) to the instance on the stack, but not the actual data. Because reference types are not always simple scalar values, automatic serialization of these types would be difficult; therefore, we must create our own.

Serialized aggregations, or types, have specific contract requirements for them to work and be used.

Format

First of all, the format option needs to be set to `Format.UserDefined` and a `MaxByteSize` set. The maximum size is 8,000 bytes, which means that using the new `MAX` data types is not possible. We'll keep this size as small as possible, keeping in mind that if we make the size too small we risk failure of the serialization. This option helps the query optimizer determine an appropriate plan for performing the aggregation.

Class Definition

When defining the class, it is also necessary to implement the `IBinarySerialize` interface. This interface exposes two methods, `Read` and `Write`. We'll use these methods to program the user-defined binary serialization in the example that follows.

Write

The `Write` method is called on the aggregate at initialization time and whenever the aggregate has finished processing a row of data and is required to send the information back to SQL Server. This method's purpose is to serialize any data required for aggregation into a binary stream.

In the example that follows, we need to do this with our `ArrayList`, using a write action for each element. However, when we reread this stream we'll need to know how many items we had in our array originally, so that we can process the correct number of elements and not read past the end of the stream. Therefore, we'll also serialize the number of elements in the array before serializing each member.

Read

As each row in a group is processed, its data will be passed into the aggregate. At that time, the aggregate will be deserialized from the binary stream through a call to the `Read` method. The stream will be received and have to be broken down in the same order in which it was written out. In our example, we first read the number of elements we're expecting, and then we loop in order to read each element. Each read action must use the same data type as that used to write it out in order to ensure that the byte stream pointer moves after each item to the correct position in the stream.

Building a Serialized UDA

This section's example implements an Excel aggregation for SQL Server 2005. We'll build an aggregation that receives a set of column data and returns the variance of the data. If you have used Excel, then you'll recognize that this example is the same as Excel's `VarP` (population variance) function.

To quickly summarize, the VarP function takes a set of scores and finds the mean of those scores. From the mean, it iterates around each of the values and subtracts the mean from that score, and squares the result and total. It then divides the total achieved so far by (the number of values – 1) and gets the square root of the result.

For this example, we'll need to have an array of data holding the values from the column we're completing a variance on. Because we're using an array—which is a reference type—we'll have to write our own serialization code. When testing the example, we build a table with five rows with the values 8, 8, 9, 12, and 13. The mean of these values is 10. If we then iterate around each value, subtracting the mean, we'll end up with five values of –2, –2, –1, 2, and 3. We square each of these values, so we get 4, 4, 1, 4, and 9, which when we total comes to 22. Finally, we divide 22 by 5, which gives us 4.4.

Let's take a look at the code for the aggregation. We'll first create a SQL Server project in VS 2005 called MyVarP and add an aggregation to it called MyVarP.cs. We're going to serialize our aggregation, so we'll need the InteropServices namespace. We'll also import the System.Collections.Generic namespace for the List<T> object that we'll use to hold the values passed in.

```
using System;
using System.Data;
using System.Data.SqlClient;
using System.Data.SqlTypes;
using Microsoft.SqlServer.Server;
using System.Runtime.InteropServices;
using System.Collections.Generic;
```

The SqlUserDefinedAggregate attribute on the aggregate class has two properties defined. We perform our own serialization using the Format.UserDefined because we're using the ArrayList. We also have a MaxByteSize property set to a value of 8,000. This indicates that any instance of this class will not exceed 8,000 bytes in length—and it cannot exceed 8,000 bytes, since that is the maximum allowed size for instances of UDAs. We set the value to the allowed maximum, as we don't know how many row instances there are and therefore how many List items there will be.

The class definition also needs to indicate that it implements the IBinarySerialize interface, because we're performing our own serialization of this array between each call.

```
[Serializable]
[SqlUserDefinedAggregate(Format.UserDefined, MaxByteSize=8000)]
[StructLayout(LayoutKind.Sequential)]
public class VarP : IBinarySerialize
```

Within the class body, define the class-scoped variables. There is only one, aValues, that is defined as a List<double>, which is a generic auto-extending array typed for doubles. Although declared, it isn't initialized at this point, as it's initialized at other points within the code. Serialized aggregations have to initialize their class fields within the Read method because they're reinstantiated between calls to Read; otherwise, their data will be lost. However, when the aggregation is constructed prior to reading in the first row, the Write method is called after the Init method, so the array list needs to be initialized for this first write action as well. Therefore, we'll initialize the variable within the Init method, too.

```
List<double> aValues;
```

The first method we'll examine is Write, which will help you understand the remainder of the assembly. This is where we serialize any data that we wish to keep between calls to the assembly. We have defined our aggregation as Format.UserDefined, so instead of SQL Server's in-process service handling the storage and retrieval of our data as we accumulate it, we have to do that ourselves. Any data item not written out here will be lost. The binary writer can write out all .NET value types but no reference types except byte and char arrays.

Prior to serializing the values in the array, we write out how many elements there are within the array so that when we come to read the stream back in, we know how many elements to read back. At the end of the Write method, the stream is closed and the SQL Server process knows to hold that data and pass it in to the assembly when it is next called through the Read method:

```
public void Write(System.IO.BinaryWriter w)
{
    // Write out how many
    w.Write(aValues.Count);

    // Write out each element
    foreach (double obj in aValues)
    {
        w.Write(obj);
    }
}
```

We now come to the Read method. This method has one input parameter: the data passed to the aggregation that was written earlier with the Write method. The Read method will never be invoked before the Write method. The binary stream of data is passed into the method as a BinaryReader, r, from which we can read the data into our List<T>. The List<T> has been defined but not initialized at this point, so we must do this before loading any information from the data stream into it. We know that the first item in the stream is a count of the number of array list items we will be reading. We also know that the count is an Int32. Once this has been defined we can loop, reading in each object in the list. Once the Read method has completed, the assembly will proceed to the next action—either the Accumulate, Merge, or Terminate method.

```
public void Read(System.IO.BinaryReader r)
{
    aValues = new List<double>();

    Int32 ii = r.ReadInt32();

    for (int i = 1; i <= ii; i++)
    {
        double dblConv = r.ReadDouble();
        aValues.Add(dblConv);
    }
}
```

Now we define our mandatory `Init` method, which will fire as the query is initialized for processing, which means that the aggregation will also be initialized for processing. Any initialization code required would be placed in here. In our scenario, we need to initialize the list because the next method to be called will be the `Write` method, which expects the array list already to have been initialized.

```
public void Init()
{
    aValues = new List<double>();
}
```

For every row returned by our query, the `Accumulate` method is called. This does include the first row, therefore showing that the first row will call two distinct methods. It is here that we perform our aggregations or storing of information for our aggregation mathematics later on.

In our aggregation, we need to hold every value entered, and we do so in a list. If we have a large rowset incoming to the aggregation, then by default we will also have a large list. Remember that as the size of the aggregate approaches 8,000 bytes, performance will decrease due to the cost of serializing and deserializing such a large number of elements. If the size exceeds 8,000 bytes, an exception will result.

```
public void Accumulate(SqlDouble lValue)
{
    aValues.Add((double)lValue);
}
```

The third mandatory method is `Merge`. This method adds all of the elements from the other group into the current group:

```
public void Merge(VarP Group)
{
    foreach (double dbl in Group.aValues)
        this.aValues.Add(dbl);
}
```

The final method is `Terminate`, which will execute when the last row has been processed and SQL Server is signaling through to the aggregation that it's moving on and therefore needs the information to process. Our example at this point would have the list containing the values that we'll be processing with. From this, we can calculate the sum of the values by iterating through the array list and adding the value of each element to a running count. We can then find out from the sum what the mean value is. Once we have the mean, we can process each item in the array list, determine its variance from the mean, square the value, and sum the result. Notice here that we use the `Math` class for mathematical functionality. Finally, we divide this value by the number of elements in the list and return it from the method.

```
public SqlDouble Terminate()
{
    double lSum = 0;

    foreach (double obj in aValues)
    {
```

```
            lSum = lSum + obj;
        }
        double lSumMeanDev = 0;
        double lMean = lSum / aValues.Count;
        double lTotMean = 0;
        foreach (double obj in aValues)
        {
            lTotMean = obj - lMean;
            lSumMeanDev = lSumMeanDev +
              (Math.Pow(Math.Abs(lTotMean), 2));
        }
        lSumMeanDev /= aValues.Count;
        return (SqlDouble)lSumMeanDev;
    }
}
```

There are no try...catch blocks of code in our example. Errors in the code will generate exceptions, and the preceding code has left our standard error handling so that when you test the aggregation, you can see this in action. However, it is still advisable to cover yourself and deal with errors in a standard fashion when writing code for production systems.

We compile the code as usual and install the assembly into the AssembliesTesting database:

```
USE AssembliesTesting
go
CREATE ASSEMBLY MyVarP
FROM 'C:\Program Files\Microsoft SQL Server\Assemblies\udaVarP.dll'
WITH PERMISSION_SET = SAFE
GO
```

Now we create the UDA in the database with the new CREATE AGGREGATE SQL statement:

```
CREATE AGGREGATE ExcelVarP(@val float)
RETURNS float
EXTERNAL NAME [MyVarP].[FatBelly.Utilities.Statistical.VarP]
GO
```

■**Note** When we create the UDA, the data type being passed in has to match the data type defined for the Accumulate and Terminate methods; otherwise, an error will occur. Another point to keep in mind about data types is that if you're passing in a string to your aggregation, then you must define the data type as nvarchar. The reason for this is that there is no mapping at this time between a non-Unicode string and a managed data type.

We then build our test table, load some values, and then call our aggregate function in a standard SELECT statement:

```
CREATE TABLE TestAgg
(AggId int,
AggValue bigint)
GO
INSERT INTO TestAgg VALUES (1,8)
INSERT INTO TestAgg VALUES (2,8)
INSERT INTO TestAgg VALUES (3,9)
INSERT INTO TestAgg VALUES (4,12)
INSERT INTO TestAgg VALUES (5,13)
GO
SELECT dbo.ExcelVarP(AggValue)
FROM TestAgg
```

The result should be

4.4

It is worth reiterating the sequence of events when performing UserDefined serialization. This will ensure that you are aware of which method fires at which point.

When the query starts to process, your aggregation is loaded into memory, ready for the first row of data to be processed. This sequence is also called on a new grouping within the GROUP BY clause. The methods called are as follows:

- Init

- Write

For the first row of data processed, and for each subsequent row processed, the following methods are executed:

- Read

- Accumulate

- Merge

- Write

Finally, once all the rows are processed and the query is terminating, the aggregation is also terminating. This sequence is also called when the grouping within the GROUP BY alters:

- Read

- Terminate

Summary

This chapter demonstrated two different methods of building aggregations: one where we had to serialize the data ourselves, and another where the serialization could be completed without any manual intervention.

The building of aggregations is normally a straightforward process, but if you need to serialize any of the accumulative data that has to be passed as each row is processed, then this adds complexity. The main point to keep in mind is that what goes in must come out. In other words the data type you write out must be the same data type you read in, and the order in which the data is placed out is the order in which you read it back.

CHAPTER 8

■ ■ ■

CLR Triggers

Prior to SQL Server 2005, a trigger would fire only in response to DML actions—in other words, it would fire in response to changes to data within a table arising from INSERT, UPDATE, or DELETE statements. If you wanted to track and audit DDL changes to system objects or monitor logins, you had to attach your trigger to system tables within your own database or within the master database. Performing such actions within the secure domain of SQL Server in any system database, such as the master database, was regarded as bad practice. It could potentially affect performance or, if a serious problem occurred during execution of the trigger, it could bring the whole server to a halt.

With CLR triggers, it is now possible to track DDL changes to tables and other database objects in a controlled and secure manner. Triggers are regarded by many DBAs as one of the most important new features of SQL Server 2005. They represent an excellent means of monitoring and auditing what goes on within a database, from either a schema or security viewpoint.

This chapter focuses on creating and using CLR triggers to monitor DLL actions. We'll cover the following topics:

- Determining when to use CLR triggers

- Understanding trigger syntax

- Looking at the XML format passed to a trigger

- Building triggers for database and server DDL events

- Dropping triggers

- Creating and using CLR triggers to monitor DML actions

By way of example, we'll take a look at building triggers that fire (and record information about the events that caused them to fire) when an object is created, modified, and deleted; when logins are created, dropped, or modified; and when stored procedures are created or modified.

The main purpose for using triggers on events such as these is to cover for potential security breaches of unauthorized user creation, to allow certain actions only at specific times of the day, or to ensure that a record is kept of previous versions of objects as they are released to production in case of the need to roll back to the original code.

When to Use CLR Triggers

CLR triggers behave in much the same way as T-SQL triggers. However, they can be written in a .NET language and possibly take advantage of resources not easily accessible from T-SQL, such as the use of regular expressions for data validation. CLR triggers can be used to define both Data Manipulation Language (DML) triggers (UPDATE, INSERT, DELETE) and Data Definition Language (DDL) triggers (CREATE TABLE).

It's important to remember that when you're working with any type of trigger—T-SQL or CLR—speed is of the essence. A trigger fires in the context of the transaction that manipulated the data. Any locks required for that data manipulation are held for the duration of the trigger's lifetime. This means that slow triggers can create blocking problems that can lead to severe performance and scalability issues. Executing a CLR trigger that performs complex processing could be more expensive than executing a standard T-SQL trigger, so more care needs to be taken.

It will probably not be an issue if an extra second is added to the execution time for certain database or server events, such as creation of a stored procedure. Although optimum code is still required, if the trade-off is a more secure environment, then there is justification for adding a trigger to that event. However, placing a trigger on a CREATE TABLE event might have a large overall increase in performance. For example, if you have an overnight process that creates and drops tables constantly in tempdb, then a trigger that fires on each CREATE and DROP—no matter how fast—would have a detrimental effect. When you're considering placing triggers on events such as CREATE and DROP TABLE, and CREATE and DROP INDEX, and you have processes that do complete a lot of creation and removal, then consider a method of suspending the trigger during those times, or ensure that you are fully aware of the performance hit. The golden rule for use of CLR triggers is, keep them simple!

CLR DDL Triggers

In many development teams, certain specific logins have database owner and full admin rights to the database. This is not ideal for an organization. It is very easy for a developer, using a T-SQL development tool that works with multiple servers, to perform a DDL action on what he thinks is a development server, but is actually a production server. Alternatively, although corporate "rules" may state that this is a serious offense, a developer with full admin rights might be tempted to create, alter, or even drop objects such as stored procedures or tables during the working day, to slip in a quick fix by the back door. In the past, only a query running against the system tables could have uncovered such an indiscretion, but often not until the following day.

It would be very useful to trap these actions as they occur so whoever is monitoring a system can be instantly alerted and take remedial action (if required) sooner rather than later. DDL triggers provide the perfect solution.

Creating CLR DDL Triggers

The syntax for creating a CLR DDL trigger is as follows:

```
CREATE TRIGGER trigger_name ON { ALL SERVER | DATABASE }
[WITH ENCRYPTION]
```

```
{ FOR | AFTER } { event_type | event_group } [,...n]
   [WITH APPEND]
   [NOT FOR REPLICATION]
{ AS
   { sql_statement [...n]  | EXTERNAL NAME <method_specifier> }
}
<method_specifier> ::= assembly_name.class_name.method_name
```

As you can see, this syntax is rather different from that used to create a conventional T-SQL trigger. We'll discuss the various new options in detail as we progress through the chapter, but we'll briefly overview them here:

- The ON clause allows you to specify the scope of the trigger. There are two options:

  - ALL SERVER: Indicates a scope of the entire database server. The trigger will fire when a relevant event, specified in the FOR|AFTER clause, occurs in any database on the server.

  - DATABASE: Indicates a scope of the current database only. The trigger will respond to an event specified in the FOR|AFTER clause when it occurs in the current database.

- In the FOR|AFTER clause (notice that you can't create a DDL INSTEAD OF trigger) you specify the events to which the trigger should respond. You can do this in two ways:

  - Using the event_type argument, which takes the form of a comma-separated list, to explicitly define the event or events for which the trigger will fire.

  - Specifying a named event_group instead of a single event type or set of event types. For example, the DDL_DATABASE_LEVEL_EVENTS group will cause the trigger to fire on every possible DDL event within a database, and the DDL_SERVER_LEVEL_EVENTS group will cause the trigger to fire on all events at the server level (such as creating or altering a database, login, or endpoint).

Defining Trigger Scope

A DDL trigger can respond either to actions in the specific database in which it was created or to events on any database in the server. It is not possible to create a trigger that fires on both server and database events, and there are specific events that can be captured at the database or server scope.

ALL SERVER Triggers

If you want your DDL trigger to fire on the defined event type, regardless of which database within the server the event arose from, then this is the option to use. The following list contains the DDL commands that have the scope of the whole server:

- CREATE|ALTER|DROP LOGIN

- CREATE|DROP HTTP ENDPOINT

- GRANT|DENY|REVOKE SERVER ACCESS

- CREATE|ALTER|DROP CERT

So, for example, the syntax to create a very basic trigger that responds to all server-scoped events is as follows:

```
CREATE TRIGGER ServerAudit
ON ALL SERVER FOR DDL_DATABASE_LEVEL_EVENTS
AS EXTERNAL NAME Apress.ServerTriggers.Auditing
```

Similarly, to create a trigger to monitor a specific event at the server level, you could simply specify comma-delimited values for the event_type parameter:

```
CREATE TRIGGER LoginAudit
ON ALL SERVER AFTER CREATE_LOGIN, ALTER_LOGIN, DROP_LOGIN
AS EXTERNAL NAME Apress.ServerTriggers.Auditing
```

The obvious place to put a DDL trigger that fires on serverwide events is within the master database, but this does have some dangers. For example, what if you have to rebuild your SQL Server installation, or you're building a failover server, and the addition of the DDL trigger is bypassed (perhaps it wasn't in the installation notes or was just forgotten)? It might be better to have a database in your server specifically for DDL triggers that fire with the ALL SERVER scope so that you know that it will be recoverable.

DATABASE Triggers

The DATABASE option restricts the CLR trigger to firing on DDL actions only within the database in which the trigger itself is created. The following list shows all the DDL database actions that can be trapped at DATABASE scope:

CREATE_TABLE	ALTER_TABLE	DROP_TABLE
CREATE_VIEW	ALTER_VIEW	DROP_VIEW
CREATE_SYNONYM	DROP_SYNONYM	CREATE_FUNCTION
ALTER_FUNCTION	DROP_FUNCTION	CREATE_PROCEDURE
ALTER_PROCEDURE	DROP_PROCEDURE	CREATE_TRIGGER
ALTER_TRIGGER	DROP_TRIGGER	CREATE_EVENT_NOTIFICATION
DROP_EVENT_NOTIFICATION	CREATE_INDEX	ALTER_INDEX
DROP_INDEX	CREATE_STATISTICS	UPDATE_STATISTICS
DROP_STATISTICS	CREATE_ASSEMBLY	ALTER_ASSEMBLY
DROP_ASSEMBLY	CREATE_TYPE	DROP_TYPE
CREATE_USER	ALTER_USER	DROP_USER
CREATE_ROLE	ALTER_ROLE	DROP_ROLE
CREATE_APPLICATION_ROLE	ALTER_APPLICATION_ROLE	DROP_APPLICATION_ROLE
CREATE_SCHEMA	ALTER_SCHEMA	DROP_SCHEMA
CREATE_MESSAGE_TYPE	ALTER_MESSAGE_TYPE	DROP_MESSAGE_TYPE
CREATE_CONTRACT	ALTER_CONTRACT	DROP_CONTRACT
CREATE_QUEUE	ALTER_QUEUE	DROP_QUEUE

CREATE_SERVICE	ALTER_SERVICE	DROP_SERVICE
CREATE_ROUTE	ALTER_ROUTE	DROP_ROUTE
CREATE_REMOTE_SERVICE_BINDING	ALTER_REMOTE_SERVICE_BINDING	DROP_REMOTE_SERVICE_BINDING
GRANT_DATABASE	DENY_DATABASE	REVOKE_DATABASE
CREATE_SECEXPR	DROP_SECEXPR	CREATE_XML_SCHEMA
ALTER_XML_SCHEMA	DROP_XML_SCHEMA	CREATE_PARTITION_FUNCTION
ALTER_PARTITION_FUNCTION	DROP_PARTITION_FUNCTION	CREATE_PARTITION_SCHEME
ALTER_PARTITION_SCHEME	DROP_PARTITION_SCHEME	

This is quite a comprehensive list and covers every database event there is. It is therefore feasible to have an assembly running against each of these events. For example, the following BigBrother trigger will fire on every event that occurs in the database that the trigger protects:

```
CREATE TRIGGER BigBrother
ON DATABASE FOR DDL_DATABASE_LEVEL_EVENTS
AS EXTERNAL NAME Apress.DatabaseTriggers.Auditing
```

There is an obvious performance overhead associated with attaching triggers to events. If you do decide to use the DDL_DATABASE_LEVEL_EVENTS group, then you may want to consider filtering particular events, if there is code specific to an event (we demonstrate how to do this a little later).

Alternatively, you can simply specify the event_type argument to make your triggers more fine-grained:

```
CREATE TRIGGER WatchProcedures
ON DATABASE FOR CREATE_PROCEDURE, DROP_PROCEDURE, ALTER_PROCEDURE
AS EXTERNAL NAME Apress.ProcedureTriggers.Auditing
```

■Note Notice that the DDL events you can trap are the same as the DDL events you can use within your T-SQL query statements. For example, in Query Analyzer you would enter CREATE PROCEDURE to create a procedure. If you created a trigger that wanted to listen to this event, then you would replace the space with an underscore (_) and create your trigger with an event_type of CREATE_PROCEDURE.

EventData

As we have noted, DDL triggers provide an excellent means of auditing and logging DDL actions. Consider the following simple example:

```
CREATE TRIGGER WatchProcedures
ON DATABASE AFTER DROP_PROCEDURE
AS INSERT INTO PROCEDURELOG VALUES ("PROCEDURE DROPPED")
```

Notice that in this case we've simply used a SQL statement, rather than a .NET assembly, to carry out the required action when the trigger fires. This trigger will fire every time a DROP PROCEDURE command is executed in the database, and it will write a simple message to a PROCEDURELOG table each time this occurs.

However, this example is of limited practical use. What we really need to do is record useful information, such as the time that the trigger fired, the type of event that caused it to fire, the username of the user who instigated the event, and so on. This is where the EventData() function comes in.

The XML EventData format does have a schema that defines its specific content depending on the event type, but for any DDL event it provides the following information:

- The type of event that fired the trigger

- The time the event occurred

- The SPID of the connection that caused the trigger to fire

- The login name and/or username of the user who executed the statement

The EventData function returns XML. The basic format of the XML is the same for each database-scoped event, with minor differences for each server-scoped event, but each trigger has specific XML nodes giving pertinent information about what has happened. Server-scoped triggers generate the following basic XML-based information:

```
<EVENT_INSTANCE>
  <EventType>name</EventType>
  <PostTime>date-time</PostTime>
  <SPID>spid</SPID>
  <ServerName>server_name</ServerName>
  <LoginName>login</LoginName>
</EVENT_INSTANCE>
```

If the trigger is database scoped, then the following syntax applies, the only minor difference being that the UserName node is also supplied:

```
<EVENT_INSTANCE>
  <EventType>name</EventType>
  <PostTime>date-time</PostTime>
  <SPID>spid</SPID>
  <ServerName>server_name</ServerName>
  <LoginName>login</LoginName>
  <UserName>user</UserName>
</EVENT_INSTANCE>
```

Dropping DDL Triggers

Unlike other DROP commands, it is necessary to include an ON clause in the DROP TRIGGER statement, indicating the option that the trigger is defined on, either SERVER or DATABASE. Failure to do so generates an error. The reason behind this is that a trigger name is unique not only by its name, but also by what level it fires at. This can prove to be dangerous, as you would expect the uniqueness to be on the name only. It also serves as a warning about naming conventions—developers or development teams should establish a set of standards right from the start.

A trigger we created earlier defined as

```
CREATE TRIGGER XMLDump
ON DATABASE FOR DDL_DATABASE_LEVEL_EVENTS
AS EXTERNAL NAME EventDataDump.Triggers.EventDataXMLDump
```

could be dropped only by

```
DROP TRIGGER XMLDump ON DATABASE
```

You can drop more than one trigger with one action within a comma-separated list, providing that they all fit within the ON option selected.

Using CLR-Based DDL Triggers

In this chapter we're interested in creating and using CLR-based DDL triggers—ones that have a special need to perform some complex processing when the trigger is activated.

We need access from our .NET code to the EventData XML-based information discussed in the previous section. Having the information in an XML format allows your assembly to leverage the simplicity and power that XML notation provides, for finding and working with the informational nodes.

We get this data via the SqlTriggerContext object, which resides in the Microsoft.SqlServer. Server namespace. We get a reference to this object through the static TriggerContext property of the SqlContext object. So for example, we use the following:

```
SqlTriggerContext sqlTrg = SqlContext.TriggerContext;
```

Once we have the SqlTriggerContext object, we can get a reference to the XML information describing the event that was fired from the EventData property of the SqlTriggerContext. This returns a value of type SqlXml, which we can convert to a string through its Value property:

```
string evData = sqlTrg.EventData.Value;
```

■**Note** When using CLR DML triggers, as you'll see later, the SqlTriggerContext object provides your code with access to the virtual inserted and deleted tables that contain the values of a row before and after the event that fired the trigger. You can also use the ColumnsUpdated method of this object to find out which columns in the table were affected by the event.

Let's now look at an example of how to retrieve this XML using our CLR-based trigger and write it to a table.

Outputting EventData XML to a Table

The EventData XML format has a schema that defines its content, which can be found in SQL Server Books Online (BOL). However, it's a distinct advantage to know the real-life values of information, such as when the trigger fired, which server the trigger fired on, and even the content of the command that caused the trigger to fire, and to be able to inspect it and know positively what your assembly is going to see. In the following example, when an event that we define for the trigger fires, we take the XML information passed to our .NET assembly and dump it to a table within SQL Server.

First we need to create a table to hold the XML data for the trigger. By storing the data in the XML data type rather than text or varchar, when the data is output using a SELECT statement, clicking the column will open up a new query window with the XML layout displayed. The table will also contain columns for the date and time the row was added to the table, and the name of the trigger:

```
USE AssembliesTesting
GO
CREATE TABLE EventDataDumpData(
  TriggerName varchar(50)  NOT NULL,
  InsertTime datetime NOT NULL  DEFAULT (getdate()),
  XMLData xml NOT NULL)
```

Next we'll create the trigger assembly itself. Create a SQL Server solution in VS and call it EventDataDump. Add a Trigger item to the solution and call it EventDataXMLDump.

We'll be working with the XML data that is sent to us, so we need to import the System.Xml namespace, and we also need the System.IO namespace for the StringReader data type:

```
using System;
using System.Data;
using System.Data.SqlClient;
using System.Data.SqlTypes;
using System.Xml;
using System.IO;
using Microsoft.SqlServer.Server;

public partial class Triggers
{
    public static void EventDataXMLDump()
    {
```

Having defined the class and the method, we need to retrieve the context details of the trigger event. We place this in a suitably named variable of type SqlTriggerContext to expose the EventData XML. Although this is XML data, it is exposed as a SqlChars object through the SqlTriggerContext's EventData property, so we can implicitly convert it to a string:

```
SqlTriggerContext sqlTrg = SqlContext.TriggerContext;
string evData = sqlTrg.EventData.Value;
```

To convert this from a string to an XML document, we simply call the LoadXml method of the XmlDocument class:

```
XmlDocument xmlDoc = new XmlDocument();
xmlDoc.LoadXml(evData);
```

Once we have an XML document, the XMLDocument class provides a number of methods available to us for working with the XML data. We need to extract the name of the trigger to insert into the table, so we'll call the SelectSingleNode method of the XmlDocument. This takes an XPath expression that points to the node in the document we want to access. In this case, we want to retrieve the text within the <EventType> element beneath the <EVENT_INSTANCE> element. The XPath expression to do this is "//EVENT_INSTANCE/EventType/text()". The final task is to perform a T-SQL insertion into the EventDataDumpData table within our database:

```
XmlNode xmlNd = xmlDoc.SelectSingleNode("//EVENT_INSTANCE/EventType/text()");
string eventType = xmlNd.Value;
using (SqlConnection cn = new SqlConnection("context connection=true"))
{
    cn.Open();
    string sql = "INSERT INTO AssembliesTesting..EventDataDumpData " +
                "(TriggerName, XMLData)  VALUES('" + eventType + "',' " +
                evData + "')";
    SqlCommand sqlComm = new SqlCommand(sql, cn);
    sqlComm.ExecuteNonQuery();
    sqlComm.Dispose();
}
}
}
```

The following code creates the trigger assembly in SQL Server 2005, which is set to fire for all events in the current database.

```
CREATE ASSEMBLY EventDataDump
AUTHORIZATION [dbo]
FROM 'C:\Program Files\SQL Server Assemblies\EventDataDump.dll'
WITH PERMISSION_SET = SAFE
GO
CREATE TRIGGER XMLDump
ON DATABASE FOR DDL_DATABASE_LEVEL_EVENTS
AS EXTERNAL NAME EventDataDump.Triggers.EventDataXMLDump
GO
```

We can test the trigger by creating a simple stored procedure that will invoke the trigger, insert the XML EventData into our table, and then list the output to a results window. Notice that we need to set QUOTED_IDENTIFIERS OFF in case there are quotation marks within the code.

```
SET QUOTED_IDENTIFIER OFF
GO
CREATE PROCEDURE FirstXML
AS
BEGIN
SELECT "Just A Test"
END
GO
SELECT * FROM EventDataDumpData
GO
```

The following is sample XML output. This is a cut and paste from the XML query pane, which is displayed when you click the XML data column.

```
<EVENT_INSTANCE>
  <EventType>CREATE_PROCEDURE</EventType>
  <PostTime>2004-10-23T22:17:10.593</PostTime>
  <SPID>55</SPID>
  <ServerName>XP-PRO</ServerName>
  <LoginName>XP-PRO\rdewson</LoginName>
  <UserName>XP-PRO\rdewson</UserName>
  <DatabaseName>AssembliesTesting</DatabaseName>
  <SchemaName>dbo</SchemaName>
  <ObjectName>FirstXML</ObjectName>
  <ObjectType>PROCEDURE</ObjectType>
  <TSQLCommand>
    <SetOptions ANSI_NULLS="ON" ANSI_NULL_DEFAULT="ON" ANSI_PADDING="ON"
                QUOTED_IDENTIFIER="OFF" ENCRYPTED="FALSE" />
    <CommandText>CREATE PROCEDURE FirstXML
AS
BEGIN
SELECT "Just A Test"
END
</CommandText>
  </TSQLCommand>
</EVENT_INSTANCE>
```

The preceding trigger would be useful in a testing database, as it allows you to create the object you are going to work with and lets you see the layout of the different event types.

■Note If you keep this trigger within the AssembliesTesting database, then you must run all your code with SET QUOTED_IDENTIFIER OFF or change the code to cope with quotation marks.

Filtering Events When Using DDL_DATABASE_LEVEL_EVENTS

The previous example used database scope and the DDL_DATABASE_LEVEL_EVENTS "catchall" so that every DDL action in the database housing the CLR trigger would cause it to fire.

Working with a catchall allows DBAs to build assemblies for monitoring events—for example, for auditing and security, but also for monitoring events related to other SQL Server services such as Service Broker, Notification Services, and so on. The listing of trappable actions presented earlier in the chapter shows that we can trap events surrounding event notifications, routes, and so forth relating to these areas of SQL Server. For example, we can have our trigger CREATE EVENT NOTIFICATION or CREATE QUEUE statements.

Events processed that would have a ripple effect can be trapped and dealt with, and events that might fire as part of a stored procedure call will also be picked up automatically. For example, you may have an overnight batch that alters a notification service. By recording actions such as this, the DBA would have a record of the event (e.g., in an event log or a SQL Server table) if a problem arose, making the debugging job a great deal easier. It is in areas such as debugging, tracking, and auditing that DDL_DATABASE_LEVEL_EVENTS on the CREATE TRIGGER statement will be mostly used.

Creating a trigger to catch all events will have an obvious performance impact and is similar to executing SELECT * from within a T-SQL query. However, it does provide certain flexibility in that if the list of events alter with a future release of SQL Server, you should not need to recompile your trigger code. The obvious danger here is that you may find that your assembly is now being executed for events that it either cannot cope with or does not want to cope with.

One possibility is to use DDL_DATABASE_LEVEL_EVENTS and then filter out those events that you don't want to monitor. Your code could inspect a table held within SQL Server to check that the event that has occurred is one the trigger should monitor. If an event fires that matches a row returned, then processing will proceed; otherwise, it will cease and the trigger will not fire for that event. Because the types of events the trigger works with are held in a database table rather than the trigger definition, you can modify the set of events without having to alter and release the trigger. This is something like working with a configuration file in normal .NET assemblies outside SQL Server.

So how do you know what event has fired if you use a catchall, or even if you have more than one event defined for the assembly? This is where the TriggerAction property of the SqlTriggerContext object comes into play. TriggerAction is an enumeration describing the event that fired the trigger.

■**Tip** As this is an enumeration, you'll obviously want to convert it to a string, via the ToString method, before displaying it.

The following example uses DDL_DATABASE_LEVEL_EVENTS, but will filter out all events except those relating to the creation or alteration of a stored procedure. If the attempt to execute such commands is being made within critical business hours, then the trigger will fire.

Specifically, our .NET code will use the TriggerAction property to determine the event that has fired and then compare that information to the list of events to which the trigger should respond, which is held in a database table. If a match is found, and we are within critical business hours, then the trigger will fire and an e-mail will be sent via Database Mail to notify the appropriate person. Prior to SQL Server 2005, such actions were difficult to monitor and even more difficult to manage.

■**Note** To run this example, you need to have Database Mail enabled and configured on your computer. You can enable Database Mail using the Surface Area Configuration tool, and you can configure it using the wizard within Management Studio (right-click the Database Mail icon in the Management folder of your server and select Configure Database Mail). You also need to set up profiles and accounts within SQL Server 2005 and have an SMTP connection defined for this example to work. This is a very simple process, and details for performing the procedure manually are provided within BOL if you do not wish to use the wizard.

The example assumes that there is a database set up that is used purely by DBAs for storing specific auditing information. In this case, we'll use our AssembliesTesting database. Within this database is a table that defines the actions we wish to monitor and the times during which these actions should be reported via e-mail. The table definition and initial data load is as follows:

```
USE AssembliesTesting
GO
CREATE TABLE AuditActions(
AuditId BIGINT IDENTITY(1,1),
TriggerName VARCHAR(100),
StartTime CHAR(5),
EndTime CHAR(5))
GO
SET QUOTED_IDENTIFIER OFF
GO
INSERT INTO AuditActions (TriggerName,  StartTime,  EndTime)
  VALUES ("AlterProcedure","07:00","18:00")
INSERT INTO AuditActions (TriggerName,  StartTime,  EndTime)
  VALUES ("CreateProcedure","07:00","18:00")
```

From Solution Explorer, create a SQL Server solution in VS 2005 and give it an appropriate name, such as TriggerAudit. Add a new Trigger item, trgTriggerAudit.cs. The only .NET namespace required beyond the standard set is System.Collections; we need this for the ArrayList object, which we'll use to hold the actions and times of the audited events.

```
using System;
using System.Data;
using System.Data.SqlClient;
using System.Data.SqlTypes;
using System.Collections;
using Microsoft.SqlServer.Server;

public partial class Triggers
{
    public static void AuditTrigger()
    {
```

AuditTrigger is the C# method that implements the trigger. Here we read in the events we want to monitor and load the array. Then, when the trigger fires, we navigate through the list of actions to see if we have a match on the trigger and the timings. We start by calling the ReadMonitoringActions method, which returns an ArrayList containing the events to monitor. We need to use an ArrayList, as we don't know in advance the number of actions in the table. An ArrayList allows a dynamic collection that can be expanded, whereas an Array has a fixed number of elements and can't be resized. However, an Array is faster to process, so we should see performance gains when moving from the ArrayList to an Array, even though there is an overhead involved in this move. We also need to get a reference to the SqlTriggerContext for the current trigger.

```
ArrayList auditActions = ReadMonitoringActions();
String[] arrActions = (String[])auditActions.ToArray(typeof(string));
SqlTriggerContext trgContext = SqlContext.TriggerContext;
```

Now we have to iterate through all the items in the array. For each item, we convert the times we stored in the auditing table for each action from strings into DateTime objects. We can then compare the short time from these variables along with the short time from Now. We also check the event to ensure that the action is one we are monitoring.

```
for (int i = 0; i < arrActions.Length; i += 3)
{
    DateTime fromDate = Convert.ToDateTime(arrActions[i + 1]);
    DateTime toDate = Convert.ToDateTime(arrActions[i + 2]);
    if (arrActions[i] == trgContext.TriggerAction.ToString() &&
        fromDate.ToShortTimeString().CompareTo(DateTime.Now.
                                        ToShortTimeString()) < 0 &&
        toDate.ToShortTimeString().CompareTo(DateTime.Now.
                                        ToShortTimeString()) > 0)
    {
```

If we pass these tests, then we want to send out an audit e-mail, so we retrieve the information about the event and call the sp_send_dbmail stored procedure that is installed with Database Mail.

```
        string evData = trgContext.EventData.Value;
        SqlPipe pipeSql = SqlContext.Pipe;
        using (SqlConnection cn = new SqlConnection("context connection=true"))
        {
            cn.Open();
            string sql = "msdb.dbo.sp_send_dbmail " +
              "@profile_name = 'APress Public Profile'," +
              "@recipients = 'robin@fat-belly.com'," +
              "@body = '" + trgContext.TriggerAction.ToString() +
              " is happening during core hours.' ," +
              "@subject = 'Trigger Action occurring'" ;
            SqlCommand sqlComm = new SqlCommand(sql, cn);
            pipeSql.Send(sqlComm.CommandText);
            pipeSql.ExecuteAndSend(sqlComm);
        }
    }
  }
}
```

The next method, ReadMonitoringActions, is where we read through the AuditActions table to create the ArrayList we use in the preceding method.

```
private static ArrayList ReadMonitoringActions()
{
```

Here we retrieve the SqlCommand object for the current context, pass in the T-SQL we wish to execute, and then execute the command. We could call a stored procedure instead, which would be the more secure option, but for the purposes of keeping the code simple to read and understand in this example we'll call the raw code:

```
ArrayList actions = new ArrayList();
using (SqlConnection cn = new SqlConnection("context connection=true"))
{
    cn.Open();
    string sql = "SELECT TriggerName,  StartTime,  EndTime " +
                 "FROM AuditActions ";
    SqlCommand sqlComm = new SqlCommand(sql, cn);
    SqlDataReader sqlTriggers = sqlComm.ExecuteReader();
```

Once we've executed the query, we need to iterate through the resulting SqlDataReader and add each column to the ArrayList. We then close the command and return the ArrayList from the method.

```
    while (sqlTriggers.Read())
    {
        actions.Add(sqlTriggers.GetString(0));
        actions.Add(sqlTriggers.GetString(1));
        actions.Add(sqlTriggers.GetString(2));
    }
    sqlTriggers.Close();
    return actions;
    }
  }
}
```

Next, we compile this into a DLL, place it into the SQL Server DLL directory, and create the assembly in SQL Server. Even although we are accessing e-mail, we are calling a procedure within SQL Server that it knows is good, and therefore we can still have a SAFE permission setting.

```
CREATE ASSEMBLY TriggerAudit
AUTHORIZATION [dbo]
FROM "C:\Program Files\SQL Server Assemblies\triggeraudit.dll"
WITH PERMISSION_SET = SAFE
GO
```

■**Note** Remember to use double quotation marks around your code if you still have the EventData example within your database.

The final task is to set up the trigger:

```
CREATE TRIGGER TriggerAuditing
ON DATABASE FOR  DDL_DATABASE_LEVEL_EVENTS
AS EXTERNAL NAME TriggerAudit.Triggers.AuditTrigger
GO
```

We can now test this trigger by performing one of the events being monitored (i.e., creating, altering, or dropping a stored procedure). It might be easier to create a simple stored procedure first, as we do in the following code. When the CREATE PROCEDURE code is executed, an e-mail will be sent from SQL Server, so we will not see it recorded in a Sent Items folder within Outlook.

■**Note** You will need to make sure that any firewall software is set up to allow you to send external mail from SQL Server.

```
CREATE PROCEDURE TrigAudTest
AS
BEGIN
SELECT "TriggerAudit Test"
END
```

A possible extension to this example is to have a second table where you can store changes that have been authorized. Once a team had DBA signoff on the change, they could place the object name within this table, and when you as a developer release the change, the trigger assembly would check this authorization table, match on the stored procedure names, and let it go through without the need to e-mail anyone. Another extension you'll see near the end of the chapter is to disallow the trigger action if it happens during times when changes aren't allowed. Instead of letting the procedure be created, we'll complete a ROLLBACK so that the change will be rejected.

Earlier in the chapter we presented an example that wrote out the XML to a table so that we could see the XML layout. Let's do a bit more work with XML in the next example and expand on the previous example by storing the event data information within a table.

Visual SourceSafe by the Back Door

Microsoft Visual SourceSafe (VSS) allows you to store multiple versions of code so that if the need arises, it is possible to return to a previous version of a set of code. VSS also allows developers to check changes that have occurred between two versions of code. This next example provides a pared-down VSS system for database objects in SQL Server.

It will store the old version of the source of a stored procedure or table when an alteration is made to either of these object types. Although with SQL Server 2005, VSS forms part of the product, it is still very easy within Query Analyzer to alter a stored procedure or other objects without using this tool. Once again, this poses a dilemma for organizations: how do you ensure that all your code within previous versions is kept safe in case a rollback is required? There is a certain amount of trust and reliance on good development techniques that code has been placed into VSS.

A good solution to this problem is to use a DDL trigger and write the old stored procedure code or table definition to a table. The only concern would be if the stored procedure were encrypted, as in this case the source would not be available. The EventData XML CommandText element would be

```
<CommandText>--ENCRYPTED--</CommandText>
```

The following example shows how to use a trigger to archive the table definition to a backup table whenever a table is created or modified. This is similar to the code in the previous example, except that now we store the code within a VSS-style table in our AssembliesTesting database instead of sending an e-mail. As you will see, it works with the XML EventData in a different way from the first example.

First, we need to create the backup table that we'll use to store the archive of table definitions:

```
USE AssembliesTesting
GO
CREATE TABLE VSS (
  VSS_Ident bigint NOT NULL IDENTITY (1,  1),
  ObjectName varchar(100)  NOT NULL,
  ObjectType varchar(20)  NOT NULL,
  LoginName varchar(80)  NOT NULL,
  DatabaseName varchar(30)  NOT NULL,
  PostTime datetime NOT NULL,
  ObjectDetails text)
GO
```

This example uses the same AuditActions table as the previous one to store the list of events we want to monitor, so we need to add a couple of rows to let our trigger know that we want to monitor all CREATE TABLE and ALTER TABLE statements:

```
INSERT INTO AuditActions (TriggerName,  StartTime,  EndTime)
  VALUES ("CreateTable","07:00","18:00")
INSERT INTO AuditActions (TriggerName,  StartTime,  EndTime)
  VALUES ("AlterTable","07:00","18:00")
```

Now we create a SQL Server project called trgSourceSafe in VS 2005 and add a trigger project. In the example, we've called the class clsSS and placed it in the Apress.SqlAssemblies. Chapter08 namespace.

```
using System;
using System.Data;
using System.Data.SqlClient;
using System.Data.SqlTypes;
using System.Xml;
using System.Collections;
using Microsoft.SqlServer.Server;
```

```
namespace Apress.SqlAssemblies.Chapter08
{
  public partial class Triggers
  {
    public static void clsSS()
    {
```

As before, we start out by getting the list of actions we want to monitor for and iterating through this list to see if the current action matches any of the events we're looking for. If it does, we load the event data for the trigger context into an XmlDocument object and pass it to the WriteOldVersion method, which contains our code to archive the original definition.

```
      XmlDocument xmlEventData;
      ArrayList auditActions = ReadMonitoringActions();
      String[] arrActions = (String[])auditActions.ToArray(typeof(string));
      SqlTriggerContext sqlTrg = SqlContext.TriggerContext;
      for (int i = 0; i < arrActions.Length - 1; i += 3)
      {
        if (arrActions[i] == sqlTrg.TriggerAction.ToString())
        {
          xmlEventData = new XmlDocument();
          xmlEventData.LoadXml(sqlTrg.EventData.Value);
          WriteOldVersion(xmlEventData);
        }
      }
    }
```

The ReadMonitoringActions method is unchanged from the previous example:

```
private static ArrayList ReadMonitoringActions()
{
  ArrayList actions = new ArrayList();
  using (SqlConnection cn = new SqlConnection("context connection=true"))
  {
    cn.Open();
    string sql = "SELECT TriggerName,  StartTime,  EndTime " +
                 "FROM AuditActions ";
    SqlCommand sqlComm = new SqlCommand(sql, cn);
    SqlDataReader sqlTriggers = sqlComm.ExecuteReader();

    while (sqlTriggers.Read())
    {
      actions.Add(sqlTriggers.GetString(0));
      actions.Add(sqlTriggers.GetString(1));
      actions.Add(sqlTriggers.GetString(2));
    }
    sqlTriggers.Close();
    return actions;
  }
}
```

We now come to the WriteOldVersion method, which will take the XML EventData, navigate through it, and store the table definition in our data table. In contrast to our first example, where we went straight to a single node, in this example we read the whole document, test each node, and store the information. First, we initialize the local variables that will hold the data we extract from the XML document:

```
private static void WriteOldVersion(XmlNode objectXML)
{
  string objectName = "";
  string objectType = "";
  string objectDetails = "";
  string loginName = "";
  string databaseName = "";
  string postTime = "";
```

Because we're going to be reading through the document in order, one node at a time, we need to use the SAX-style parser of the XmlNodeReader class for this example instead of the DOM-style XmlDocument. As we read each node, we test that it is an element (as opposed to any other type of node, such as a text node) and compare its name to the elements we're looking for. If we find a match, a further read is required to move the XmlNodeReader to the next node— the text node that contains the actual content of the element—and we store the details in the appropriate local variable. Then, when we've read through the whole document, we close the XmlNodeReader:

```
XmlNodeReader xmlDetails = new XmlNodeReader(objectXML);

while (xmlDetails.Read())
{
  if (xmlDetails.NodeType == XmlNodeType.Element &&
      xmlDetails.Name == "ObjectName")
  {
    xmlDetails.Read();
    objectName = xmlDetails.Value;
  }
  if (xmlDetails.NodeType == XmlNodeType.Element &&
      xmlDetails.Name == "ObjectType")
  {
    xmlDetails.Read();
    objectType = xmlDetails.Value;
  }
  if (xmlDetails.NodeType == XmlNodeType.Element &&
      xmlDetails.Name == "LoginName")
  {
    xmlDetails.Read();
    loginName = xmlDetails.Value;
  }
  if (xmlDetails.NodeType == XmlNodeType.Element &&
      xmlDetails.Name == "DatabaseName")
```

```
    {
      xmlDetails.Read();
      databaseName = xmlDetails.Value;
    }
    if (xmlDetails.NodeType == XmlNodeType.Element &&
          xmlDetails.Name == "PostTime")
    {
      xmlDetails.Read();
      postTime = xmlDetails.Value;
    }
    if (xmlDetails.NodeType == XmlNodeType.Element &&
          xmlDetails.Name == "CommandText")
    {
      xmlDetails.Read();
      objectDetails = xmlDetails.Value;
    }
  }
  xmlDetails.Close();
```

Now that we have the information, we write it out to the table:

```
  SqlPipe pipeSql = SqlContext.Pipe;
  using (SqlConnection cn = new SqlConnection("context connection=true"))
  {
    cn.Open();
    string sql = "INSERT INTO VSS " +
                 "(ObjectName,ObjectType,LoginName,DatabaseName," +
                 " PostTime,ObjectDetails)  " +
                 "VALUES('" + objectName.Trim() + "','" + objectType.Trim() +
                 "','" + loginName.Trim() + "','" + databaseName.Trim() +
                 "','" + postTime.Trim() + "','" + objectDetails.Trim() + "')";
    SqlCommand sqlComm = new SqlCommand(sql, cn);
    pipeSql.Send(sqlComm.CommandText);
    pipeSql.ExecuteAndSend(sqlComm);
  }
 }
}
}
```

We can now create the assembly and trigger. Again, the assembly can be given the
SAFE permission set, as it doesn't access any outside resources. The trigger is executed on
DDL_DATABASE_LEVEL_EVENTS, so we can control what objects to keep backups of through the
AuditActions table, rather than having to alter and release the trigger.

```
CREATE ASSEMBLY trgSourceSafe
AUTHORIZATION [dbo]
FROM 'C:\Program Files\SQL Server Assemblies\trgSourceSafe.dll'
WITH PERMISSION_SET = SAFE
```

```
go
CREATE TRIGGER trgVSS
ON DATABASE FOR DDL_DATABASE_LEVEL_EVENTS
AS EXTERNAL NAME trgSourceSafe.[Apress.SqlAssemblies.Chapter08.Triggers].clsSS
```

To test this, you can create a table either in code or graphically, or, if you have left the other rows in the AuditActions table from the previous example, create or modify a stored procedure. When the trigger fires, you can then see the results within the VSS table we created.

CLR DML Triggers

As well as DDL triggers, you can, of course, also write DML triggers in .NET. Doing so allows you as a developer to extend traditional triggers with greater functionality, as you found with stored procedures.

Up until SQL Server 2005, triggers were, in the main, used for auditing and recording before and after images of records, or to reflect changes completed in the triggered table onto another disassociated table. Examples could be found in order processing, where a trigger would fire when an order was placed, reducing the amount of stock. The trigger would check stock levels and create an order to a supplier for more stock if required. This was powerful and very useful functionality.

Through the use of .NET, we can now extend this functionality. For example, we can open up a second connection directly to a supplier's database and place the order straight into that supplier's system.

Creating DML Triggers

The syntax for creating CLR DML triggers is as follows:

```
CREATE TRIGGER trigger_name
ON { table | view }
[WITH [ENCRYPTION] [,]
        [EXECUTE AS CALLER | SELF | OWNER | 'username']]
{ FOR | AFTER | INSTEAD OF }
{ [INSERT] [,] [UPDATE] [,] [DELETE] }
[WITH APPEND]
[NOT FOR REPLICATION]
AS EXTERNAL NAME assembly_name.class_name.method_name
```

This syntax is nearly the same as that for DDL CLR triggers, except it's created on a table or view, rather than on the whole database or server. In addition, there's a much more restricted set of events that you can fire the trigger on, and you have the extra option of INSTEAD OF as well as FOR and AFTER, where the trigger is executed instead of the statement that caused it to fire.

Using CLR DML Triggers

When using CLR DML triggers, it is still possible to test whether a specific column has been updated through the IsUpdatedColumn method of the SqlTriggerContext class, which works in the same way as the UPDATED(column) method available in T-SQL.

Also available are the two logical tables, inserted and deleted. However, retrieval of this information does require a call back to SQL Server. Unlike EventData, which for DML triggers will be set to a value of NULL, this information is not passed through to your CLR trigger when the trigger is fired. This is quite a sensible move, as passing large rows of data when there is no guarantee that the assembly will use them could involve a large overhead.

IsUpdatedColumn

IsUpdatedColumn works like UPDATED in T-SQL triggers. It takes an int representing the zero-based ordinal of the column and returns a bool value signifying whether or not that column has been changed. The number of columns can be retrieved through the ColumnCount property of the SqlTriggerContext class, and this allows you to loop through the columns to test which ones have been updated.

Using ColumnsUpdated

In this section, we'll build a very simple trigger that illustrates the use of the IsUpdatedColumn method and demonstrates how to retrieve data from the inserted table. We don't do anything with the information except to place the output in the EventLog, where it can be easily inspected.

Create a new SQL Server project in VS and call it DMLTrigger. Add a new trigger and call it ColsUpdDemo, and add the following code, as always starting with the using directives:

```
using System;
using System.Data;
using System.Data.SqlClient;
using System.Data.SqlTypes;
using System.Diagnostics;
using Microsoft.SqlServer.Server;
```

The only new namespace here is System.Diagnostics, which contains the classes we use for writing to the EventLog. This provides an easy way for us to inspect output from the trigger and to list which columns have been updated.

The code in the method that implements the trigger starts by getting a reference to the Application log and writing an entry to it to indicate that our trigger is starting. (We'll look at writing to the Windows event logs in detail in Chapter 9.)

```
public partial class Triggers
{
  public static void ColsUpdDemo()
  {
    SqlTriggerContext sqlTrg = SqlContext.TriggerContext;

    EventLog ev = new EventLog("Application",".","ColsUpdated");
    ev.WriteEntry("Starting");
```

Next, we loop through the columns in the data table bound to the trigger. For each column, we write a new entry to the Application log containing the current iteration number for the loop (i.e., the index number for the column) and a string representation of the Boolean value indicating whether that column has been updated.

```
for (int i = 0; i < sqlTrg.ColumnsUpdated.Length - 1; i++)
{
  ev.WriteEntry(string.Format("Column {0}, updated: {1}",i,
    sqlTrg.IsUpdatedColumn(i).ToString()));
}
```

In the next section of the example, we retrieve the top row from the inserted logical table as a SqlDataReader object. We can then get to each column in the row by using the indexer or, as shown in the following code, by explicitly getting the column information via the GetString method. Once again, we know the number of fields that are held within the table via the SqlDataReader's FieldCount property, allowing the trigger to cope with any additional columns added to the triggering table. We retrieve the value of the second column from the inserted table and write this to the event log together with the number of columns in the trigger table:

```
SqlPipe pipeSql = SqlContext.Pipe;
using (SqlConnection cn = new SqlConnection("context connection=true"))
{
  cn.Open();
  string sql = "SELECT * FROM inserted";
  SqlCommand sqlComm = new SqlCommand(sql, cn);
  SqlDataReader dr = sqlComm.ExecuteReader();
  dr.Read();
  string col1 = dr.GetString(1);
  ev.WriteEntry(string.Format("Inserted {0}, {1}", dr.FieldCount, col1));
  dr.Close();
}
}
}
```

The following code simply creates the assembly and the trigger in SQL Server, and adds a row to the AuditActions table we created earlier in the chapter. This will fire the trigger, which will write the details to the event log.

```
USE AssembliesTesting
go
CREATE ASSEMBLY DMLTrigger
AUTHORIZATION [dbo]
FROM "C:\Program Files\SQL Server Assemblies\DMLTrigger.dll"
WITH PERMISSION_SET = EXTERNAL_ACCESS
GO
CREATE TRIGGER ColsUpd
ON AuditActions FOR INSERT
AS EXTERNAL NAME DMLTrigger.Triggers.ColsUpdDemo
GO
INSERT INTO AuditActions (TriggerName, StartTime, EndTime)
  VALUES ("DropProcedure","06:00","20:00")
```

Summary

Triggers acting on DDL events are considered by some to be the most powerful addition to SQL Server 2005 assemblies from an organizational viewpoint. Having the ability to monitor accurately and instantly actions that are being performed on database objects and giving management information of core hour changes that are forbidden would be enough to deter anyone from even contemplating a quick fix.

DML triggers using assemblies could be just as powerful, but you must be careful here, as there will be extra overhead to go back to the server to get the logical tables, so only use assemblies when you really need to.

CHAPTER 9

■ ■ ■

Error Handling and Debugging Strategies

Now that you've seen examples of all the different types of database objects it's now possible to build in .NET, we can zoom in on some of the practical issues you'll encounter with whatever type of object you're creating. In the next chapter, we'll examine some of the security issues involved in writing database objects in .NET, but first, in this chapter, we'll look at two separate but closely related issues: exception handling and debugging.

At face value, of course, the two techniques are entirely unrelated. *Exception handling* is about dealing with more-or-less predictable events that may prevent your code from running (such as the failure to connect to a linked server), whereas *debugging* is about ensuring that no bugs remain in the assembly when it's deployed. However, in both cases, you rely heavily on the exceptions thrown by .NET, so it makes sense to cover the two topics in a single chapter.

This chapter covers the following topics:

- Debugging SQL assemblies, both in Visual Studio (VS) and using the command line

- Understanding structured exception handling in .NET

- Using the `SqlException` class

We'll then take a look at two ways in which we can inform users that a problem has arisen:

- Sending e-mails from .NET code

- Writing entries to the Windows event log

Debugging SQL Assemblies

As with all programming languages, the .NET languages distinguish between two types of error that can occur:

- Compile-time errors that are detected by the compiler and prevent the compilation of the assembly

- Runtime errors that the compiler can't detect and that therefore only manifest themselves at runtime

In this section, we'll concentrate on debugging runtime errors, as compile-time errors are usually fairly straightforward to solve. The C# compiler error messages are generally quite descriptive, and since they point to the exact line where the compiler encountered the error, it's usually relatively easy to get to the source of the problem and correct it.

Runtime errors mostly derive from incorrect data held in a variable, so the single most useful debugging technique is to step through code one line at a time, to see the changing values of variables as the code executes. This is, of course, easy to do with VS, but it's also possible to a degree using only the tools that ship with the .NET Framework SDK.

Debugging with Visual Studio

To debug a SQL assembly in VS, you need to create a SQL Server project—it's not possible to attach the debugger to the sqlsrver.exe process and debug a DLL that way.

■**Note** You need to be running under a Windows administrator account to debug SQL assemblies. This is because debugging stops the entire SQL Server process, so it's worth stressing once again that you should *never* debug on a live server.

To see how debugging SQL assemblies works in VS, create a new SQL Server project in VS called VSDebugExample and add a reference to the AdventureWorks database. Then add a new stored procedure item (we've called ours GetContactData.cs) to the project, and add some code to the body of the method. It doesn't really matter what code you add for this example, as long as it compiles; however, for this instance we've used the following code:

```
using System;
using System.Data;
using System.Data.SqlClient;
using System.Data.SqlTypes;
using Microsoft.SqlServer.Server;

public partial class StoredProcedures
{
    [Microsoft.SqlServer.Server.SqlProcedure(Name="uspGetContactData")]
    public static void GetContactData(int id)
    {
        try
        {
            using (SqlConnection cn = new SqlConnection("context connection=true"))
            {
                cn.Open();
                string sql = @"SELECT Title, FirstName, MiddleName, LastName,
                            Suffix FROM Person.Contact WHERE ContactID = @id";
                SqlCommand cmd = new SqlCommand(sql, cn);
                cmd.Parameters.AddWithValue("@id", id);
                SqlDataReader reader = cmd.ExecuteReader();
```

```
        SqlContext.Pipe.Send(reader);
        SqlContext.Pipe.Send("Command executed successfully.");
      }
    }
    catch (Exception e)
    {
      SqlContext.Pipe.Send(e.Message);
    }
  }
}
};
```

This procedure simply returns the name details of a contact from the `Person.Contact` table in AdventureWorks based on the ID passed into the procedure and returns the data to SQL Server through the `SqlPipe.Send` method.

To test debugging, add a breakpoint by clicking in the left-hand margin next to one of the first lines of code, as shown in Figure 9-1.

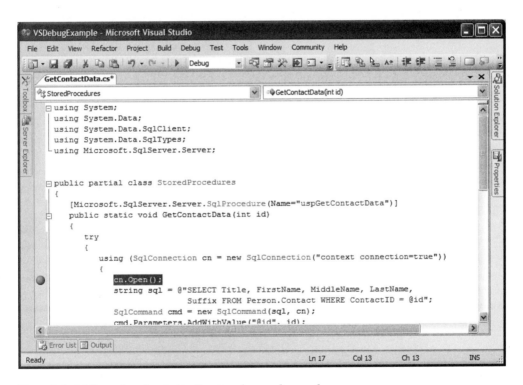

Figure 9-1. *Adding a breakpoint to the stored procedure code*

Before debugging is allowed within the SQL Server process, you need explicitly to enable it. To do this, open Server Explorer, expand the Databases node, and then right-click the node for the AdventureWorks database. In the context menu, ensure that Allow SQL/CLR Debugging is checked, as shown in Figure 9-2.

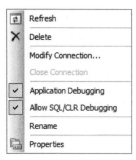

Figure 9-2. *Enabling debugging*

When the stored procedure is created, VS adds a SQL script called `test.sql` that runs the procedure using an `EXEC` command. You'll need to add an appropriate value here, for example:

```
EXEC uspGetContactData 1
```

As you learned in Chapter 2, VS SQL Server projects are deployed automatically to the database, so you don't need to write the `CREATE ASSEMBLY` or `CREATE PROCEDURE` statement. Simply click the Start button on the main menu, and the procedure will start to execute, pausing when the breakpoint is reached. You can now step through the code, line by line. VS provides three windows that allow you to examine the contents of variables as the code is running:

- *Autos window*: This window contains variables relating to the line that's just been executed. As the window's name implies, VS adds these variables to the Autos window automatically.

- *Locals window*: This window shows the values of all variables that are local to the currently executing method (i.e., variables declared in the body of the method and parameters that are passed into it).

- *Watch windows (VS allows four of these)*: These windows show the values of expressions that the developer wants to track. Add an expression to a Watch window by selecting Debug ➤ Quick Watch from the main menu.

The Whidbey version of VS has several improvements for debugging. Far more information is available on the values of variables, for example, allowing you to view the individual objects in a collection when you hover the cursor over a variable. To see this in action, step through the code until the following line is highlighted:

```
SqlDataReader reader = cmd.ExecuteReader();
```

At this point, the `Parameters` collection of the `SqlCommand` object has been populated. VS provides information about the collection that you can access through the debugging windows or (new to VS 2005) by hovering the cursor over the word `Parameters` on the previous line. If you open the node for `cmd.Parameters` in the Autos window, VS will display the values of its public and nonpublic properties. To examine the `SqlParameter` object that our code added to the collection, open the "Non-Public members" node and then the "_items" node. We added only one parameter, so it appears as item [0], which you can see in Figure 9-3.

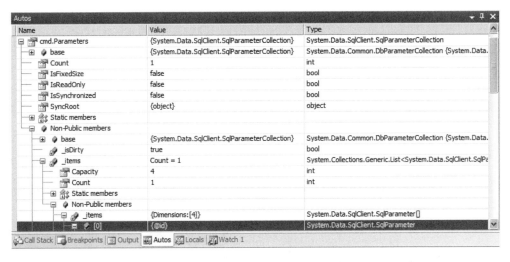

Figure 9-3. *Viewing the contents of the Parameters collection in the Autos window*

Extra information is also available on exceptions, and this too can be accessed inside a catch block within the debugging environment. The easiest way to see this is to deliberately throw an exception, so stop the debugger and add the following lines to the code at the start of the try block:

```
int i = 0;
int z = 1 / i;
```

Attempting to divide any number by zero will cause a DivideByZeroException to be thrown, so this will allow you to see the exception helper. Now set a breakpoint in the catch block, by clicking the left margin by the following line:

```
pipe.Send(e.Message);
```

Run the code, and it will stop at the breakpoint. You can, of course, access the information in the Exception object like any other local variable, but VS also provides a new exception helper. Hover the cursor over the line in the code that contains the catch statement, and an exclamation point will appear near the cursor. Click this exclamation point to open the exception helper, which is shown in Figure 9-4.

ⓘ **DivideByZeroException was caught**   ✕

Attempted to divide by zero.

Troubleshooting tips:

Make sure the value of the denominator is not zero before performing a division operation.

Get general help for this exception.

Search for more Help Online…

Actions:

View Detail…

Copy exception detail to the clipboard

Figure 9-4. *The VS exception helper*

Here you can get information about what caused the exception and hints on how to avoid the exception occurring (in this case, naturally enough, the suggestion is that you shouldn't divide by zero). There are also links to help on the exception and to examine the contents of the Exception object and its members.

Debugging from the Command Line

Even if you don't have the full version of Visual Studio 2005 installed, you can still step through your code line by line. SQL Server 2005 comes with a pared-down version of VS, which you can use to debug code (it seems to be very similar in debugging functionality to the CLR debugger of previous .NET versions). You can't use this debugger directly with SQL assemblies (attempts to launch it are simply ignored), but it is possible to get around this by debugging your .NET code outside SQL Server before deploying the assembly. You'll see how to do this later in the chapter.

The debugger can be launched programmatically by calling the Launch method of the System.Diagnostics.Debugger class, or it is launched automatically whenever an unhandled exception is thrown by a program. When either of these two events occurs, the user will be given the chance to select a debugger and start debugging, using any of the debuggers installed on the system, as shown in Figure 9-5.

Figure 9-5. *Choosing a debugger*

If you select "New instance of Visual Studio 2005" on this screen, you will be able to step through the code and set breakpoints and watches, exactly as you would in the full version of VS (see Figure 9-6).

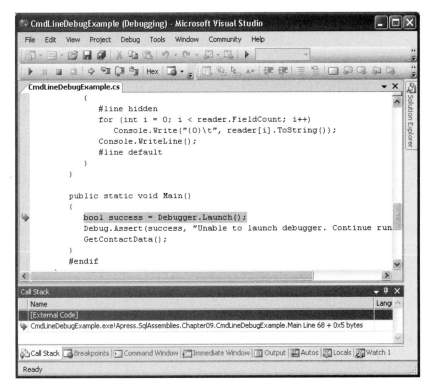

Figure 9-6. *Using the Visual Studio debugger*

Unfortunately, however, assemblies that are running within SQL Server can't be debugged in this way. This means that if you're not using VS, it may make sense to debug your assembly (or at least as much of the key code as you can) outside SQL Server before testing it in SQL Server. It's useful to look in this context at a couple of .NET debugging tricks that allow you to execute different code when you're debugging to the code in the release build, so you can create a single set of source code files that need only be recompiled to be installed into SQL Server. These techniques can be useful even if you're using VS, as it's convenient to make sure your .NET code works properly in a stand-alone setting, before having to worry about integrating it with SQL Server.

Using Preprocessor Directives

The most obvious of the aforementioned techniques is to take advantage of C#'s *preprocessor directives*. These are commands used to instruct the compiler to perform certain actions—in particular, to compile blocks of code only under certain conditions. You can take advantage of these to make your assembly handle exceptions in a different way when it's being debugged to the final release version. For example, you can send diagnostic information, such as the values of particular variables, to the user only when the debug build of the assembly is being executed. Conditional compilation also allows you to add a Main method to a DLL assembly so that it can be tested as a stand-alone program or to test a module that accesses SQL Server data over the context connection outside SQL Server using a standard ADO.NET connection. We'll present an example of these techniques shortly.

Preprocessor directives work by allowing us to define (or "undefine") symbols such as DEBUG. These are arbitrary names—something like Boolean variables in .NET code. We use the #define directive to define a symbol, and then, inside our code, we can check to see whether this symbol is defined using the #if...#endif directive; the code in this block will only be compiled if the symbol is defined. This block can also contain #elif directives to check for further conditions and an #else directive. All #define and #undef directives must appear before any .NET code in the source code file (not including other directives), for example:

```
#define DEBUG
#define TRACE
// ... .NET code here
#if DEBUG
// Code that will be compiled if DEBUG is defined
#elif TRACE
// Code that will be compiled if TRACE but not DEBUG is defined
#else
// Code that will be compiled if neither is defined
#endif
```

You can combine symbols with the && and || operators, check that symbols are not defined using !, and combine conditions using parentheses, for example:

```
#if (!DEBUG && !TRACE) || RELEASE
// Code will compile only if neither DEBUG nor TRACE are defined,
// or if RELEASE is defined.
#endif
```

You can also define a symbol using the command-line compiler by including the /define or /d option:

```
csc /d:DEBUG sourcefile.cs
```

If you're using VS, by default both the DEBUG and TRACE symbols will be defined for debug builds, while only TRACE will be defined for release builds. You can change this on the Build section of the Properties page for the project.

When you want to mark the symbol as undefined, simply change the #define directive to #undef:

```
#undef DEBUG
```

Although preprocessor directives must precede any .NET code in a source file (so you can't undefine a symbol halfway through a method), .NET assemblies can consist of multiple source files, so you can have a symbol defined for some but not all files. This is useful if you want to debug different parts of your assembly separately.

You can also generate custom compiler warnings and errors using the #warning and #error directives:

```
#if DEBUG
#warning Debug build
#endif
```

Finally, the #line directive allows you to change the line numbering as displayed in compiler errors and warnings, or to hide certain lines from the debugger. To change the line numbering, use #line followed by a number, and to reset it to the normal numbering according to the line's actual position in the source file, use #line default:

```
#line 100
// This line appears as line 100
// This line appears as line 101
#line default
// Normal numbering restored from this point.
```

To hide lines from the debugger, use #line hidden. The debugger will step over the following lines until another #line directive is reached. You can use this feature to avoid stepping through code that you've already debugged.

The Conditional Attribute

Another way of adding code to your assembly that won't be included in the release build is to use the Conditional attribute. If this attribute is applied to a method, that method will still exist in the compiled code, but it will be called only if a given symbol is defined at the point in the code where the method is called. An assembly can consist of several source code files, so if a symbol is defined in the file where the method is defined, that doesn't mean that it will necessarily be defined in a file where the method is called.

An example might make this clearer. Suppose you have two C# code files, Class1.cs and Class2.cs. Class1.cs contains a class with an entry-point Main method and a conditional method named Print. The Main method calls Print and then calls a method of Class2, which is defined in the second source code file:

```
// Class1.cs
#define DEBUG

using System;
using System.Diagnostics;

class Class1
{
    static void Main(string[] args)
    {
        Print("In Main method"); // Called because DEBUG is defined
        Class2.DoStuff();
    }

    [Conditional("DEBUG")]
    public static void Print(string msg)
    {
        Console.WriteLine(msg);
    }
}
```

Notice the `using` directive for the `System.Diagnostics` namespace, as that's where the `Conditional` attribute resides.

`Class2` has just one method, which just calls the `Class1.Print` method and returns. However, because the `DEBUG` symbol isn't defined in this file, the conditional `Print` method won't actually be called.

```
// Class2.cs
#undef DEBUG
public class Class2
{
   public static void DoStuff()
   {
      Class1.Print("Doing stuff"); // Not called
      // Do stuff...
   }
}
```

Note that conditional methods must be `void` and cannot be implementations of interface methods.

The Debug and Trace Classes

The last .NET debugging tools we'll look at are the `Debug` and `Trace` classes. These classes both live in the `System.Diagnostics` namespace and provide ways to debug your code and to trace its execution. These classes contain a number of static methods that can be used to emit messages if certain conditions are met. The methods of both classes are conditional, the principal difference between the classes being that the methods of `Trace` will be called only if `TRACE` is defined, whereas those of `Debug` are conditional on the `DEBUG` symbol.

These two classes allow you to configure `TraceListeners` that specify an output stream to which debugging information is sent, and then to write information to the listeners. These are particularly useful when debugging UDFs and UDT methods that can't send messages directly to the caller using the `SqlPipe.Send` method.

There are predefined `TraceListener` subclasses that send output to an event log (`EventLogTraceListener`) or to an I/O stream, such as a file or the console (`TextWriterTraceListener`). For example, to configure debugging information to be written to a text file, you can use code like this:

```
Debug.AutoFlush = true;
Debug.Listeners.Add(new TextWriterTraceListener("C:\\Apress\\" +
    "SqlAssemblies\\Chapter09\\DebugExample\\DebugLog.txt"));
Debug.WriteLine("Debugging configured.");
```

Note that the `AutoFlush` property is set to `true` before writing any text to the listener. This ensures that all information will actually be written; otherwise, the buffer may not be flushed and data could be lost.

Another useful method of the `Debug` and `Trace` classes is `Assert`. This allows you to pop up a message box if a certain condition isn't met, displaying an error message and the current call stack trace. For example, you can use the following to display an error message if the value of a certain variable is `null`:

```
Debug.Assert(myvar == null, "Warning: myvar is null");
```

Debugging Example

To see some of the techniques just described in action, we'll create a CLR procedure that uses the DEBUG symbol to include a Main method and to choose whether to access data using the context connection or an external connection, so that we can test and debug the assembly from the command line before recompiling it as a DLL and installing it into SQL Server.

As always, we begin with the using statements. There are three we'll include in both debug and release builds: the standard System namespace, the System.Data.SqlClient namespace for accessing SQL Server data, and the System.Diagnostics namespace, which contains the classes used for debugging.

```
using System;
using System.Data.SqlClient;
using System.Diagnostics;
```

If the DEBUG symbol isn't defined, we'll want to use the extensions to the SQL Server .NET provider, so we need to import the Microsoft.SqlServer.Server namespace:

```
#if !DEBUG
using Microsoft.SqlServer.Server;
#endif
```

We'll add the SqlProcedure attribute to the method that implements our procedure only if it's not a debug build:

```
namespace Apress.SqlAssemblies.Chapter09
{
    public class CmdLineDebugExample
    {
        #if !DEBUG
        [SqlProcedure]
        #endif
        public static void GetContactData()
        {
```

Next, we define the connection string. For release builds, we'll be running inside SQL Server, so we use the context connection, but if we're running outside SQL Server, we have to use a standard ADO.NET connection string:

```
        try
        {
            string connStr;
            #if !DEBUG
```

```
connStr = "context connection=true";
#else
connStr = "Database=(local);Initial Catalog=AdventureWorks;" +
          "Integrated Security=true";
#endif
```

The lines to access and process the data will be the same, regardless of whether or not we're running inside SQL Server. In this example, we just want to get the data into a reader, to send straight back to SQL Server. We start by creating a new SqlConnection object based on whichever connection string was defined and opening this connection. Then we define a query to return the top ten names from the Person.Contact table of the AdventureWorks database, create a new SqlConnection object using this query and our SqlConnection object, and finally call its ExecuteReader method:

```
using (SqlConnection cn = new SqlConnection(connStr))
{
    cn.Open();
    string sql = @"SELECT TOP 10 FirstName, LastName
                   FROM Person.Contact";
    SqlCommand cmd = new SqlCommand(sql, cn);
    SqlDataReader reader = cmd.ExecuteReader();
```

If we're running in SQL Server, we just send the results straight back to the pipe. Otherwise, we'll create a method called WriteData to write the results to the console window:

```
    #if DEBUG
    WriteData(reader);
    #else
    SqlContext.Pipe.Send(reader);
    #endif
    }
}
```

If any exceptions occur, we'll send them either to the command window or to SQL Server, as appropriate:

```
catch (Exception e)
{
    #if DEBUG
    Console.WriteLine(e.Message);
    #else
    SqlContext.Pipe.Send(e.Message);
    #endif
    }
}
```

If we're in debug mode, we need a method to display the results that would otherwise be sent to the SQL Server pipe. This method takes a SqlDataReader as a parameter and simply iterates through each column of each row in the reader, writing the contents of that cell to the console window, followed by a tab character. This iteration through the reader is hidden from the debugger, so as to avoid having to step through every row and every column when we're debugging. At the end of every row, we begin a new line:

```
#if DEBUG
private static void WriteData(SqlDataReader reader)
{
    while (reader.Read())
    {
        #line hidden
        for (int i = 0; i < reader.FieldCount; i++)
            Console.Write("{0}\t", reader[i].ToString());
        Console.WriteLine();
        #line default
    }
}
```

For this assembly to be executable from the command line, it also needs a Main method. We won't need this when we're running inside SQL Server, so we include it in the same #if DEBUG block as the previous method. This method starts up the debugger, so the developer can step through the code; if the debugger fails to start, we use the Debug.Assert method to ask the user whether or not to continue with the program. If the user elects to go on, we call the method that implements our stored procedure.

```
public static void Main()
{
    bool success = Debugger.Launch();
    Debug.Assert(success, "Unable to launch debugger. Continue running?");
    GetContactData();
}
#endif
    }
}
```

To compile this into a stand-alone executable, we use the following command-line statement:

```
csc /d:DEBUG /DEBUG CmdLineDebugExample.cs
```

Note that, as well as defining the DEBUG symbol with the /d:DEBUG option, we also include the /DEBUG option, which causes the C# compiler to emit debugging information, which the debugger needs to step through the source code. When you run this example from the command line, you will be asked which debugger you want to use. Select the Microsoft CLR Debugger 2005 option and the debugger will open with the following line highlighted in green:

```
bool success = Debugger.Launch();
```

Click the Step Into button to start debugging, and much of the power of VS's debugging features will be available, including the ability to step through code a line at a time and to set watches and breakpoints.

Once you've finished debugging the assembly, you can install it into SQL Server by recompiling it as a DLL without the DEBUG symbol defined:

```
csc /t:library CmdLineDebugExample.cs
```

When all the debugging information is omitted, this is a completely standard SQL assembly, so the SQL statements for creating the assembly and the procedure in the AdventureWorks database have nothing new to be remarked upon:

```
USE AdventureWorks
GO

CREATE ASSEMBLY CmdLineDebugExample
FROM 'C:\Apress\SqlAssemblies\Chapter09\CmdLineDebugExample\CmdLineDebugExample.dll'
WITH PERMISSION_SET = SAFE;
GO

CREATE PROCEDURE uspGetContactData
AS
EXTERNAL NAME CmdLineDebugExample.[Apress.SqlAssemblies.Chapter09.
CmdLineDebugExample].GetContactData;
GO

EXEC uspGetContactData
```

.NET Exception Handling

You've seen numerous examples of basic .NET exception handling in previous chapters, so here we'll focus on two particular aspects:

- Using the SqlException object, which is thrown whenever errors occur during execution of a SQL statement

- Creating custom exception classes

We'll spend the rest of the chapter looking at some of the actions we can take when exceptions occur.

Using SqlException

When errors occur executing a SQL statement, an exception of type SqlException will be thrown. As more than one error can occur in the execution of a single command, a standard .NET exception class can't hold all the necessary information. To get around this, the SqlException class gives access to a SqlErrorsCollection that provides information about all the errors that occurred. Unfortunately, you can't throw your own instances of SqlException, as the class has no public constructor (and it's also sealed, so you can't create your own subclasses of it either). It would perhaps have been useful when we access an external data source using a

.NET API (such as the DirectoryServices API you encountered in Chapter 5) to provide the same level of information that SQL Server provides, so that external applications calling the procedure could handle .NET errors in the same way as SQL Server errors. However, for the moment at least, it's not possible to do this.

You can use the information in the SqlErrorsCollection to fine-tune how you handle errors. Each error is uniquely identified by an error number, so you can take specific actions when you know a particular error has occurred. For example, the error with number 229 occurs when users attempt to access a database object for which they don't have permission, and error 156 indicates a SQL syntax error. In the former case, you may want to log the unsuccessful access attempt, while the latter could imply a bug in a module that generates a SQL command dynamically, so you may want to inform the programmer via e-mail.

■**Note** The messages associated with individual message numbers can be found via the sys.messages system view.

```
catch (SqlException e)
{
    foreach (SqlError err in e.Errors)
    {
        switch (err.Number)
        {
            case 229:
                // Write entry to event log
                break;
            case 156:
                // E-mail .NET programmer with details of error
                break;
            default:
                // Handle any other SQL errors
                break;
        }
    }
}
catch (Exception e))?
    // Handle any non-SQL exceptions here.
    // We can have multiple catch blocks for each try block,
    // and the first one that matches the exception thrown
    // will be executed, so subclasses should always precede
    // the classes they inherit from, and hence System.Exception
    // should come last.
}
```

We'll look at the .NET code for writing entries to the Windows event logs and for sending e-mails later in this chapter.

A single SQL command can generate multiple errors, so we have to iterate through each `SqlError` in the `SqlException.Errors` collection to see if it matches the number we're looking for.

Related errors can be handled in a single block using multiple `case` statements:

```
case 14126:
case 14260:
case 20047:
case 229:
case 230:
    // Handle permission errors
    break;
```

Throwing Your Own Exceptions

As well as handling exceptions thrown by the methods you call in your code, you'll sometimes need to throw your own exceptions. If your code is unable to complete execution, you need to indicate this to the calling application, which will assume that everything went according to plan if an exception isn't thrown. In some cases, it may be acceptable simply to let an exception bubble up to the caller by rethrowing it in a `catch` block or by just not handling it. Generally, though, you'll want a greater degree of control over the information passed back to the user, so you'll want to throw a new exception.

There are two possibilities for throwing your own exceptions in .NET code: you can throw a new instance of a built-in class from the Framework Class Library (FCL), or you can create an exception class of your own by inheriting from `System.Exception` or one of its derived classes. To throw an exception, you simply create a new instance of the exception class and pass it to the `throw` keyword:

```
ArgumentNullException e = new ArgumentNullException(
    "Parameter 'name' cannot be null");
throw e;
```

The trick is obviously in choosing which exception type to throw. All .NET exceptions derive from the `System.Exception` class, which has two major subclasses: `System.SystemException` and `System.ApplicationException`. In theory, only the runtime itself is supposed to throw instances of `SystemException` or derived classes, and application code should throw subclasses of `ApplicationException`. In practice, however, this stricture is rarely upheld. It doesn't make much sense to reinvent the wheel, and Microsoft has created a whole range of exceptions deriving from `SystemException` that are suitable for most occasions. For example, if you need to throw an exception when a null value is passed into a method, it makes sense to throw a new instance of `ArgumentNullException`, rather than defining a new class that inherits from `ApplicationException`.

In general, it makes sense to throw the most specific type of exception that's available and applicable to the circumstances, so that calling classes can decide on the granularity of the exception handling they require. In the previous example, this would mean throwing an `ArgumentNullException` rather than an `ArgumentException`, as that allows the calling method to handle all `ArgumentExceptions` together, or to handle `ArgumentNullExceptions` separately. Throwing new instances of `Exception` or `SystemException` in particular is a bad practice that should be avoided (and throwing instances of `ApplicationException` isn't much better), because these exceptions give the caller no information at all about what went wrong.

Creating Custom Exception Classes

If, instead of throwing one of the built-in exceptions, you need to create a custom exception class, it's also recommended by Microsoft to derive it directly or indirectly from ApplicationException, but again, this is a rule observed almost as much in the breach as in the adherence. In practice, it's common to take advantage of the existing SystemException-derived classes in the FCL to create subclasses that provide a general description of the problem. However, you shouldn't derive exceptions directly from either Exception or SystemException; if you're not subclassing a specific exception type, it makes more sense to derive from ApplicationException, as this makes it clear to callers that the exception originated in your application and isn't something generated within the runtime itself.

Apart from selecting the correct base class to derive from, there are two other things you need to do to adhere to the best practices for custom exception classes. First, all exception classes should have names ending in Exception. And second, they should implement three recommended constructors:

- *Zero-parameter constructor:* This should provide a default error message for exceptions of this type.

- *Single-parameter constructor:* This takes a string parameter containing the message for the exception.

- *Two-parameter constructor:* This takes a string containing the message and an Exception instance representing the inner exception—an exception that was caught in the current method and that the method is passing back to the caller wrapped in the current exception instance.

Other than these simple recommendations, there's very little for you to do; all the work is done by the base Exception class, so you just need to call the appropriate base constructor (things get a bit more complicated if the exception needs to be usable from COM clients, but that's not an issue for SQL assemblies). For example, the following code defines an exception that could be thrown when a SQL syntax error occurs:

```
public class InvalidSqlException : ApplicationException
{
    InvalidSqlException() : base("Invalid SQL syntax")
    {
    }

    InvalidSqlException(string message) : base(message)
    {
    }

    InvalidSqlException(string message, Exception innerException) :
                                        base(message, innerException)
    {
    }
}
```

This class can be used in the same way as any other exception class:

```
throw new InvalidSqlException("Invalid SQL command: " + sql);
```

Recording Errors

When errors do occur, you have three basic options for handling them. First, you can simply pass the problem back to the calling application to deal with—for example, by throwing an exception or by just sending an error message back to the user. This could be a good option in circumstances where you suspect that the user is at fault (i.e., if a query is based on mistyped information), and you need to get the user to try again. Second, you could try to correct the problem on the spot by performing an alternative action (such as redirecting a query to a mirror server). Finally, you can record the error, either by making an entry in a log file or by e-mailing information to the DBA or system administrator, so that he can take appropriate action (e.g., if a linked server is down).

These techniques are, of course, not mutually exclusive, and if you detect a serious problem, it's very likely that you'd want to both inform the administrator immediately by sending an e-mail and log the error for future reference, and you may well also want to attempt an alternative operation.

For the remainder of the chapter, we'll look at a couple of ways to record errors in SQL assemblies: by sending an e-mail or by writing an entry to a Windows event log.

E-mailing Error Information

The ability to send an e-mail from a module such as a stored procedure isn't anything new, of course: you can send an e-mail directly from T-SQL if SQLMail or Database Mail is enabled in the database. However, you'll also need to e-mail directly from your CLR modules, in which case it makes sense to use .NET's own features for sending e-mails. E-mailing obviously comes with an overhead and has security implications, as the DBA has no control over the information sent out of the database in an e-mail, so this technique is probably best used to draw attention to issues that need immediate action, such as the detection of a server being down.

Sending an e-mail from .NET code is an extremely straightforward affair, so we'll keep this example very simple. We'll write a stored procedure that takes an ID and a list of column names and uses those to create on the fly a SQL statement that accesses the HumanResources.Employee table of the AdventureWorks database. Dynamic SQL is one area where there's a clear advantage to using .NET code, even though it's also possible in T-SQL—string manipulation in C# is much easier to write and maintain than in T-SQL and also potentially more efficient. For example, we can split a comma-delimited list of values into its constituent parts in a single line of .NET code.

In this stored procedure, we'll pass in a comma-delimited list that contains the names of the columns we want to return as the first parameter, and the ID of the employee as the second. We'll use these values to create a SQL statement and then execute that statement, returning a single row of data. Finally, we'll send this row back to the caller. We'll look out for both SqlExceptions and general .NET exceptions. If any SqlExceptions are thrown, it's very likely because an invalid column name was included in the list of columns, so we won't bother sending an e-mail (although it could also be because the user executing the procedure doesn't have permission to access the Employee table). However, if any other exception occurs, something unexpected has happened, and we'll notify the administrator via e-mail.

As always, we start with the using directives. Apart from the usual suspects, we have System.Text, where the StringBuilder lives, and System.Net.Mail, which we need to send e-mails from .NET code.

```
using System;
using System.Data.SqlClient;
using System.Net.Mail;
using System.Text;
using Microsoft.SqlServer.Server;
```

Within the code for the stored procedure, we start by instantiating the StringBuilder we'll use to create the SQL statement and the SqlPipe that we'll use to communicate with the caller, as we need to access these objects in both the try and catch blocks that surround our code:

```
namespace Apress.SqlAssemblies.Chapter09
{
    public class EmailExample
    {
        [SqlProcedure]
        public static void GetEmployeeData(string columnList, int id)
        {
            StringBuilder sb = new StringBuilder();
            SqlPipe pipe = SqlContext.Pipe;
```

Our first task within the try block is to create the SQL statement. We start by removing any square brackets from the column list, as we'll add our own around each of the column names. This helps to secure against SQL injection, because anything within the square brackets will be interpreted as part of a column name and therefore won't be executed as a SQL command:

```
            try
            {
                columnList = columnList.Replace("[", "");
                columnList = columnList.Replace("]", "");
```

We start building the statement by adding a SELECT command to the StringBuilder, and then we split the list of column names into a string array using the String.Split method. This takes a char array containing the characters where we want to split the string (in our case, just a comma):

```
                sb.Append("SELECT ");
                string[] columnNames = columnList.Split(new char[] { ',' });
```

Now that we have the column names as individual strings within an array, we can iterate through that array, adding each name to our StringBuilder. Each name is surrounded by square brackets and followed by a trailing comma and space. We call `Trim` on the column name before appending it to the `StringBuilder` so that any whitespace included in the list of column names is removed:

```
foreach (string column in columnNames)
{
    sb.Append("[");
    sb.Append(column.Trim());
    sb.Append("], ");
}
```

To finish off the SQL statement, we remove the final comma and space from the `StringBuilder`, and then add the `FROM` and `WHERE` clauses. The ID of the employee we want to find will be passed into the statement as a parameter, rather than built into the statement programmatically:

```
sb.Remove(sb.Length - 2, 2);
sb.Append(" FROM HumanResources.Employee WHERE EmployeeID=@id");
```

Now we open the context connection, create a new `SqlCommand` object for the SQL statement we've just built, and add to it the `@id` parameter together with the value that was passed into the stored procedure. Then we execute the command by calling the `ExecuteReader` method and send the results back to the caller:

```
using (SqlConnection cn = new SqlConnection("context connection=true"))
{
    cn.Open();
    SqlCommand cmd = new SqlCommand(sb.ToString(), cn);
    cmd.Parameters.AddWithValue("@id", id);
    SqlDataReader reader = cmd.ExecuteReader();
    pipe.Send(reader);
    pipe.Send("Command executed successfully.");
}
```

If any SQL exceptions occur, we simply send the SQL statement that we created on the fly back to the caller, together with the messages from the `SqlErrors` in the `SqlException`'s `Errors` collection, so that the user can see what went wrong and correct the parameters:

```
catch (SqlException e)
{
    pipe.Send("Invalid SQL statement: " + sb.ToString());
    foreach (SqlError err in e.Errors)
        pipe.Send(err.Message);
}
```

If any other exceptions occur, we'll send an e-mail to an administrator's account, so that the problem will be detected immediately and can be put right. We'll create a separate method to do the actual e-mailing, so here we'll simply call this method, passing in the body, subject, and list of recipients for the e-mail:

```
catch (Exception e)
{
    EmailExceptionInfo(e.Message,
                       "Exception in stored procedure GetEmployeeData",
                       "sqlassemblies@apress.com");
    pipe.Send(e.Message);
}
```

The method to send the e-mail is very simple. We just set the SMTP server to use by creating a new SmtpClient object, passing in the name of the server (alternatively, we could use its IP address; we can also pass in the TCP port that the SMTP service is running on if it's not the default). We then create a new MailMessage instance, passing in the From e-mail address, the list of recipients, the e-mail's subject, and finally the body of the message. Once we have this, we can simply pass it into the SmtpClient's Send method:

```
private static void EmailExceptionInfo(string body, string subject,
                                       string recipients)
{
    // Change the string in the following line to refer to a valid and
    // accessible SMTP server
    SmtpClient client = new SmtpClient("SmtpServer");
    MailMessage msg = new MailMessage("EmailExampleAssembly@apress.com",
                                      recipients, subject, body);
    client.Send(msg);
}
}
}
```

It goes without saying that the SQL Server machine needs to be able to access an SMTP server in order to send e-mails.

Next, we compile the C# file as usual:

```
csc /t:library EmailExample.cs
```

The SQL script to install and execute this stored procedure contains few surprises:

```
USE AdventureWorks
GO

CREATE ASSEMBLY EmailExample
FROM 'C:\Apress\SqlAssemblies\Chapter09\EmailExample\EmailExample.dll'
WITH PERMISSION_SET = UNSAFE;
GO
```

```
CREATE PROCEDURE uspGetEmployeeData(@columnList nvarchar(1000), @id int)
AS
EXTERNAL NAME EmailExample.[Apress.SqlAssemblies.Chapter09.EmailExample].
GetEmployeeData;
GO

EXEC uspGetEmployeeData 'NationalIDNumber', 1;
```

Naturally, our EmailExample assembly requires the EXTERNAL_ACCESS permission set as it is sending data out of the server. Also notice that our code will send an e-mail only if something unpredictable happens (in this case, a non-SQL exception is thrown). In this very simple example, that's highly unlikely to happen, so an e-mail will be sent only if you deliberately tamper with the code to cause a non-SQL exception (e.g., by dividing by zero within the try block).

Writing to an Event Log

An alternative approach to recording errors is to write an entry to a Windows event log. You've already seen simple examples of this in Chapter 8, but we haven't yet shown how to take full advantage of the event log. In this section, we'll take a more detailed look at event logs and examine how to use them to their full potential from .NET code.

Event Logs and Windows Event Viewer

Windows Event Viewer provides a single place where administrators and users can view the log files of all the applications running on a server. Where simple text log files provide a long list of entries that are very difficult to browse through, Event Viewer provides facilities to categorize and filter entries, so an administrator can easily find important entries. It separates out the different components of an entry, such as the time it was written and its severity, and these components can be used to sort and filter the log.

However, writing to a log file that Event Viewer can read involves more work than writing a line to a text file. An application must register as an event source for a particular log to write entries to that file, and as well as the message for the entry you can specify its type (e.g., whether it's an error or a warning), an event ID that identifies the specific type of event that occurred, and a category ID that indicates a more general category the event belongs to. When the log is viewed in Event Viewer, Windows searches for a set of text files associated with the log that contain information describing the event and, if it belongs to a category, about that category.

These files are compiled into resource DLLs that Event Viewer uses to display information about errors. .NET provides a default message DLL (EventLogMessages.dll), and, if no other DLL is associated with the event source, the error message you pass into the method used to write the log entry will be displayed as part of this default message. However, this default behavior is somewhat inflexible. It doesn't allow you to assign your log entries to particular categories, which can be used to filter the entries in Event Viewer, and it provides a default (and hence pretty useless) URL for the user to click to receive more information about the error. It also doesn't provide a convenient way to manage event messages in different languages, so if this is necessary you'd need to create resource files anyway. To get the most out of the Windows event log, you therefore need to create your own message DLLs.

Writing the .NET Code

To demonstrate advanced event log usage in .NET, we'll create a simple CLR stored procedure that selects all the data from the Employee and Contact tables for any employee with a specific name. We'll create a new event log for this procedure, and whenever it's executed, we'll write an entry to the log that indicates the results of the query: whether or not the query executed successfully, and if it did, whether or not it returned any rows. Running the procedure will create the log file itself, but we'll need to create the related text files manually and then compile them into resource DLLs. We'll also need to modify the registry entries for the log in order to point to these files.

The .NET code starts by creating the SQL command to get the contact details for a person; this is very straightforward, so we'll pass over it very quickly. The only thing to notice in the first part of our example is that we include a using directive for the System.Diagnostics namespace, as this is where the EventLog class resides.

```
using System;
using System.Data.SqlClient;
using System.Diagnostics;
using System.Text;
using Microsoft.SqlServer.Server;

namespace Apress.SqlAssemblies.Chapter09
{
    public class EventLogExample
    {
        [SqlProcedure]
        public static void GetDataForNamedEmployee(string name)
        {
            // Open the context connection
            using (SqlConnection cn = new SqlConnection("context connection=true"))
            {
                cn.Open();

                // Define our SQL statement
                string sql = @"SELECT * FROM HumanResources.Employee e
                            INNER JOIN Person.Contact c
                            ON c.ContactID = e.ContactID
                            WHERE c.FirstName + ' ' + c.LastName = @name";
                SqlCommand cmd = new SqlCommand(sql, cn);

                // Add the @name parameter and set its value
                cmd.Parameters.AddWithValue("@name", name);

                // Get the SqlPipe to send data/messages back to the user
                SqlPipe pipe = SqlContext.Pipe;
```

Once we've configured the command, the real fun begins! The remaining code in this method is placed within a try...catch block, and if anything goes wrong we'll need to catch the error and log it. First, we execute the command to get a SqlDataReader:

```
try
{
    SqlDataReader reader = cmd.ExecuteReader();
```

Once we have the reader, we take note of whether it has rows or not (if it doesn't, we'll log a different event). We need to do this right away, before it's sent back to the user, because the HasRows property will always return false after that. Then (if all's still going well) we send the data in the reader back to the caller:

```
bool hasRows = reader.HasRows;
pipe.Send(reader);
```

Next, we'll add an entry to the log and send a message to the user. We'll vary the log entry and the message according to whether the query returned any rows or not. If it didn't, we'll add a log entry of type warning and send a message saying that no rows were found; otherwise, we'll add an informational entry and send a message to indicate that the command completed without problems.

```
if (!hasRows)
{
    WriteLogEntry(name, EventLogEntryType.Warning, 2000, 1);
    pipe.Send("No matching rows found.");
}
else
{
    WriteLogEntry(name, EventLogEntryType.Information, 1000, 1);
    pipe.Send("Command executed successfully.");
}
```

The actual writing of the entry is performed in a method called WriteLogEntry, which we'll look at shortly. This method needs four pieces of data: the string that will be passed into the message for the particular entry type and displayed as part of the message in Event Viewer, the EventLogEntryType enum value for the entry type, the ID for the event, and the ID for the category that we want this entry to belong to.

If an exception occurs, we'll add a log entry detailing what went wrong, and we'll also send the information to the user. If the exception is a SqlException, we'll iterate through all the SQL errors in its Errors collection and add information about each error to the message:

```
catch (SqlException e)
{
    // Build the log entry from the SqlErrors
    StringBuilder sb = new StringBuilder();
    foreach (SqlError err in e.Errors)
        sb.AppendFormat("Error {0}\nSeverity {1}\nState {2}\n{3}\n\n",
                        err.Number, err.Class, err.State, err.Message);
```

```
                // Write the entry and send a message to the caller
                WriteLogEntry(sb.ToString(), EventLogEntryType.Error, 3000, 2);
                pipe.Send("SQL errors occurred executing the stored procedure.");
                pipe.Send(sb.ToString());
            }
```

We use a StringBuilder in this instance to create the message containing the SQL error information, as we don't know how many errors the collection will contain. The information about each error is added to the StringBuilder using the AppendFormat method, which allows us to incorporate parameters into the string, in much the same way as we would with a Console.WriteLine call.

If any other exception occurs, we will simply embed the error message into the message defined in our message file:

```
            catch (Exception e)
            {
                WriteLogEntry(e.Message, EventLogEntryType.Error, 4000, 2);
                pipe.Send("Unknown error occurred executing the stored procedure.");
                pipe.Send(e.Message);
            }
        }
    }
```

The WriteLogEntry method, where the actual entry is written, is very simple. First, we check whether our assembly is already registered as an event source, and if not, we register it as a source for the SQL Assemblies Log custom event log:

```
    private static void WriteLogEntry(string message, EventLogEntryType entryType,
                                      int msgId, short categoryId)
    {
        if (!EventLog.SourceExists("EventLogExample"))
            EventLog.CreateEventSource("EventLogExample", "SQL Assemblies Log");
```

If the custom log doesn't already exist, creating an event source associated with it will also cause the log to be created. This has two effects: it creates an event log file (.evt) to contain any entries added to the log, and it creates a registry entry for the log. This entry will point to the default .NET message DLL, although at the time of this writing, it failed to specify the correct path in .NET 2.0, so the entry appeared in the Event Viewer with a message explaining that the event ID wasn't recognized. We'll need to modify this registry value to point to our custom message DLL, and we'll also need to add another couple of values to the key. We'll show shortly how to get Event Viewer to find and use our custom message DLLs.

Once we know the source is registered, we can instantiate a new EventLog object representing our custom log, then use this to write an entry to the log, and finally close the log:

```
            EventLog log = new EventLog("SQL Assemblies Log");
            log.Source = "EventLogExample";
            log.WriteEntry(message, entryType, msgId, categoryId);
            log.Close();
        }
    }
}
```

Notice that we need to set the `Source` property before writing to the log, as each entry must be written by a registered source. The `WriteEntry` method itself has many overloads; in our case, we specify the message, the entry type (as an `EventLogEntryType` enum value), the ID for the message, and the ID for the category. These IDs are defined in our message file, so let's look at that next. But first compile the C# file as usual using the following command:

```
csc /t:library EventLogExample.cs
```

Creating Message Files

Message files define the event types that an event source can generate and provide information about them that Event Viewer uses to display the event. Note that Event Viewer looks up the message DLL; the information in this file isn't written to the log file, so if it's changed, entries already written to the log will also change. Message files are designed primarily for use with unmanaged C++ code, so we won't include everything here that can go in a message file. A message file consists of up to three parts: an optional header, which contains metainformation about the event types such as definitions of the languages the message file supports; the definitions of any entry categories used by the event source (these can also be stored in a separate file); and the definitions of the entry messages themselves.

■**Note** A complete description of message text files is impossible here, but for full details see http://msdn.microsoft.com/library/default.asp?url=/library/en-us/tools/tools/ message_text_files.asp.

The event categories can be placed in the same file as the events themselves, or they can be in a separate file. The format for both is the same, but if the event categories are placed in the message file, the categories must precede the events. In both cases, each message consists of a set of name/value pairs, and each pair must be placed on a separate line. The first value must be the `MessageId`, and this is the only mandatory value we need to define. Note that, because they're defined in the same way, the `MessageIds` for categories can't be the same as those for events. The section for each message ends with the message text, followed by a line containing just a period.

Most of the values that can be given in a message file are in fact ignored when the entries are written in .NET code: they are overridden by the values passed into the `WriteEntry` method. The only values we need to concern ourselves with here are the `MessageId`, the `Language` for the message, and of course the message itself. The language names that can be included are specified in the header section of the file before the first message, together with an arbitrary number that is used as the language identifier in the resource table, for example:

```
LanguageNames=(English=1:MSG00001)
LanguageNames=(German=2:MSG00002)
```

By default, only English is defined (with the ID 1:MSG00001). If messages in more than one language are included, separate the text for each language with a line containing a single period:

```
MessageId=1
Language=English
The operation could not be carried out.

.

Language=German
Die Operation konnte nicht ausgeführt werden.

.
```

We can include parameters in the message text using %1, %2, etc., but unfortunately the .NET EntryLog.WriteEntry method allows us to pass in only one parameter. (This is the message string that is passed into the WriteEntry method, and it will be inserted into the message at the appropriate place in the text.) Any carriage returns in the message text will be replaced with a space, so if you want to add a line space in the message, you need to replace it with the sequence %r. For a full list of the other escape sequences used in message text files, please see the link cited at the beginning of this section. Finally, any URLs prefixed with http:// will automatically be converted to hyperlinks when the message is displayed in Event Viewer, so we can include links to web sites where more information about the error is given.

Here, then, is our message text file (EventLogMessages.mc). Notice that the event categories are defined in exactly the same way as the individual messages and that they are placed first in the file (for this simple, monolingual example, we don't need a header section).

```
; // Event categories
MessageId=1
Language=English
Execution completed

.

MessageId=2
Language=English
Execution failed

.


; // Event messages
MessageId=1000
Language=English
Successfully retrieved data for employee %1%r
For more information, please refer to the website%r
http://www.JulianSkinner.com/books/SqlAssemblies/ErrorMessages.aspx?id=3000

.

MessageId=2000
Language=English
No rows found for employee %1%r
For more information, please refer to the website%r
http://www.JulianSkinner.com/books/SqlAssemblies/ErrorMessages.aspx?id=2000
```

```
.
MessageId=3000
Language=English
SQL errors occurred executing stored procedure:%r%1%r
For more information, please refer to the website%r
http://www.JulianSkinner.com/books/SqlAssemblies/ErrorMessages.aspx?id=3000
.
MessageId=4000
Language=English
An unknown error occurred executing stored procedure:%r%1%r
For more information, please refer to the website%r
http://www.JulianSkinner.com/books/SqlAssemblies/ErrorMessages.aspx?id=4000
.
```

That completes the message text file, but for Event Viewer to be able to use it, we must first compile it into a resource DLL. There are three steps to this process, using three different command-line tools. As we've already mentioned, the Windows event log system is designed primarily to be used from unmanaged C++ code, so these tools don't all ship with the .NET SDK. However, they ship with all versions of Visual Studio, and because you're working with C++ rather than .NET code, you don't need to use Visual Studio 2005. You can access these tools from the Visual Studio command prompt (in the Visual Studio Tools menu under Microsoft Visual Studio in the Start menu), so open this command prompt and change to the directory where you saved the .mc file.

The first step is to compile the text file into an .rc file using the message compiler (mc.exe):

```
mc EventLogMessages.mc
```

This generates (among other things) an .rc file with the same name as the .mc file (in our case, EventLogMessages.rc). Next, we have to compile this into a resource file (.res), using the resource compiler (rc.exe):

```
rc -r EventLogMessages.rc
```

Again, this generates a file with the same name as the input file (EventLogMessages.res). If you want the .res file to have a different name, use the -fo option:

```
rc -r -fo:EventLogExampleMessages.res EventLogMessages.rc
```

The final step to generating a message DLL is to compile the resource file into a DLL. To do this, we use the C++ linker, link.exe:

```
link -dll -noentry -out:EventLogMessages.dll EventLogMessages.res
```

This generates a warning that we haven't specified a processor type to optimize for:

```
LINK : warning LNK4068: /MACHINE not specified; defaulting to X86
```

However, since our DLL doesn't contain any code—just resources—this isn't a problem.

We've now compiled the .res file into EventLogMessages.dll, but before Event Viewer can use it, we need to configure the registry entry for the log. The easiest way to do that is to run our stored procedure, which will create the registry entry and the .evt file for the log, and then modify the registry using regedit. If the event log will be stored on a computer other than your development machine, you'll also need to copy the message DLL to the event log machine.

Creating the Stored Procedure

The next step is to install the assembly into SQL Server and create the stored procedure in the AdventureWorks database:

```
USE AdventureWorks;
GO

CREATE ASSEMBLY EventLogExample
FROM 'C:\Apress\SqlAssemblies\Chapter09\EventLogExample\EventLogExample.dll'
WITH PERMISSION_SET = UNSAFE;
GO

CREATE PROCEDURE uspGetDataForNamedEmployee(@name nvarchar(512))
AS
EXTERNAL NAME EventLogExample.[Apress.SqlAssemblies.Chapter09.EventLogExample].
GetDataForNamedEmployee;
GO
```

This code should need no explanation by now, but notice that we have to define the PERMISSION_SET as UNSAFE, as accessing the event log requires special permissions that aren't granted to SAFE or EXTERNAL_ACCESS assemblies (we'll look at code access security in the next chapter).

Finally, run the stored procedure (you should see a message saying that no rows were returned, as Carla Adams isn't an employee):

```
EXEC uspGetDataForNamedEmployee 'Carla Adams';
```

Modifying the Registry

In the previous sections we covered how to create our custom event log, but we haven't told Event Viewer where to find the messages and categories, so it can't yet correctly display the entries in the log. To rectify this, open up regedit (select Run from the Start menu and then enter **regedit** in the text box) and navigate to the HKEY_LOCAL_MACHINE\SYSTEM\ CurrentControlSet\Services\EventLog entry. You should see that a new subentry has been created here for the SQL Assemblies Log, and this entry itself has two subentries, EventLogExample and SQL Assemblies Log, as shown in Figure 9-7. These are the two event sources registered for this log (a default source with the same name as the log is automatically registered).

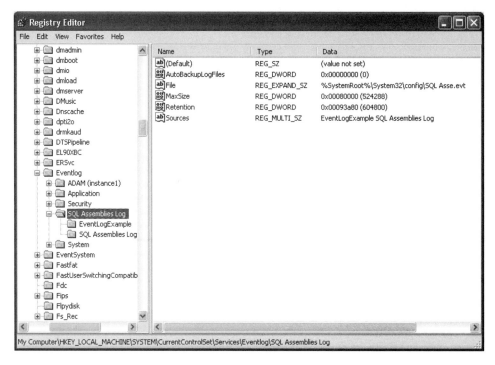

Figure 9-7. *Modifying the registry entry for the log*

For each of these two subentries, if a value called `EventMessageFile` doesn't already exist, right-click the node in the left hand pane and select New ➤ Expandable String Value, and name the new value **EventMessageFile**. Once the value exists, right-click it and select Modify. In the dialog box that appears, enter the path to the message DLL, as shown in Figure 9-8.

Figure 9-8. *Defining the path to the message DLL*

Now repeat this process again for both subentries, to create a new expandable string value called `CategoryMessageFile`. We defined our categories in the same file as the event messages, so again set the value to the path of the `EventLogMessages.dll` file. You should now have created four registry values, two each for the `EventLogExample` and `SQL Assemblies Log` subentries under the SQL Assemblies Log entry.

If you open Event Viewer now, you should see the entry created earlier displayed correctly, as shown in Figure 9-9.

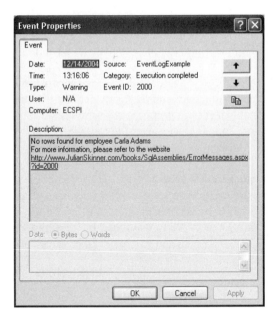

Figure 9-9. *Viewing an entry in Event Viewer*

If the user clicks the hyperlink, she will be presented with a dialog box warning her that information will be sent over the Internet, as shown in Figure 9-10.

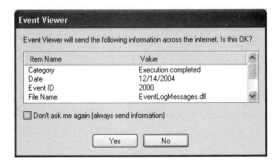

Figure 9-10. *Dialog warning box*

If the user clicks Yes here, the requested page will be displayed in Windows Help and Support Center.

Summary

The .NET environment, both inside and outside of the Visual Studio (VS) 2005 IDE, provides many tools for debugging. The VS IDE provides a very rich debugging environment that would merit a book in itself, so here we had to content ourselves with a very quick look at its basic features. Even if you don't have the full version of VS 2005, however, it's still possible to step through code in a visual debugger, as SQL Server 2005 ships with a pared-down version of VS 2005. Unfortunately, you can't use this pared-down version with an assembly that's running inside SQL Server, but you can use it to debug .NET assemblies before they're installed in the database.

Besides these visual tools, .NET comes with a number of classes and language constructs you can use to aid debugging, including preprocessor directives and the Conditional attribute, which allow you to compile code or call methods only if certain preprocessor symbols are defined, and thus provide a convenient way to write code that compiles differently in debug and release builds. You can use these features to compile debug versions of your assemblies that can be tested outside SQL Server.

In the second part of the chapter, we took a quick look at exception handling in SQL assemblies, and in particular we examined using the SqlException class and throwing new exceptions. When exceptions are caught in SQL assemblies, you will often need to record the problem, and we looked in detail at two ways of doing this in .NET assemblies: by sending an e-mail or by writing an entry to the event log.

CHAPTER 10

■■■

Security

The ability to execute .NET code within SQL Server brings with it many new challenges and responsibilities, as well as new opportunities. This is especially true in the area of security. The fact that .NET code can perform many tasks that are impossible with T-SQL necessarily means that it also introduces a lot of potential new security pitfalls. Fortunately, however, .NET also comes with its own powerful security mechanisms—namely, role-based security and code access security—that responsible developers can use to ensure their code isn't put to malicious use, and that system administrators can use to restrict the rights of potentially dangerous code. In this chapter we'll look closely at these two features and see how they apply in the context of SQL Server assemblies.

We've already shown how DBAs can restrict the permissions for a particular assembly using the PERMISSION_SET clause of the CREATE ASSEMBLY statement (in fact, this feature is based on code access security). In this chapter, we'll look in more detail at these permission sets, and discuss the advantages and issues with each setting.

This chapter covers the following topics:

- Using role-based security to ensure that SQL assemblies don't allow users to access Windows resources they're not entitled to

- Managing code access security and setting the permissions for groups of assemblies

- Using code access security in code to ensure that .NET code can't be abused to perform actions it wasn't intended to do

- Working with the different permission sets of SQL Server assemblies

.NET Security

As previously mentioned, the .NET security model relies on two fundamental concepts: role-based security and code access security. *Role-based security* (in the System.Security. Principal namespace) allows code to authorize actions for a particular user or for a role to which the user belongs, or to impersonate a particular Windows user account. *Code access security* (in the System.Security.Permissions namespace), on the other hand, is used to determine what actions a *block of code* may perform.

Role-Based Security

Role-based security is relevant for SQL Server because SQL Server runs under a specific user account—specified when SQL Server is first installed—and not under the account of the user who is currently connected (the current server login). Users can therefore potentially access through a SQL assembly a resource for which they have no permissions, and thus bypass Windows security. Using role-based security, an assembly can check whether the current server login belongs to a particular Windows role, or it can impersonate the Windows user that the login represents, so that no actions can be performed that would ordinarily be forbidden for that user by Windows security. In both cases, of course, this is only possible if the current login is a Windows login rather than a SQL Server login.

For example, suppose SQL Server is configured to run under an account called `SqlServerProcessAccount`. This account has access to an XML file on a network share, `S:\myfile.xml`, which is accessed by a SQL assembly called `ReadMyFile`. However, not all SQL Server users are entitled to view this file, so you need a way to stop nonauthorized users from bypassing Windows security by accessing the file through the `ReadMyFile` assembly in SQL Server. Using role-based security within the `ReadMyFile` assembly, you can retrieve the credentials for the user who is actually executing the assembly, and so ensure that that user has read permission on the `S:\myfile.xml` file. However, if the user is logged on with a SQL Server login, you won't be able to retrieve the Windows user account, so you will need to deny access.

Role-based security uses two objects to perform these checks:

- The *identity* object, which represents a particular user account

- The *principal* object, which represents the current security context and encapsulates both the identity and the roles to which that user belongs

These objects are defined by the `IIdentity` and `IPrincipal` interfaces, and the .NET Framework Class Library provides two implementations of each of these: a `GenericIdentity` and `GenericPrincipal`, which aren't tied to any particular authentication system, and a `WindowsIdentity` and `WindowsPrincipal`, which represent Windows users and roles. We're concerned with these latter classes here. You would use the generic classes if you wanted to authenticate users against a custom authentication system, rather than using Windows authentication.

Checking for Role Membership

You can retrieve the `WindowsIdentity` for the Windows login of the current user through the `SqlContext.WindowsIdentity` property. If the current login uses SQL Server rather than Windows authentication, this will return `null`.

```
WindowsIdentity winId = SqlContext.WindowsIdentity;
```

Once you have this identity, you can create the corresponding `principal` object, passing in the identity:

```
WindowsPrincipal principal = new WindowsPrincipal(winId);
```

You can now use this object to check whether the current user is in a particular Windows role by calling its IsInRole method. This method has three overloads, which provide different ways to specify the Windows role to which you want to check that the user belongs:

- If the role is a built-in role, you can pass in a WindowsBuiltInRole enumeration value, such as WindowsBuiltInRole.Administrator.

- You can specify the name of the role (e.g., "BUILTIN\Administrators").

- You can specify the role ID as an integer.

For example, to check whether the current user is a member of the Administrators role, you would use the following:

```
if (principal.IsInRole(WindowsBuiltInRole.Administrator))
{
    // User is a member of the Administrators role
}
```

Alternatively, you can check for role membership using declarative security. To do this, you add an attribute to mark code that can be executed only by a certain user account or role:

```
[PrincipalPermission(SecurityAction.Demand, Role="BUILTIN\Administrators")]
void DoSomething()
{
    // Method body
}
```

We'll look at declarative security later in the chapter, when we discuss code access security. However, in the case of role-based security, the declarative approach has a major drawback. For security reasons, the default principal object provided by the CLR is unauthenticated; this helps prevent potentially malicious code from discovering what authentication method is being used. This means that a PrincipalPermissionAttribute demand with a specific role will cause an exception, even if the user is in that role. It is possible for trusted code to get around this by explicitly setting the principal policy for the current application domain before accessing the principal:

```
' Get a reference to the current AppDomain
AppDomain currDomain = AppDomain.CurrentDomain;

' Set the AppDomain's principal policy to Windows principal
currDomain.SetPrincipalPolicy(PrincipalPolicy.WindowsPrincipal);
```

This requires the UNSAFE permission set to execute in a SQL assembly.

■Note The PrincipalPermissionAttribute is in the System.Security.Permissions namespace (where most of the permissions used by code access security reside), *not* in System.Security.Principal.

Impersonating a Windows User

The Impersonate method of the WindowsIdentity object allows you to execute code under the user account associated with that identity, rather than the process under which SQL Server is running. This returns an object of type WindowsImpersonationContext, which you can use when you want to revert to the original account (the user account under which the SQL Server process is executing):

```
// Impersonate the Windows account of the current server login
WindowsImpersonationContext impContext = winId.Impersonate();

// Code here will execute under the user account of the current login

// Stop impersonating the server login account
impContext.Undo();

// Code here will execute under the SQL Server service account
```

The ability to do this is vital if an assembly accesses Windows resources such as files on the network, because this technique ensures that users won't be able to access, through a SQL Server assembly, resources that would normally be forbidden to them. Of course, it's theoretically possible to prevent this anyway by setting the execution rights on the assembly in SQL Server, but that would entail placing what are effectively system administration duties in the hands of the DBA. This might work on a very small system, but isn't feasible in an enterprise environment.

Role-Based Security Example

To demonstrate this, we'll write a .NET UDF that reads memos stored on the network in a predefined RTF format. The memos contain the name of the author, the intended recipients, a subject, and a body, as shown in Figure 10-1.

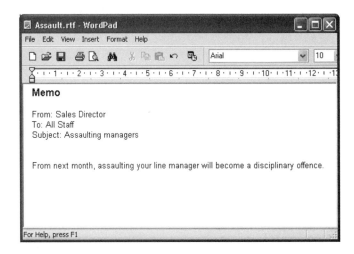

Figure 10-1. *A sample memo*

Our UDF will read the From, To, and Subject lines and the first paragraph of the memo body, and return these as a table. The code that reads the memos will use impersonation to ensure that the currently logged-in Windows user will be able to read only those files to which he has access under standard Windows security. Using impersonation also means that users will be able to read the files they have access to, even if the SQL Server process account doesn't have access to them.

The code consists of two .NET DLL assemblies: the UDF assembly calls into an assembly called MemoReader, which performs the actual reading of the RTF file. This assembly contains two classes: a class called MemoReader, which has a public method that reads all the RTF files in a given directory, and Memo, which represents an individual memo and has public properties that return the memo's body, subject, and so forth.

Reading the RTF Files

The first C# source code file we need to write is called MemoReader.cs, which contains two classes that will be called from our SQL Server assembly. As usual, we start the file with the using directives:

```
using System;
using System.Collections;
using System.IO;
using System.Security.Principal;
using System.Text.RegularExpressions;
```

As well as the standard System namespace and the System.Security.Principal namespace that contains the classes needed to implement role-based security, we import the System.IO namespace for reading the files, the System.Collections namespace for the ArrayList class (which we'll use to store a collection of all the Memo objects from a directory), and the System.Text.RegularExpressions namespace. We need this because we'll be using a regular expression to extract the individual bits of information from each RTF file.

The first class in this file is the Memo class. This class contains very little code: it has four private fields to hold the recipient, sender, subject, and body of the memo, and public read-only properties to expose these private fields. The public constructor for the class takes four parameters of type string, and uses this information to populate the private fields:

```
namespace Apress.SqlAssemblies.Chapter10
{
   public class Memo
   {
      private string recipient;
      private string sender;
      private string subject;
      private string body;

      public Memo(string recipient, string sender, string subject, string body)
      {
         this.recipient = recipient;
         this.sender = sender;
```

```
      this.subject = subject;
      this.body = body;
   }

   public string Recipient
   {
      get { return recipient; }
   }

   public string Sender
   {
      get { return sender; }
   }

   public string Subject
   {
      get { return subject; }
   }

   public string Body
   {
      get { return body; }
   }
}
```

The second class, MemoReader, is the one that does all the hard work. It contains two methods, ReadRtfFile and ReadAllMemos. The ReadRtfFile method takes a string parameter containing the filename (including the path) of the RTF file to read and uses the information in this file to create a new Memo object, which is returned from the method.

We start by checking that the filename passed in has the extension .rtf; if not, we throw an exception. If it does, we instantiate a new StreamReader object for the file, read its entire contents into a string, and close the reader:

```
public class MemoReader
{
   private static Memo ReadRtfFile(string filename)
   {
      if (!filename.EndsWith(".rtf"))
         throw new IOException("Wrong file type: not an RTF file.");
      StreamReader sr = new StreamReader(filename);
      string memoContents = sr.ReadToEnd();
      sr.Close();
```

Our next task is to extract the required information from the file contents. RTF is a text-based format, so the easiest way to do this is to use a regular expression. We're not going to write a full RTF parser (which would be very complex), so we're assuming a fairly rigid adherence to a predefined format for all the memos. In this format, the From, To, and Subject fields all appear on a single line followed by a paragraph mark and start with the name of the field followed by a colon. Any whitespace around the field will be ignored. These fields are followed by two blank lines and then the body of the memo.

In RTF, a paragraph mark is represented by the string \par, so what we're looking for is something like this (there may also be additional whitespace in the text):

```
\par
From:<sender field>\par
To:<recipient field>\par
Subject:<subject field>\par
\par\par
<body field>\par
```

We want to capture the individual fields into named groups in our regular expression. In regular expression (RE) language, we do this using the string (?<*capture name*>*match*), where *match* contains the characters we want the capture to match. All the fields could contain any characters except for a newline character, so the match for these is .+ (the period represents any character other than a newline, and the plus sign indicates that we're looking for one or more instances of this). When we've allowed for the possibility of whitespace characters around the field names and values, the actual regular expression we use looks like this:

```
\\par\s*From:\s*(?<sender>.+)\s*\\par\s*To:\s*(?<recipient>.+)\s*\\par\s*Subject:\s*
(?<subject>.+)\s*\\par\s*\\par\s*\\par\s*(?<body>.+)\\par\r\n
```

The sequence \s represents any whitespace character in RE language, and we use a following asterisk (*) to indicate that there could be zero or more instances of these. Note also that we need to escape the backslash in the RTF sequence \par, because the backslash is an escape character in RE as well as RTF.

We create a new Regex object to represent this expression (also specifying that the expression should be compiled), and call its Match method, passing in the string containing the contents of the RTF file. This method returns a Match object that contains details of the match, and we check its Success property to see if the string did match our expression. If it didn't, this will be because the RTF file wasn't in the correct memo format, and we return null. Otherwise, we instantiate a new Memo object from the data stored in the named captures of our Match object. We retrieve these by calling the Match object's Result method, passing in the name of the captured group we want in the format ${*capture name*}, and returning the Memo from the ReadRtfFile method:

```
        Regex re = new Regex(@"\\par\s*From:\s*(?<sender>.+)\s*\\par\s*To:\s*
            (?<recipient>.+)\s*\\par\s*Subject:\s*(?<subject>.+)\s*\\par\s*
            \\par\s*\\par\s*(?<body>.+)\\par\r\n", RegexOptions.Compiled);
        Match match = re.Match(memoContents);
        if (!match.Success)
            return null;
        return new Memo(match.Result("${recipient}"), match.Result("${sender}"),
            match.Result("${subject}"), match.Result("${body}"));
    }
```

The second method in the MemoReader class, ReadAllMemos, takes the path of a directory and calls the ReadRtfFile method on each file in this directory with the extension .rtf. It also takes a WindowsIdentity object, which we'll use to impersonate a given Windows user account. When we call this method from our UDF assembly, we'll pass in the identity we get from the SqlContext.WindowsIdentity property.

The reason that we're performing the impersonation here rather than in the SQL assembly itself is that impersonation requires the UNSAFE permission set. We can therefore install this assembly into SQL Server with the UNSAFE permission set and assign the UDF assembly itself the more restrictive EXTERNAL ACCESS permission set. This may seem to be a case where everything will balance out in the end, but there is some advantage to this: although the assembly will be installed into SQL Server, there will be no modules that call it directly. Therefore, if the DBA trusts this assembly, any assemblies that call it can be given a reduced permission set. The alternative of performing the impersonation in the SQL assembly itself would require giving the assembly that is called directly from SQL Server the UNSAFE permissions, and if the MemoReader assembly were called from any other assemblies, they too would need UNSAFE permissions. The approach we've taken therefore potentially reduces the number of unsafe assemblies in the database, which makes managing them a little easier.

Most of the code in this method will be contained within a try...catch...finally block. Because the finally block will undo the impersonation to restore the current identity to the SQL Server process account, it will need to access the WindowsImpersonationContext object returned from the call to Impersonate. This means that we need to declare and initialize our local WindowsImpersonationContext variable before the start of the try block:

```
public static ArrayList ReadAllMemos(string folder, WindowsIdentity winId)
{
    WindowsImpersonationContext impersCtxt = null;
```

Within the try block, we call the Impersonate method of the WindowsIdentity object that was passed into our method to switch the security context to that of the actual Windows user, rather than the SQL Server process account under which it's currently running. Then we instantiate a new ArrayList object to hold all the Memo objects and get a reference to the DirectoryInfo object that represents the folder we want to read the files from. We then call the GetFiles method on this object to retrieve an array of FileInfo objects with the extension .rtf in the folder:

```
try
{
    impersCtxt = winId.Impersonate();

    ArrayList memos = new ArrayList();
    DirectoryInfo dir = new DirectoryInfo(folder);
    FileInfo[] files = dir.GetFiles("*.rtf");
```

Once we have this array, we can iterate through all the files and call our ReadRtfFile on each one. This call to ReadRtfFile is wrapped in a nested try block with an empty catch block, because if the user doesn't have permission to read this file, we just want to ignore the file, so the user won't even be aware of its existence. If ReadRtfFile returns null, this is because the file isn't in the correct format, and we couldn't extract the appropriate information, so we don't add the Memo to our ArrayList:

```
for (int i = 0; i < files.Length; i++)
{
    // Ignore any files we can't read
    try
    {
        Memo memo = ReadRtfFile(files[i].FullName);
        if (memo != null) memos.Add(memo);
    }
    catch {}
}
```

When we've finished iterating through the files, we simply return our populated `ArrayList` from the method:

```
    return memos;
}
```

If any exceptions occur, we just throw a new `IOException`, including the original exception as its `InnerException`:

```
catch (Exception e)
{
    IOException ex = new IOException("Cannot read directory", e);
    throw ex;
}
```

After these blocks have finished executing, the `finally` block will always execute. Here we ensure that the impersonation context is reset by calling the `Undo` method on the `WindowsImpersonationContext` object that was returned from the `Impersonate` method, so long as this isn't `null`:

```
            finally
            {
                if (impersCtxt != null)
                    impersCtxt.Undo();
            }
        }
    }
}
```

The UDF Assembly

Our second C# source file, `RbsExample.cs`, contains the code for the UDF assembly itself. This is very simple, because most of the code is in `MemoReader.cs`. We start as usual with the using directives. As well as the standard `System` and SQL Server-related namespaces, we need to import `System.Collections` for the `IEnumerable` interface, `System.IO` and `System.Security` for typed exceptions that we'll throw if the directory passed into the function doesn't exist or if SQL Server authentication is being used, and System.Security.Principal, where the WindowsIdentity class resides:

```
using System;
using System.Collections;
using System.Data;
using System.Data.Sql;
using System.Data.SqlTypes;
using System.IO;
using System.Security;
using System.Security.Principal;
using Microsoft.SqlServer.Server;
```

As with other .NET table-valued UDFs, the RbsExample assembly consists of a public class with two public methods: one (ReadMemos) that is called when the function is initialized, and another (GetMemo) that is called to retrieve the fields for an individual row.

The ReadMemos method is decorated with a SqlFunction attribute that has its FillRowMethodName property set to tell SQL Server the name of the method that will read the fields from a row (in our case, GetMemo). ReadMemos takes single string parameter—the name of the directory to read the RTF files from—and returns an implementation of the IEnumerable interface, which SQL Server will use to iterate through each row of our data (i.e., each Memo object) in turn:

```
namespace Apress.SqlAssemblies.Chapter10
{
    public class RbsExample
    {
        [SqlFunction(FillRowMethodName="GetMemo")]
        public static IEnumerable ReadMemos(string directoryName)
        {
```

Within the method body, we first check to see whether the directory passed into the method actually exists. If it doesn't, we throw an exception; otherwise, we retrieve the WindowsIdentity representing the user account for the current Windows login. If this is null, it means that the current login uses SQL Server authentication; if it isn't null, we'll pass it, together with the name of the directory we want to read files from, into the ReadAllMemos method of our MemoReader class. As shown earlier, this returns an ArrayList of Memo objects, and since ArrayList implements IEnumerable, we can just return this from the method. If any exceptions occur, we simply throw a new exception, passing in the original exception as its InnerException (remember that UDFs don't have access to a SqlPipe to send messages back to the user):

```
        try
        {
            if (Directory.Exists(directoryName))
            {
                WindowsIdentity winId = SqlContext.WindowsIdentity;
                if (winId == null)
                    throw new SecurityException(
```

```
                              "Won't work with SQL Server authentication");
                return MemoReader.ReadAllMemos(directoryName, winId);
            }
            else
            {
                throw new IOException("Directory doesn't exist");
            }
        }
        catch (Exception e)
        {
            throw new IOException("Can't read files from the directory", e);
        }
    }
```

The final method we need to write for this example is GetMemo, which is called by SQL Server to retrieve the fields for an individual row of data. The method must return void, and it has one input parameter: the object representing the current row extracted from the IEnumerable implementation that was returned from the ReadMemos method. This will be an instance of our Memo object, but it is passed in as an object and needs to be cast to a Memo before we can access its properties. The method also has a number of output parameters—one for each field in our data. Within our method, we therefore just need to populate the output parameters with the values of the properties of our Memo object, typing them to the appropriate SQL types:

```
    public static void GetMemo(object o, out SqlChars sender,
                out SqlChars recipient, out SqlChars subject, out SqlChars body)
    {
        Memo memo = (Memo)o;
        sender = new SqlChars(memo.Sender);
        recipient = new SqlChars(memo.Recipient);
        subject = new SqlChars(memo.Subject);
        body = new SqlChars(memo.Body);
    }
  }
}
```

That completes the .NET code for this example, so compile the two C# files into DLLs. On Julian's system, the command is as follows:

```
csc /t:library MemoReader.cs
csc /t:library /r:MemoReader.dll RbsExample.cs
```

Installing and Testing the Assembly

Once you've compiled the files, the next task is to install the assemblies into SQL Server. We'll add the UDF to the AssembliesTesting database and, as we mentioned earlier, we'll install the

MemoReader assembly with the UNSAFE permission set and the RbsExample assembly with the EXTERNAL ACCESS permission set:

```
USE AssembliesTesting
GO

CREATE ASSEMBLY MemoReader
FROM 'C:\Apress\SqlAssemblies\Chapter10\RbsExample\MemoReader.dll'
WITH PERMISSION_SET = UNSAFE
GO

CREATE ASSEMBLY RbsExample
FROM 'C:\Apress\SqlAssemblies\Chapter10\RbsExample\RbsExample.dll'
WITH PERMISSION_SET = EXTERNAL_ACCESS
GO

CREATE FUNCTION ReadMemos(@directoryName nvarchar(256))
RETURNS TABLE
(
    Sender     nvarchar(256),
    Recipient  nvarchar(256),
    Subject    nvarchar(256),
    Body       nvarchar(4000)
)
AS
EXTERNAL NAME RbsExample.[Apress.SqlAssemblies.Chapter10.RbsExample].ReadMemos
GO
```

The owner of the AssembliesTesting database must have the permissions to install unsafe and external access assemblies for this code to run, and the database itself will need its TRUSTWORTHY property set to ON. Please see the section "Configuring a Database to Allow Nonsafe Assemblies" at the end of this chapter for more information about installing assemblies that require a nonsafe permission set.

Before testing the assembly, make sure that you've copied the three RTF files from the Apress download into a directory on your system. To test that role-based security is working, you need to ensure that read permissions for one of the files are denied to the Windows account that you use to access SQL Server. To do this, right-click the file in Windows Explorer, select Properties from the context menu, and open the Security tab. Here, click the Add button to add your user account so that you can set the permissions specifically for that account, and you will be presented with the dialog shown in Figure 10-2.

Enter the local machine or the domain that the account belongs to, or select it by clicking the Locations button, and enter the name of the account you want to set the permissions for. You can also click Check Names to ensure you've entered a valid account name (enter it in the form **DOMAIN_NAME\username** for an Active Directory user or **LOCAL_MACHINE_NAME\username** for a local account). Once you're done, click OK to return to the file's Properties dialog. Select the user account you just added to the list, and then check the Deny check box for the Read permission, as shown in Figure 10-3.

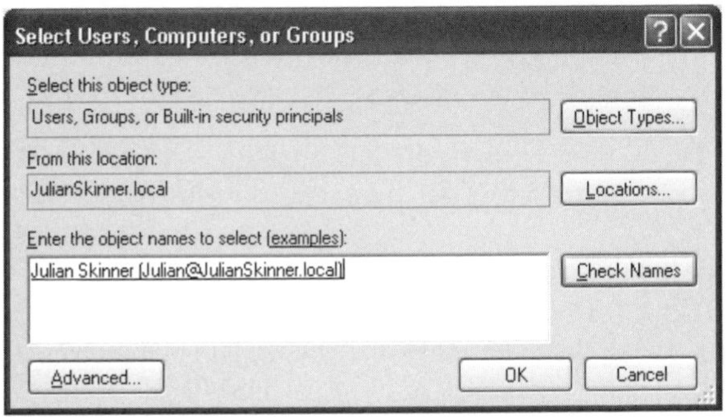

Figure 10-2. *Selecting a user account to set its permissions for a file*

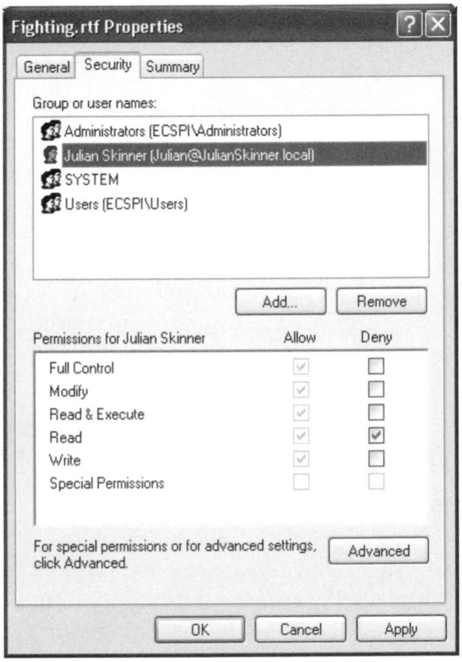

Figure 10-3. *Denying Read permission on a file for a user*

Click Apply and confirm the change in the warning dialog box that Explorer displays, and you're now ready to test the UDF. Go back to Management Studio and run a SELECT command to test the function, passing in the name of the directory where you saved the RTF files:

```
SELECT * FROM ReadMemos('C:\Apress\SqlAssemblies\Chapter10\RbsExample')
```

You should see something like Figure 10-4, with the information from the two files that you didn't restrict access to, but without any information from the third file.

	Sender	Recipient	Subject	Body
1	Sales Director	All Staff	Assaulting managers	From next month, assaulting your line manager will become a disciplinary offence.
2	Head Office	All Managers	Binge drinking	Please refrain from binge drinking during office hours from Monday to Thursday.

Figure 10-4. *The results of the ReadMemos UDF*

If you want to check that the assembly would have access to the file without role-based security, comment out the line where the call to the WindowsIdentity.Impersonate method is made, recompile the C# source files, and reinstall the assemblies and the UDF in SQL Server. Then run the SELECT command again, and (so long as the SQL process account has access to all three files) you'll see that the UDF can read all three files.

On a final note before we leave the topic of role-based security, you can use this impersonation technique not only to deny access to files that the SQL Server process account can access, but also to grant access to files that it can't. This means that you can restrict the permissions of the SQL Server process account while still allowing users who have the necessary permissions to access the files through SQL Server.

Code Access Security

The second strand in .NET security is code access security (CAS). CAS is the .NET security mechanism that controls the permissions available to specific pieces of code. It allows you to define what actions a specific block of code may perform, such as which Windows resources it can access, or whether it is permitted to access unmanaged code. You can set permissions in your code for a specific method or for specific lines of code, or you can set permissions administratively for whole groups of assemblies. To manage these permissions for groups of assemblies, .NET introduces the concept of *code groups*.

Code Groups

Code groups define the security status of a particular set of assemblies. Each code group has a *membership condition*, which defines which assemblies belong to that group, and a *permission set*, which specifies the actions that assemblies in the group are permitted to perform. Code groups can be nested within other code groups and are scoped to the entire enterprise, to the local machine, or to a specific user. Permissions can also be granted at the application domain level for code that is running within a host application (such as IIS or IE). Each of these levels has its own hierarchy of code groups so, for example, all managed code executing in a domain that has a common enterprise security policy will be within the enterprise All_Code group and also the All_Code group for the local machine.

A code group's membership condition specifies the criterion an assembly must meet in order to belong to that group. For example, you can stipulate that a group should include all code that's installed into the global assembly cache (GAC), code that's signed with a particular certificate, or code that's downloaded from a specific URL. There are a number of these built-in membership conditions that will cover most typical requirements, but it's also possible to define your own conditions, in .NET code, by writing a class that implements the IMembershipCondition interface. Note that code will belong to a code group only if it also belongs to the group's parent group; if an assembly doesn't match a particular group, it won't belong to any of that group's children. Since an assembly can belong to multiple code groups, the permissions it receives will be calculated from the union of these groups.

Apart from the top-level All_Code group at the enterprise and user levels, the default built-in code groups are all at the machine level. These groups are based on the *zone* in which the code originated. For example, an assembly executed on the local machine belongs to the My_Computer_Zone code group. The other zones are taken from Internet Explorer's settings, so, for instance, code that originated from a site listed as restricted in Internet Explorer will belong to the Restricted_Zone group. By default, code from this group isn't allowed to run at all.

Evidence

To determine whether an assembly belongs to a specific code group, the CLR uses the *evidence* presented by the hosting application or by the CLR class loader. The types of evidence available include digital signatures, strong names, and the URL or zone of origin of the assembly, although it's also possible to create custom forms of evidence. The CLR uses this evidence to determine whether the assembly meets the membership condition of a code group. If it does, the assembly will be included in that group.

Managing CAS Permissions

The security policies that define the code groups, membership conditions, and named permission sets for a level are stored in XML files, which can be configured manually (and this is the only way to achieve some tasks, such as creating a custom membership condition), but generally security policy is managed through one of two .NET tools:

- The .NET Framework Configuration tool (mscorcfg.msc). This tool provides a convenient MMC-style GUI for managing the enterprise, machine, and user security policies, as well as configuring the GAC, .NET remoting, and individual assemblies and applications.

- The Code Access Security Policy tool (caspol.exe). This command-line utility allows you to view and configure code groups and permission sets and resolve security policy issues.

■**Note** The locations of the XML security policy files can be found by selecting the appropriate node for that level in the .NET Framework Configuration tool.

The easiest way to configure security policy is undoubtedly using mscorcfg, so we'll use that to demonstrate how to configure the permissions available to a specific SQL Server assembly. You'll see later how you can use CAS to request (or deny) specific permissions in code. For this example, we'll create a stored procedure assembly that reads a web page and prints out its source code to the SQL pipe. This isn't in itself particularly useful, but for this example we wanted to keep the code as simple as possible and focus on the administrative tasks of using mscorcfg to restrict the assembly's access to the Apress web site, and prevent it accessing any other site.

The code for the assembly is contained in a file named AssemblyPermissionsExample.cs. We start by importing four namespaces. As well as the usual System and Microsoft.SqlServer. Server namespaces, we import System.IO and System.Net, which contain the classes we need to read a web page from the Internet:

```
using System;
using System.IO;
using System.Net;
using Microsoft.SqlServer.Server;
```

Our assembly consists of a single class with just one method: the ReadWebPage method that implements our stored procedure. This method has a string parameter containing the URL of the page we want to connect to. We open up an HttpWebRequest to this page, get the HttpWebResponse that is sent back, and then get a reference to the underlying stream so that we can read the contents:

```
namespace Apress.SqlAssemblies.Chapter10
{
    public class AssemblyPermissionsExample
    {
        [SqlProcedure]
        public static void ReadWebPage(string url)
        {
            SqlPipe pipe = SqlContext.Pipe;
            try
            {
                HttpWebRequest req = (HttpWebRequest)HttpWebRequest.Create(url);
                HttpWebResponse resp = (HttpWebResponse)req.GetResponse();
                Stream stm = resp.GetResponseStream();
```

The SqlPipe.Send method, which we'll use to send the contents of the page back to SQL Server, can cope with only up to 4,000 characters in one go, so we need to read 4,000 characters from the stream at a time. To do this, we open up a StreamReader based on the response stream, and call its Read method, passing in a 4,000-element char array, which we then convert to a string and send to SQL Server via the SqlPipe.Send method. Read returns the actual number of characters read, so we need to continue reading until this is 0, which indicates that the end of the stream has been reached:

```
            StreamReader sr = new StreamReader(stm);
            int bufferSize = 4000;
            int charsRead = 0;
            char[] buffer = new char[bufferSize];
            do {
                charsRead = sr.Read(buffer, 0, bufferSize);
                pipe.Send(new string(buffer, 0, charsRead));
            } while (charsRead > 0);
```

To finish up, we close the open objects and handle any exceptions that occurred simply by sending the error message back to SQL Server:

```
        sr.Close();
        stm.Close();
        resp.Close();        }
    catch (Exception e)
    {
        pipe.Send(e.Message);
    }
  }
 }
}
```

As usual, we need to compile this C# source file into a DLL. However, the compilation process is slightly different from previous examples, as we're going to create a new code group based on a strong name, so we need to create a key file first, and then use this to strongly name the assembly using the /keyfile compilation option. To create the key file, we use the utility sn.exe, which comes with the .NET Framework. This program is found in the <Program Files>\Microsoft Visual Studio 8\SDK\v2.0\Bin folder, so make sure that this folder is in your PATH environment variable, and run the following command:

```
sn -k AssemblyPermissionsExample.snk
```

Now compile the C# source code, including the /keyfile option pointing to the file that was just created by sn.exe:

```
csc /t:library /keyfile:AssemblyPermissionsExample.snk AssemblyPermissionsExample.cs
```

This creates a DLL signed with a strong name that we can use as a membership condition, so we're now ready to create a new code group to which this assembly will belong. To start with, then, start up mscorcfg by selecting Programs ➤ Administrative Tools ➤ Microsoft .NET Framework 2.0 Configuration from the Start menu (or open up the tool from the Administrative Tools applet in the Control Panel). The security policy settings are available under Runtime Security Policy, so expand that node, and you'll see nodes for the three levels: Enterprise, Machine, and User. Since the default security policy is set entirely at the machine level, expand the Machine node. This has three subnodes; besides Code Groups and Permission Sets, there is a node for Policy Assemblies (assemblies that contain implementations of custom permissions or membership conditions).

Before we create the code group that will include our SQL assembly, we'll first create the permission set that will stipulate what permissions the group will have available to it. There are a number of built-in named permission sets, as shown in Figure 10-5, and they range from Everything, which includes almost every built-in permission (the exception is SkipVerification), to Nothing. Code with the latter permission set has no permissions at all, so it can't execute. Besides Everything there's also the Full Trust permission set (the default for My_Computer_Zone). This doesn't actually contain any permissions: code with Full Trust doesn't need specific permissions, as it isn't subject to any CAS restrictions.

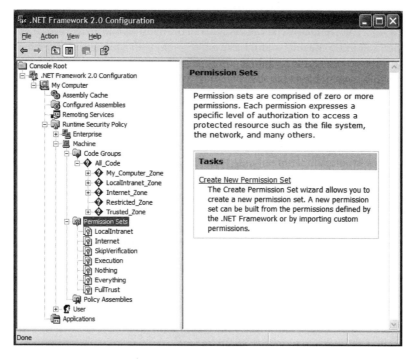

Figure 10-5. *The .NET Framework Configuration tool*

However, rather than using a built-in permission set, we want to create a new one. To do this, right-click Permission Sets under the Machine node, and select New. This starts the Create Permission Set Wizard and displays the dialog shown in Figure 10-6.

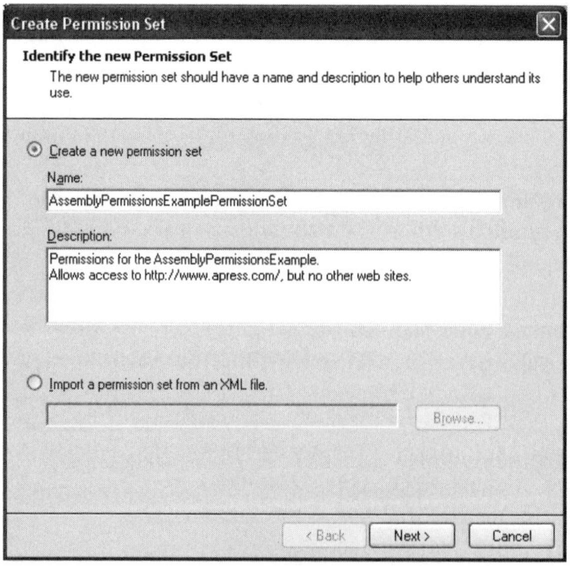

Figure 10-6. *The Create Permission Set Wizard*

Enter the name, and optionally a description, of the new permission set. (Here we've called it `AssemblyPermissionsExamplePermissionSet` to avoid any possible confusion.) If you already have a permission set that's been exported to an XML file, you can also use this dialog to import it, rather than creating a completely new permission set.

Clicking Next brings up the screen in Figure 10-7, which allows us to specify the permissions that code with this permission set will have.

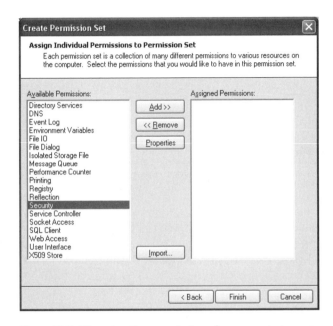

Figure 10-7. *Choosing the permissions for a permission set*

Each "permission" actually contains a number of more specific permissions; for example, the Security permission contains subpermissions to allow execution of the assembly, to allow .NET verification to be skipped, to allow the assembly to call unmanaged code, and so on. Other permissions can either allow a blanket authorization or permit access simply to one resource; for instance, the `Registry` permission can grant access to the entire registry or merely to named keys. Note that some of the built-in permission sets may be altered, while others can't, so how the permission properties look when you open the property dialogs of the permissions in a named permission set can vary considerably. Note also that in addition to the built-in permissions, it's possible to create custom permissions in .NET by inheriting from the `CodeAccessPermission` class.

To execute at all, our assembly will need the `Execute` security permission, so select Security in the left-hand pane and click the Add button. This brings up the Permission Settings dialog shown in Figure 10-8, which allows you to select the individual subpermissions you want to include.

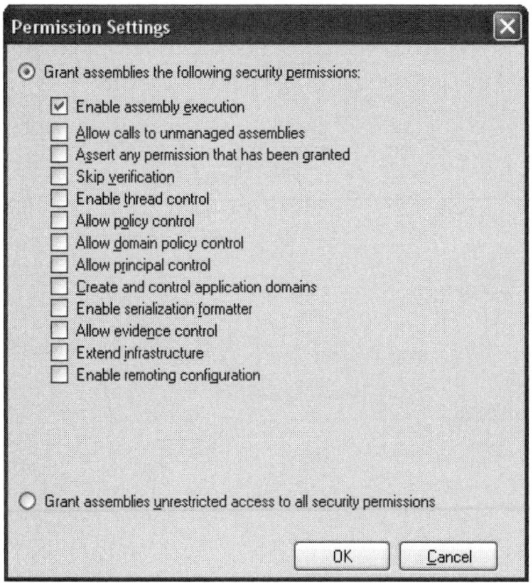

Figure 10-8. *The Security permission settings*

The only security permission our assembly needs is Execute, so tick the first check box, and click OK.

The next permission we need to add is Web Access, so select this and again click Add. This brings up the settings dialog for the Web Access permission, as shown in Figure 10-9.

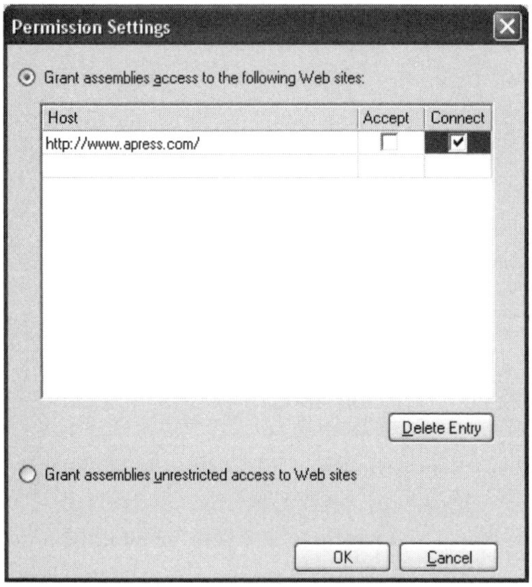

Figure 10-9. *The Web Access permission settings*

The only site we're going to permit access to is the Apress web site, so enter http://www.apress.com in the top row and tick the Connect check box, leaving the Accept check box clear (because our assembly has no reason to accept incoming connections from this or any other site).

When you've configured this permission, click OK to return to the Assign Permissions screen. Those are the only two permissions our assembly needs, so click Finish to create the permission set.

The next task is to create the code group that will include our SQL assembly. This code group will be associated with the permission set that we've just created and will have a membership condition based on the strong name of our SQL assembly. Again, we'll add the code group at the machine level, and as all code groups must come within the All Code group, we'll start the Create Code Group Wizard by right-clicking the node for the All Code group in mscorcfg and selecting New from the context menu.

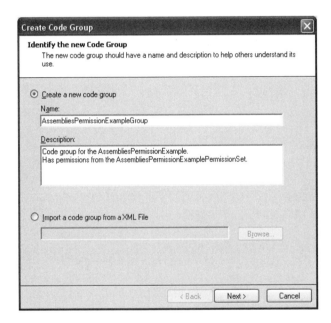

Figure 10-10. *The Create Code Group Wizard*

Again, as well as entering a name and optionally a description for the new code group, we can also opt to import a code group that was previously saved in XML format. However, we're creating a new code group from scratch, so ensure that the "Create a new code group" option is selected, enter **AssembliesPermissionExampleGroup** in the Name field, and, if you like, insert an appropriate description in the Description field, and then click Next.

The next screen, shown in Figure 10-11, allows us to select the membership condition that stipulates what evidence will cause an assembly to be included in this group.

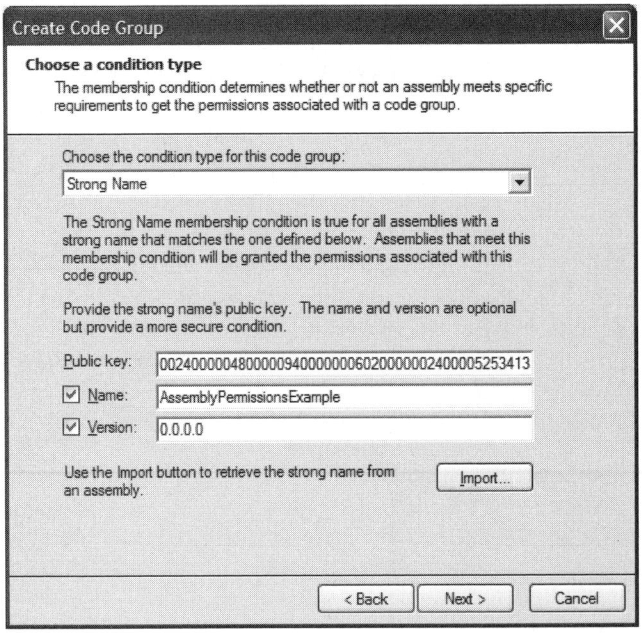

Figure 10-11. *Choosing the membership condition for a code group*

Here you can specify the criterion that code must meet to belong to this group. The range of criteria extends from the general, such as All Code or GAC (i.e., all code running in assemblies installed into the GAC), to the very specific. You can stipulate, for example, that the code group include assemblies downloaded from a certain URL or code that is signed with a particular strong name or certificate.

We want code to be placed in this group that has been signed with the `AssemblyPermissionsExample.snk` key file, so select Strong Name from the drop-down box, and the wizard will provide text boxes to enter the public key, and (optionally) name and version, for the strong-named assembly. You could write some .NET code to extract the public key from the assembly, but the easiest way to get this information is just to click the Import button and browse to the DLL we created earlier. This will populate the three text boxes, but leave the Name and Version check boxes clear. Selecting these options improves security, because it restricts the membership condition to a specific version of a specific assembly, so the flip side is that you shouldn't select these if you want all code signed with a specific key to belong to this group. We have only the one assembly, so we've gone for the improved security in this example.

Clicking Next takes us to the Assign a Permission Set to the Code Group screen shown in Figure 10-12. Here we can either select an existing named permission set or create a new one.

We of course want to use the permission set we've just created, so ensure the first option is chosen, select `AssemblyPermissionsExamplePermissionSet` from the drop-down list, and click Next. The final screen of the Create Code Group Wizard displays, as shown in Figure 10-13.

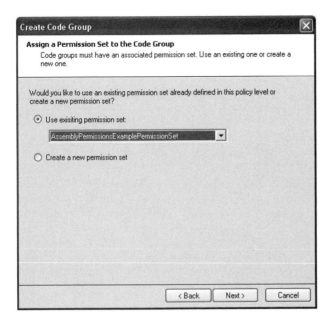

Figure 10-12. *Choosing the membership condition for a code group*

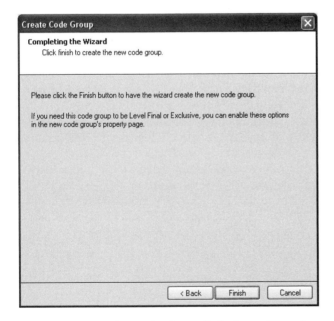

Figure 10-13. *Completing the Create Code Group Wizard*

Click Finish to create the code group, and it will now appear in mscorcfg with the name Copy of AssembliesPermissionExampleCodeGroup. However, we still need to make a couple of alterations to it, so right-click the group and select Properties. This displays the property dialog for the group, as shown in Figure 10-14.

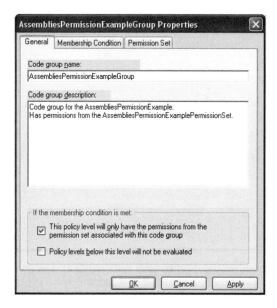

Figure 10-14. *The general properties for the new code group*

This dialog has three tabs, the second two of which allow us to modify the membership condition and permission set associated with the group, and are the same as the corresponding screens from the Create Code Group Wizard. However, as well as setting the name and description of the group, the General tab allows us to specify that the code group is to be *exclusive* and/or *level-final*. Exclusive code groups do not receive any other permissions from other code groups at the same level (the machine level in this case). If a group is level-final, permissions defined at a lower level in the hierarchy (in this case, that would mean permissions assigned at the user level) will be ignored if the membership condition for this code group is met. To stop the assembly from receiving additional permissions (and hence being able to access other web sites), you need to select the top check box to make the code group exclusive.

Also, while you're in the property dialogs for the code group, rename the group to delete "Copy of", so that it's just called AssembliesPermissionExampleCodeGroup.

SQL Server won't be aware of the new code group until it's been restarted, so before installing the assembly into the database, restart the database engine. Now open up Management Studio and run the following script to install and test the stored procedure:

```
USE AssembliesTesting;
GO

CREATE ASSEMBLY AssemblyPermissionsExample
FROM 'C:\Apress\SqlAssemblies\Chapter10\AssemblyPermissionsExample\
AssemblyPermissionsExample.dll'
WITH PERMISSION_SET = EXTERNAL_ACCESS;
GO

CREATE PROCEDURE uspReadWebPage(@url nvarchar(256))
```

```
AS
EXTERNAL NAME AssemblyPermissionsExample.
[Apress.SqlAssemblies.Chapter10.AssemblyPermissionsExample].ReadWebPage;
GO
```

```
EXEC uspReadWebPage 'http://www.apress.com/';
```

Since the assembly accesses the Internet, we need the `EXTERNAL_ACCESS` SQL Server permission set. When this script is run, you should see the HTML source for the Apress web site in the results pane in Management Studio. However, if you run the example with a different web page, you will see an error message. For example, if you run the following command:

```
EXEC uspReadWebPage 'http://www.JulianSkinner.com/'
```

you will see this error message:

```
Request for the permission of type 'System.Net.WebPermission, System,
Version=2.0.0.0, Culture=neutral, PublicKeyToken=b77a5c561934e089' failed.
```

By insisting on having assemblies signed with strong names or certificates, DBAs can use CAS in this way to control the precise permissions available to SQL assemblies, without writing a single line of code. However, developers can also make use of CAS to ensure that their code isn't abused by code that calls into it, and we'll spend most of the rest of the chapter looking at how to use CAS in .NET code. However, first we need to explain how CAS permissions combine within a chain of method calls.

Permissions and the Call Stack

The actual permissions any assembly receives are dependent on a couple of things. First, most assemblies will belong to more than one code group, so the permissions received will be the union of the permission sets for all the code groups that the assembly matches, on all levels that apply. This behavior can be changed by marking the assembly as exclusive and/or level-final. If you want to ensure that an assembly receives exactly the permissions of a specific code group, mark that group as both exclusive and level-final.

Second, assemblies are very frequently called from other assemblies, in a long chain of method calls, and the caller and callee very likely have different permission sets. This is where code access security at the programmatic level comes in. There are four actions that .NET assemblies can perform to check or modify the permissions that assemblies further up or down the call stack will receive:

- Demand: An assembly demands a particular permission to ensure that all calling assemblies have the right to perform a particular action. When a Demand is made, .NET will check all methods further up the call stack to make sure that they too have permission to perform this operation. If they don't, an exception will be thrown. For example, suppose you build a library with methods to read and update files from the Windows file system. This would be called from other assemblies, some of which may be written by other people and potentially malicious. By demanding the File IO permission in our code, you ensure that your method can only be called by assemblies that themselves have the right to access the file system. The .NET Framework Class Libraries make very frequent use of this, so as you'd expect the file I/O classes in the System.IO namespace demand the File IO permission before they perform any file access.

- `Assert`: When an assembly asserts a permission, it is claiming that it is safe for any callers to perform an action, regardless of whether or not they have permission to perform it. If you have a DLL that stores information in a specific key in the registry, accessing only a hard-coded key, you know it's safe for any callers to execute this method, even those that don't have the right to access the registry. By asserting the `Registry` permission, you declare that all callers may perform this operation. The stack walk will be stopped at this point, and the permissions of callers further up the call stack won't be checked. In order to assert a permission, your assembly must have that permission itself, and also the "assertion" security permission. SQL Server assemblies can never assert permissions.

- `Deny`: If you want to prevent methods that you're calling into further down the call stack from performing specific operations, you can deny a permission. In this case, if any method further down the call stack requests that permission, it will be refused. However, note that, because an assertion stops the stack walk, denying a permission won't prevent a method further down the call stack from performing an action if an assertion is made anywhere between the two methods.

- `PermitOnly`: This action prevents a permission being granted further down the call stack for any resource except the one(s) named. For example, you can use `PermitOnly` to ensure that a method can be used only to access a particular file or group of files. As with `Deny`, a `PermitOnly` will be ignored if an `Assert` occurs further down the call stack.

Using CAS in .NET Code

There are two ways to use code access security in .NET code: *imperatively*, by instantiating .NET classes that implement `IPermission` and calling methods on them, and *declaratively*, by adding attributes to a method that indicate the security actions to apply to that method.

Imperative Security

To use code access security imperatively, we simply instantiate the appropriate permission class and call the required method on it. For example, to ensure that our code has permission to open a file with the path `C:\info.txt` for reading, we would use this code:

```
FileIOPermission perm = new FileIOPermission(FileIOPermissionAccess.Read,
                                             "C:\\Info.txt");
perm.Demand();
```

The parameters passed into the constructor naturally differ for each permission type, so you'll need to consult the MSDN documentation for details on instantiating a specific permission object.

There is, however, one complication. If a method performs an `Assert`, `Deny`, or `PermitOnly`, a stack walk modifier is placed on that method to indicate what action should be performed when a stack walk occurs. Only one modifier of each type can be placed on a given method, so we can't, for example, make two asserts within the same method. Instead, we need to use a permission set if we want to assert two separate permissions. Permission sets are represented in .NET code through the `PermissionSet` class in the `System.Security` namespace.

To see how to use the PermissionSet class, suppose you have an assembly that you don't really trust that has a method that downloads a text file from the Web and saves it in the local file system. You want to call into this assembly, but you don't want to give it permission to access any more resources than it absolutely needs. To do this, you have to create a new instance of the PermissionSet class with no permissions, and then add a WebPermission that allows the assembly to connect to the named web site and a FileIOPermission that allows it to write to a named file. Once the permission set has been configured, you can call PermitOnly on it to permit access only to the named resources:

```
PermissionSet perms = new PermissionSet(PermissionState.None);
WebPermission webPerm = new WebPermission(NetworkAccess.Connect,
        "http://www.apress.com/");
perms.AddPermission(webPerm);
FileIOPermission filePerm = new FileIOPermission(FileIOPermissionAccess.Write,
        "C:\\temp.txt");
perms.AddPermission(filePerm);
perms.PermitOnly();
```

This ensures that any methods lower down the call stack won't be able to connect to any other web sites, read any local files, or write to any files except the one specified in your code (C:\temp.txt). If it attempts to do any of these things, a SecurityException will be thrown.

Tip If you're having trouble getting permissions to perform as expected, you can convert the permission to XML format by calling its ToXml method, and compare that with the XML of the failed permission displayed in the message of the SecurityException. We had lots of fun trying to work out why we weren't allowed to connect to the web site http://www.apress.com, even though we'd granted permission to connect to it. A closer look at the XML in the exception message finally revealed that the HttpWebRequest was actually requesting http://www.apress.com/, with a trailing slash.

Declarative Security

The second way to use CAS is declaratively, by attaching .NET attributes to methods in your code. The permission attributes have the same name as the corresponding class, and the action to take is passed in as a SecurityAction enum value, together with any additional information that would be passed into the class constructor in imperative security. For example, to specify that a method should demand read access to the file C:\temp.txt, we would define it with the following attribute:

```
[FileIOPermission(SecurityAccess.Demand, Read="C:\\temp.txt")]
public static string ReadFile(string filename)
{
    // Method body
}
```

The main advantage of declarative security is that specifying the required permissions in the metadata allows other assemblies to determine what permissions the method/class needs without actually calling it. It also has a couple of extra actions, besides the familiar `Demand`, `Assert`, `Deny`, and `PermitOnly`:

- `InheritanceDemand`: If applied to a class, all derived classes must have the permission. If applied to a method, all overrides of the method must have the permission. These checks are performed when the class is loaded by the CLR.

- `LinkDemand`: Only the immediate caller is required to have the permission; callers higher up the call stack aren't checked. This check is performed during JIT compilation rather than at runtime.

All these actions can be applied either to classes or to methods. However, there are three extra actions that are applied at the assembly level:

- `RequestMinimum`: Requests the minimum permissions that are required for the assembly to execute; without these, the code won't run

- `RequestOptional`: Requests optional permissions that aren't required to run the code, but that would be useful (e.g., for extra functionality)

- `RequestRefuse`: Requests the refusal of permissions that could be misused if they were granted

CAS Example

To demonstrate CAS in a SQL Server assembly, we'll create a stored procedure that reads the stock price for a particular company from a CSV file on the Internet and stores the data in a table called `StockPrices` in the AssembliesTesting database. In general, you would probably run code like this periodically in an external application such as a Windows service on another machine, but there could be circumstances in which you want to be able to access it from within SQL Server. For example, you might want to update the prices from within a stored procedure called to perform analytical calculations based on the fluctuations of stock prices, or from within a trigger called every time a new row is added to a table containing details of companies whose stock prices are to be monitored.

For this example, our assembly will get the data from `http://finance.yahoo.com`. This site makes stock prices available as a CSV file. The company symbol (e.g., MSFT for Microsoft) and the fields you want returned are passed to the site as parameters in the query string. In our case, we'll retrieve the current stock price, the time and date for the price, the opening price for the day, the change over the day, and the volume of sales traffic. The details returned from the Yahoo site aren't absolutely current (you need a subscription for that), but they illustrate the point nicely.

The definition for the table where we store this data is

```
CREATE TABLE StockPrices
(
    id        int identity primary key,
    symbol    nchar(4),
    price     float not null,
    tradetime datetime not null,
```

```
   change    float not null,
   openprice float not null,
   volume    int not null
);
```

HttpFileReader.cs

The .NET code for this example is contained within two C# source files, HttpFileReader.cs and CasExample.cs, both of which will be compiled into DLLs. The first of these contains a class named HttpFileReader with a single method, ReadFile, which takes a URL as a string parameter and reads the file from that URL, returning each line as a separate string within a string array. As always, we start with the using directives:

```
using System;
using System.Collections.Specialized;
using System.IO;
using System.Net;
```

Besides System, we import System.Collections.Specialized (for the StringCollection class), System.IO (for stream handling), and System.Net (where the classes we use to connect to the web site reside). The WebPermission class also lives in System.Net, so we don't need to import the System.Security.Permissions namespace.

Within the ReadFile method, the first thing we do is to demand permission to connect to the URL passed in as a parameter (we're using imperative security for this example):

```
namespace Apress.SqlAssemblies.Chapter10
{
    public class HttpFileReader
    {
        public static string[] ReadFile(string url)
        {
            WebPermission webPerm = new WebPermission(NetworkAccess.Connect, url);
            webPerm.Demand();
```

The WebPermission is required to connect to a web site using the HttpWebRequest class (to connect directly using TCP, use the SocketPermission class instead). The WebPermission constructor takes two parameters: a NetworkAccess enum value that can be either Connect (to connect to a site on the Internet and read data from it) or Accept (to accept incoming HTTP connections), and a string specifying the URL to connect to/accept connections from. Once we've created the WebPermission object, we call its Demand method to ensure that our code has that permission. If it doesn't, a SecurityException will be thrown (we haven't included exception handling in this class, because we just want any exceptions to bubble up to the calling assembly).

Next, we make the HTTP request and read the downloaded file into a string array using a StreamReader. We make the request by calling the static HttpWebRequest.Create method, passing in the URL we want to connect to. We then call the GetResponse method of this object to retrieve the HTTP response returned back from the web server. The HttpWebRequest and HttpWebResponse classes that we use to read the file are slightly counterintuitive in that when we get the objects, they're returned as instances of the WebRequest/WebResponse parent classes, so they need to be cast to the appropriate subclasses:

```
HttpWebRequest request = (HttpWebRequest)HttpWebRequest.Create(url);
HttpWebResponse response = (HttpWebResponse)request.GetResponse();
```

To read the data from the response, we retrieve the response stream and then instantiate a StreamReader to read this stream. The StreamReader has a ReadLine method that allows us to read a whole line in one go. This returns the line as a string, or null when the end of the file has been reached, so we read from the stream until we get back null. Each line is stored in a StringCollection—one of the built-in typed collection classes in the FCL.

```
Stream stream = response.GetResponseStream();
StreamReader sr = new StreamReader(stream);
StringCollection strings = new StringCollection();
string line = sr.ReadLine();
while (line != null)
{
    strings.Add(line);
    line = sr.ReadLine();
}
```

Once we've finished reading the data, we close the open objects, copy the StringCollection into a string array, and return that from the method:

```
            sr.Close();
            stream.Close();
            response.Close();
            string[] lines = new string[strings.Count];
            strings.CopyTo(lines, 0);
            return lines;
        }
    }
}
```

Then we save this file as HttpFileReader.cs and compile it into a DLL:

```
csc /t:library HttpFileReader.cs
```

CasExample.cs

The second C# source file contains the code for the stored procedure itself. This calls into the HttpFileReader class to read the CSV file containing the stock prices from the Internet, parses the data returned from the ReadFile method, and then stores that to the StockPrices table in the database.

Along with the usual SQL Server namespaces, we again import the System.Net namespace, as it contains the WebPermission class. We also need the System.Security and System.Security.Permissions namespaces to set up the permissions for the assembly:

```
using System;
using System.Data;
```

```
using System.Data.Sql;
using System.Data.SqlClient;
using System.Data.SqlTypes;
using System.Net;
using System.Security;
using System.Security.Permissions;
using Microsoft.SqlServer.Server;
```

This assembly contains one class with one method: the InsertLatestStockPrice method that implements our stored procedure. This has one parameter—a string that contains the stock exchange symbol for the company we want to get the stock price of.

```
namespace Apress.SqlAssemblies.Chapter10
{
    public class CasExample
    {
        [SqlProcedure]
        public static void InsertLatestStockPrice(string symbol)
        {
```

Within this method, we start by constructing the URL that we'll access to get the stock price information. We then instantiate a WebPermission to allow access to this URL. We need to access SQL Server data through ADO.NET, so we'll need the SqlClientPermission as well, granting access to the context connection only. We do this by instantiating a SqlClientPermission with no permissions and then calling its Add method to allow it to connect with a specific connection string. Add takes three parameters: the connection string to grant access on, a string containing additional connection properties, and a KeyRestrictionBehavior value to indicate whether these properties are the only ones allowed (AllowOnly) or are explicitly prohibited (PreventUsage). Because the context connection doesn't require any extra properties, we'll add a blank string for the second parameter and KeyRestrictionBehavior.AllowOnly for the third.

We combine these two permissions into a PermissionSet and call PermitOnly on it in order to ensure that the DLL we're calling (the HttpFileReader assembly) can't access any other web sites, before we call the ReadFile method. This ensures that if the ReadFile method does try to access any other web site (or SQL Server with any other connection), an exception will be thrown. This restriction could only be bypassed if the called assembly had the "assertion" security permission, which no assembly called from SQL Server may be granted.

```
            try
            {
                PermissionSet perms = new PermissionSet(PermissionState.None);
                string url = "http://finance.yahoo.com/d/quotes.csv?s=" + symbol +
                        "&f=sl1d1t1c1ov";
                WebPermission webPerm = new WebPermission(NetworkAccess.Connect, url);
                perms.AddPermission(webPerm);

                SqlClientPermission sqlPerm = new SqlClientPermission(
                                            PermissionState.None);
                sqlPerm.Add("context connection=true", "",
                        KeyRestrictionBehavior.AllowOnly);
```

```
perms.AddPermission(sqlPerm);
perms.PermitOnly();
string[] data = HttpFileReader.ReadFile(url);
```

Because the CSV file returned from our web request has just one line, the ReadFile method will return a one-string array. We can separate this into the various fields by calling the String class's Split method. This takes a char array containing the characters we want to split the string at—in this case, just a comma. There are seven fields in the returned data, so the Split method returns a seven-element string array. These string values need to be converted to the appropriate types before we can insert the values into the database. The date and time are enclosed in quotation marks, so we need to remove those before creating a DateTime object. We also need to check whether an opening price is returned; if it isn't, we'll get the string "N/A" instead. If it does contain this value, we want to insert a null value rather than zero into the database. The standard C# double type doesn't have a way of representing null, so we'll go straight to the SqlDouble type instead, setting our openprice local variable to SqlDouble.Null. Otherwise, we call the SqlDouble's Parse method, passing the value in from the cols string array. The other values can be passed straight into the Parse method for the appropriate .NET type:

```
string[] cols = data[0].Split(new char[] { ',' });

string date = cols[2].Substring(1, cols[2].Length - 2);
string time = cols[3].Substring(1, cols[3].Length - 2);
DateTime tradetime = DateTime.Parse(date + " " + time);

double price = Double.Parse(cols[1]);
double change = Double.Parse(cols[4]);
SqlDouble openprice = cols[5] == "N/A" ? SqlDouble.Null :
                                         SqlDouble.Parse(cols[5]);
int volume = Int32.Parse(cols[6]);
```

Once we have the typed data, we can insert a new row into the StockPrices table:

```
using (SqlConnection cn = new SqlConnection("context connection=true"))
{
    cn.Open();
    string cmdStr = "INSERT INTO StockPrices VALUES
                        (@symbol, @price, @tradetime,
                         @change, @openprice, @volume)";
    SqlCommand cmd = new SqlCommand(cmdStr, cn);
    cmd.Parameters.AddWithValue("@symbol", symbol);
    cmd.Parameters.AddWithValue("@price", price);
    cmd.Parameters.AddWithValue("@tradetime", tradetime);
    cmd.Parameters.AddWithValue("@change", change);
    cmd.Parameters.AddWithValue("@openprice", openprice);
    cmd.Parameters.AddWithValue("@volume", volume);
    cmd.ExecuteNonQuery();
}
}
```

If any exception occurs (e.g., if the web site can't be reached, or the string passed in isn't a valid company symbol), we'll just send the error back to the caller:

```
      catch (Exception e)
      {
         SqlPipe pipe = SqlContext.Pipe;
         pipe.Send(e.Message);
      }
   }
}
}
```

Save this file as CasExample.cs and compile it into a DLL:

```
csc /t:library /r:HttpFileReader.dll CasExample.cs
```

Deploying and Testing the Procedure

The CREATE ASSEMBLY and CREATE PROCEDURE statements for the example require little explanation. Of course, we need to set the PERMISSION_SET to EXTERNAL_ACCESS because we're accessing external data:

```
CREATE ASSEMBLY CasExample
FROM 'C:\Apress\SqlAssemblies\Chapter10\CasExample\CasExample.dll'
WITH PERMISSION_SET = EXTERNAL_ACCESS;
GO

CREATE PROCEDURE uspInsertLatestStockPrice(@symbol nchar(4))
AS
EXTERNAL NAME
 CasExample.[Apress.SqlAssemblies.Chapter10.CasExample].InsertLatestStockPrice;
GO
```

Finally, test the stored procedure by executing it with a valid symbol such as 'MSFT', and check that a row was successfully inserted into the StockPrices table:

```
EXEC uspInsertLatestStockPrice 'MSFT';
SELECT * FROM StockPrices;
GO
```

Partially Trusted Code

When we looked at the CAS permission sets earlier in the chapter, we mentioned that the Full Trust permission set was different from the others in that it didn't include any permissions, but bypasses CAS so no permissions are needed. In fact, CAS makes a significant distinction between fully trusted code that has this permission set and all other, partially trusted code (including code that has the Everything permission set). The most obvious distinction between them is that partially trusted code isn't by default permitted to call into assemblies that are strong named. This is because such assemblies are usually installed into the GAC and shared between many applications (remember that this includes all the .NET Framework Class Libraries), and if code that isn't fully trusted has access to them, it could potentially do a great deal of damage, especially as assemblies in the GAC by default have full trust.

These restrictions on partially trusted code are of particular importance when writing and deploying SQL Server assemblies, because SQL assemblies aren't fully trusted. This means that if you want to call into the FCL, you need to create a private copy. There are two ways to do this: you can install the library into SQL Server using another CREATE ASSEMBLY statement, or you can copy the library into the same directory as your own assembly, in which case SQL Server will detect it as a dependency when you install your assembly and install it automatically. The former solution is generally preferred as less likely to cause versioning confusion.

It is possible, however, when you write a strong-named assembly to stipulate that it may be called from partially trusted callers, by applying the AllowPartiallyTrustedCallers attribute at the assembly level. Thankfully, this has been placed on several of the most frequently used assemblies that make up the FCL (including mscorlib.dll, System.dll, System.Data.dll, and System.Xml.dll), so these can all be called from SQL Server assemblies without creating private copies. This covers, *inter alia*, basic file I/O and the HttpWebRequest and HttpWebResponse classes we used in the preceding example.

SQL Server Assembly Permission Sets

We saw in Chapter 2 that when an assembly is deployed to SQL Server, the DBA must specify the permission set for the assembly in the CREATE ASSEMBLY statement. These are normal code access security permission sets, and can be one of SAFE, EXTERNAL_ACCESS, or UNSAFE. While this obviously gives a greater degree of control to the DBA than traditional extended stored procedures (which were effectively all unsafe), in practice much of the extra functionality that makes SQL assemblies so attractive in the first place requires at least the external access, and often the unsafe, permission set to run. At the moment, many of the .NET class libraries are little more than wrappers over the native Windows APIs, and so accessing them requires unsafe permissions. Hopefully this will change in Longhorn and later operating systems, where the native API *is* .NET, and so we will need much less access to unmanaged code.

In the meantime, you don't need the UNSAFE permission set to call into those assemblies that allow partially trusted callers and that you can therefore run from the GAC, but you will need it for the other assemblies in the FCL. Also, note that the permissions available to an assembly can't be increased, because even unsafe assemblies don't have the "assertion" security permission, so there's no way to add a permission to the permission set or to override the denial of a permission. Every assembly you call into will be bound by the same restrictions as the SQL Server assembly itself; the only way this can be subverted within .NET code is if the assembly calls into an assembly in the GAC, which by default will have full trust. This is why it's so important that access to assemblies in the GAC is restricted, and why it's vital that you only install assemblies into the GAC if you're absolutely sure that you can trust them completely.

The Safe Permission Set

Restricting an assembly to run with the SAFE permission set allows roughly the same functionality as a T-SQL stored procedure. Safe assemblies are permitted to access the computational features of .NET, but not to access external data sources. Although your DBA may be keen to restrict you to safe assemblies, in practice this security level is of relatively little use: in most circumstances where this can be used, it would be better to use T-SQL. The only situation in which it would be appropriate to use a CLR assembly with this permission set is if you're performing extensive calculations such as string manipulation for which T-SQL wasn't designed, and using .NET will improve the performance and readability of the code.

The External Access Permission Set

This is perhaps the permission set that you'll use the most, as it allows access to external resources, but still protects against many of the dangers of unmanaged code such as memory leaks. This level permits everything allowed by the safe permission set, as well as access to external data sources, such as file I/O, Internet, and e-mail access. It doesn't permit assemblies to contain unsafe or unverifiable . NET code, or to call into unmanaged code (e.g., using P/Invoke).

■Note Accessing external resources will fail if the current login is a SQL Server rather than a Windows login, or if the caller is not the original caller.

The Unsafe Permission Set

The unsafe permission set allows almost complete access to all the functionality of .NET, including access to external resources and unsafe and unmanaged code. Assemblies with this permission set *don't* have full trust, so there are some restrictions. However, because this permission set includes the right to call unmanaged code (which of course isn't subject to CAS), there are effectively no limits to what an unsafe assembly can do. Also, because unsafe assemblies can use .NET pointers in C# or C++ code, and can use direct memory access in unmanaged code, there's no absolute protection against memory leaks or buffer overflows.

Installing Nonsafe Permission Sets

Because of the security risks associated with installing unsafe and external access assemblies into a database, by default these types of assemblies can't be installed into a database. To get around that, we must do one of two things:

- Set the database's TRUSTWORTHY property to ON and grant the owner of the database the EXTERNAL ACCESS ASSEMBLY/UNSAFE ASSEMBLY permission as appropriate (if it doesn't already possess that permission).

- Sign the assembly with a certificate or asymmetric key associated with a login with the appropriate ASSEMBLY permission.

Let's look at these two options in turn.

Configuring a Database to Allow Nonsafe Assemblies

To install an unsigned assembly into a database with UNSAFE or EXTERNAL ACCESS, that database needs to be configured to allow such assemblies to run. In the first place, this means the database must have its TRUSTWORTHY property set to ON. We can do this through the ALTER DATABASE command (only members of the sysadmin fixed server role can run this statement):

```
ALTER DATABASE AssembliesTesting
SET TRUSTWORTHY ON;
```

As well as allowing nonsafe assemblies to be installed in the database, this also means that impersonation contexts from this database will be permitted within the SQL Server instance, so long as the owner of the database is trusted as an authenticator in the target scope. The implication of this is that it won't be possible to mark all databases that need to access nonsafe assemblies as trustworthy, so for some databases, you will have no option but to sign nonsafe assemblies.

The second condition for installing an unsigned nonsafe assembly is that the owner of the database into which it's being installed must have the EXTERNAL ACCESS ASSEMBLY or UNSAFE ASSEMBLY permission as appropriate. You can grant these permissions using a standard GRANT statement, for example:

```
USE master
GO

GRANT EXTERNAL ACCESS ASSEMBLY
TO [Apress\AssembliesTestingDbo];
GO
```

This grants the EXTERNAL ACCESS ASSEMBLY permission to a login called Apress\AssembliesTestingDbo.

Signing Assemblies

The second option is to sign the assembly you wish to install with a certificate or asymmetric key, and then to associate this certificate or key with a login that has the appropriate EXTERNAL ACCESS ASSEMBLY or UNSAFE ASSEMBLY permission.

For example, to install the MemoReader assembly from the first example in this chapter into the AssembliesTesting database, use the following procedure. First, create a key with which to sign the file using the command-line utility sn.exe:

```
sn -k MemoReader.key
```

Next, compile the source code file into a DLL, signing it with the key that's just been created:

```
csc /t:library /keyfile:MemoReader.key MemoReader.cs
```

Now import the key into the master database, use it to create a new login, and grant the UNSAFE ASSEMBLY permission to that login:

```
USE master
GO
```

```
CREATE ASYMMETRIC KEY MemoReaderKey
FROM FILE = 'C:\Apress\SqlAssemblies\Chapter10\RbsExample\MemoReader.key';
GO

CREATE LOGIN MemoReaderLogin
FROM ASYMMETRIC KEY MemoReaderKey;
GO

GRANT UNSAFE ASSEMBLY
TO MemoReaderLogin;
```

You can now install the assembly into the AssembliesTesting database:

```
USE AssembliesTesting
GO

CREATE ASSEMBLY MemoReader
FROM 'C:\Apress\SqlAssemblies\Chapter10\RbsExample\MemoReader.dll'
WITH PERMISSION_SET = UNSAFE;
GO
```

Summary

This chapter has been dominated by code access security (CAS), because CAS is the corner-stone of SQL Server assembly security and the foundation on which the SQL Server permission sets that are granted to assemblies are built. However, CAS isn't the only component of .NET security, and we began the chapter with a look at role-based security, which allows you to ensure that certain operations are performed only by Windows user accounts in a certain role or to impersonate the Windows account of the current login (rather than executing under the fixed SQL Server user account). We went on to look at CAS, introducing the concepts of code groups and permission sets, and exploring how to use the .NET Framework Configuration tool to apply a specific set of permissions to an assembly or group of assemblies. Then we showed how to use CAS in code, both declaratively and imperatively, and discussed issues with partially trusted code. We ended the chapter by looking at how SQL Server uses permission sets to restrict the access rights of SQL Server assemblies.

■ ■ ■

CHAPTER 11

Integrating Assemblies with Other Technologies

We've now covered all the basic issues involved in working with assemblies in SQL Server, so in this, the last chapter of the book, we'll concentrate entirely on two examples that demonstrate the integration of SQL assemblies with other technologies. The first example illustrates integration with another technology associated closely with .NET—XML web services—and demonstrates how we can use a SQL assembly as a web service client and so integrate SQL Server data with data taken from the Web. The second example looks at integration with a SQL Server technology—the new Service Broker message queuing system—and shows how we can use .NET assemblies to facilitate the creation of Service Broker applications.

This chapter covers the integration of assemblies for the purposes of

- Consuming web services from a database

- Gathering, sending, and storing database usage statistics using Service Broker

Web Services

One major advantage of CLR assemblies is the ability to consume web services from within the database. This wouldn't be easy with T-SQL, and would also require a lot of work in an unmanaged extended stored procedure. With .NET, it's almost as simple as accessing a local DLL: there are just a couple of extra command-line utilities we need to run to be able to access web services from within a SQL assembly:

- `wsdl.exe`: This utility examines the Web Service Description Language (WSDL) file for the web service and generates from it a source code file that performs the actual web access. We simply compile this file into our assembly and we can use the classes in it to access the web service just like a local assembly. If you use Visual Studio instead of the command-line compiler, you can omit this step, and instead simply add a web reference to your project in the VS IDE.

- `sgen.exe`: By default, .NET web services use dynamic XML serialization to encode .NET types for transmission over the Web. Dynamic code generation would be a security liability within SQL Server, and therefore isn't permitted for SQL assemblies. The `sgen.exe` utility is used to generate the XML serialization code for an assembly before installing it into SQL Server. At the time of writing, this step must be performed at the command prompt, and isn't available within the VS IDE.

■**Note** These tools are supplied only with the .NET SDK and Visual Studio 2005—they *aren't* shipped with the distribution version of the .NET Framework that comes with SQL Server 2005. So, if you don't have a copy of Visual Studio 2005, you'll need to download the full version of the .NET 2.0 SDK.

For this example, we'll use an existing public web service: the TerraServer-USA web service, which returns information about locations in the United States as well as aerial images provided by the U.S. Geological Survey (USGS). You can find out more about TerraServer-USA at http://www.terraserver-usa.com.

Our example resides in the AdventureWorks database, and it consists of a stored procedure that takes as a parameter the ID for a row in the Person.Address table. It uses this value to look up the row and select the city name, state or province, and country for the address. We then pass this information to the TerraServer-USA web service, and retrieve a list of matching places. For each of these, it queries the web service again to retrieve the image associated with the place, and then inserts a new row into a table, CityDetails, in the database containing the binary data for the image and other information about the place.

This is admittedly code that could be placed outside the database, in an external business object written in .NET, but there are two advantages to creating this as a SQL assembly. First, having the code inside the database allows it to be called from within other stored procedures, triggers, and so on. This means that it can be called, for example, whenever a new row is inserted into the Person.Address table. Second, the assembly performs several database queries, so we reduce network traffic by performing this within the database itself.

■**Note** At first sight, this looks like code that might be more usefully placed in a table-valued UDF to enable reuse. Unfortunately, however, the tables returned from table-valued functions aren't permitted to contain columns of type image. Columns of type varbinary are allowed, but this data type simply isn't big enough for our purposes.

Storing Data from the Web Service

Before we get down to writing the code, let's first create the CityDetails table where we'll store the data from the web service. This should be created in the AdventureWorks database, and in the Person schema:

```
USE AdventureWorks;
GO

CREATE TABLE Person.CityDetails
(
    CityDetailsID int IDENTITY PRIMARY KEY,
    AddressID    int FOREIGN KEY REFERENCES Person.Address(AddressID),
    Name         nvarchar(256),
    Latitude     float,
```

```
   Longitude     float,
   Population    int,
   Image         varbinary(max),
   CONSTRAINT UNQ_NameLatLong UNIQUE (Name, Latitude, Longitude)
);
GO
```

The only major point to note here is that, to avoid duplicate data being entered, we'll add a UNIQUE constraint based on the longitude and latitude coordinates of the city and the city name, as many places in the TerraServer-USA database seem to be duplicated. Specifying all three of these for the constraint will allow near duplicates to be entered (e.g., Seattle Center beside Seattle), and also ensure that different places that share the same name can be entered.

Writing the .NET Code

The next task is to write the .NET code that implements our stored procedure. In this case, with stunning originality, we've called the source code file WebServiceExample.cs. As usual, we start with the using directives; the only namespaces we need to import are the usual suspects for SQL Server assemblies (System, the System.Data namespaces, and Microsoft.SqlServer.Server):

```
using System;
using System.Data;
using System.Data.Sql;
using System.Data.SqlClient;
using System.Data.SqlTypes;
using Microsoft.SqlServer.Server;
```

The code for the stored procedure will be contained in a single method, GetCityData. This takes one parameter—the ID of the address for which we want to get the city details. We'll start by getting the city, state, and country for this address via the in-process provider, so we first need to open up the context connection to SQL Server:

```
namespace Apress.SqlAssemblies.Chapter11
{
   public class WebServiceExample
   {
      [SqlProcedure]
      public static void GetCityData(int addressID)
      {
         using (SqlConnection cn = new SqlConnection("context connection=true"))
         {
            cn.Open();
```

Next, we need to build the SQL command to perform this query. The city, state, and country are all in different tables in the AdventureWorks database, so our query contains a couple of inner joins. We also need to add a single parameter to the command—the ID for the address we want the data for. We won't be reusing this command, so we simply add the parameter and its value at the same time by calling the SqlParametersCollection's AddWithValue method. Once we've done this, we call the SqlCommand.ExecuteReader method to retrieve the data from the database:

```
string selectQuery = @"SELECT a.City, s.Name As State, c.Name As Country
                       FROM Person.Address a
                       INNER JOIN Person.StateProvince s
                       ON a.StateProvinceID = s.StateProvinceID
                         INNER JOIN Person.CountryRegion c
                         ON s.CountryRegionCode = c.CountryRegionCode
                       WHERE a.AddressID = @addressID";
SqlCommand selectCmd = new SqlCommand(selectQuery, cn);
selectCmd.Parameters.AddWithValue("@addressID", addressID);
SqlDataReader reader = selectCmd.ExecuteReader();
```

Now that we have the data as a SqlDataReader, we need to extract the names of the city, state, and country into local variables. First we check that the address ID supplied did match an address in the database, and so the reader contains data. If it does, we call Read to move to the first row, and then get the data from the three columns. The query should return only a single row, so we don't need to call Read more than once. After we've done that, we close the SqlDataReader, as it's no longer needed:

```
if (reader.HasRows)
{
   reader.Read();
   string city = (string)reader[0];
   string state = (string)reader[1];
   string country = (string)reader[2];
   reader.Close();
```

Once we have this information, we concatenate it into a single string (separated by commas); this is the form in which we'll pass the data to the web service. Then we'll instantiate the web service and call its GetPlaceList method. This method takes the name of the city (the string we've just constructed), the maximum number of entries to return, and a Boolean parameter to indicate whether only entries with an associated image are to be returned, and it returns an array of PlaceFacts objects. The PlaceFacts struct is a custom type used by the web service, and the code for this class will be generated when we run wsdl.exe on the TerraServer-USA web service.

```
string placeName = city + ", " + state + ", " + country;
TerraService terraService = new TerraService();
PlaceFacts[] places = terraService.GetPlaceList(placeName, 100,
                                                false);
```

■**Note** As we're calling wsdl.exe from the command line, we can place the TerraService class in the same namespace as the rest of our code. However, if you're using VS, it will by default be placed in the namespace com.terraserver-usa.www, so you'll need to either add a using directive for this namespace at the start of the code, or fully qualify the names of all the TerraServer-specific types.

Next we'll create the command to insert a new row into the `CityDetails` table. This command will be executed for each `PlaceFacts` object in the `places` array that we got back from our first call to the web service. As we'll be calling this multiple times with different values, we need to set up `SqlParameter` objects for each column value that we'll be inserting into the table, and then add these to the `SqlCommand` object through the `Parameters.AddRange` method. The one value that will always be the same is the associated address ID from the `Person.Address` table, so we can set this right away:

```
string insertQuery = @"INSERT INTO Person.CityDetails
                          VALUES (@addressID, @name, @longitude,
                             @latitude, @population, @image)";
SqlCommand insertCmd = new SqlCommand(insertQuery, cn);
SqlParameter addressIDParam = new SqlParameter("@addressID",
                                                SqlDbType.Int);
SqlParameter nameParam = new SqlParameter("@name",
                                            SqlDbType.NVarChar, 256);
SqlParameter longParam = new SqlParameter("@longitude",
                                            SqlDbType.Float);
SqlParameter latParam = new SqlParameter("@latitude",
                                            SqlDbType.Float);
SqlParameter popParam = new SqlParameter("@population",
                                            SqlDbType.Int);
SqlParameter imgParam = new SqlParameter("@image", SqlDbType.Image);

insertCmd.Parameters.AddRange(new SqlParameter[] { addressIDParam,
            nameParam, longParam, latParam, popParam, imgParam });
addressIDParam.Value = addressID;
```

The other parameter values will vary for each of the `PlaceFacts` objects in the array, so we iterate through these, retrieve the information, and call the insert command for each one. The `PlaceFacts` struct has a property called `Center`, which returns a `LonLatPt` object that encapsulates the longitude and latitude of the center of the place that the `PlaceFacts` represents. From this, we can retrieve the longitude and latitude as floating-point numbers, so we'll use these to set the values of two of our parameters to the insert command.

We can also use this `LonLatPt` to find out which image we need to download, as the image data itself isn't included in the `PlaceFacts` object. Each image is regarded as a tile in the map of the United States, so we need to find out which tile we want. To do this, we call the `GetTileMetaFromLonLatPt` method, which takes three parameters:

- The `LonLatPt` that we want the tile for

- The type of image we want, as an integer from 1 to 4

- The scale of the image as a `Scale` enum value

Here we've gone for image type 1 (aerial photograph), and a scale of `Scale8m`, which is the highest resolution available for nonsubscribers. This returns an object of type `TileMeta`, containing the metadata for the selected tile, which we can use to get the image data itself. The `TerraService` has a method called `GetTile`, which takes as its parameter the ID for the tile we want to retrieve, and we can pass into this the value of the Id property of our TileMeta object. This returns the binary image data as a byte array.

We also get a couple of other bits of information from the PlaceFacts object—the population of the place (although this has always been zero in the places I've seen), and the name of the place from the City property of the Place object associated with the PlaceFacts (the Place struct simply contains string properties returning the city, state, and country of the place). Once we've used this information to set the values of the parameters to our insert command, we simply execute the command:

```
foreach (PlaceFacts facts in places)
{
    LonLatPt coords = facts.Center;
    TileMeta metadata = terraService.GetTileMetaFromLonLatPt(coords,
                                                  1, Scale.Scale8m);
    byte[] image = terraService.GetTile(metadata.Id);
    nameParam.Value = facts.Place.City;
    longParam.Value = coords.Lon;
    latParam.Value = coords.Lat;
    popParam.Value = facts.Population;
    imgParam.Value = image;
    insertCmd.ExecuteNonQuery();
}
```

Once we've finished iterating through the PlaceFacts array and inserting rows into the table, we clean up the resources and send a message to the user:

```
SqlContext.Pipe.Send("Command executed successfully.");
terraService.Dispose();
}
```

If no rows were found matching the supplied AddressID in our original database query, we'll also clean up resources and send a message to the user informing them of this fact:

```
else
{
    reader.Close();
    SqlContext.Pipe.Send(
            "No addresses in the database match the specified ID.");
}
        }
    }
}
}
```

Generating the Custom Types Used by the Web Service

That completes the .NET code that we'll be writing for this example. However, before we compile it, we need to run wsdl.exe to generate the custom types that are used by the web service, including the `TerraService` class itself. The `wsdl` command-line tool takes as input the WSDL file that defines the web service (in the case of .NET web services, this is the `.asmx` file). In our case, we also want to pass in a couple of other options:

- `/o`: The name of the source code file that will be generated

- `/n`: The namespace that the code will be placed in

Because the default language for the generated source code is C#, we don't need to specify the language. However, if you want the code to be in another language, you'll also have to include the `/l` option. The possible values for this are `CS` (C#), `VB` (Visual Basic), `JS` (JScript), or `VJS` (J#).

Our call to `wsdl` therefore looks like this:

```
wsdl /o:TerraService.cs /n:Apress.SqlAssemblies.Chapter11 http://www.terraserver-
usa.com/TerraService2.asmx
```

This will generate a C# source code file called `TerraService.cs`, and you should now see the message:

```
Writing file 'TerraService.cs'
```

Compiling the Code

The next step is to compile our .NET code into a DLL assembly, including the `TerraService.cs` file we've just generated:

```
csc /t:library WebServiceExample.cs TerraService.cs
```

For a normal .NET assembly not hosted in SQL Server, we wouldn't need to do any more than this. However, as we noted at the start of this example, for security reasons SQL Server assemblies aren't allowed to use the default dynamically generated XML serialization assembly, and we need to generate a static serialization assembly, by calling the command-line tool `sgen.exe`:

```
sgen /a:WebServiceExample.dll
```

The only option we need is `/a`, which indicates the name of the assembly we want to generate the XML serialization classes for. This generates a serialization assembly with the name `WebServiceExample.XmlSerializers.dll`. If you want to overwrite an existing serialization assembly, you can use the `/f` option to force `sgen` to overwrite an existing file; if this option isn't included and the file already exists, `sgen` will throw an error.

■Note If you recompile the assembly for any reason, you need to run `sgen` on it again before redeploying the assemblies to SQL Server.

Deploying the Assemblies

We're now ready to deploy these assemblies (WebServiceExample and WebServiceExample. XmlSerializers) to SQL Server. The WebServiceExample assembly needs to be deployed first, as the serialization assembly references it (if you deploy the serialization assembly first, it creates a hidden copy of the WebServiceExample assembly, which you then can't use to create the stored procedure).

The code generated by wsdl contains synchronization attributes, and therefore the assembly must be installed with the UNSAFE permission set:

```
CREATE ASSEMBLY WebServiceExample
FROM 'C:\Apress\SqlAssemblies\Chapter11\WebServiceExample\WebServiceExample.dll'
WITH PERMISSION_SET = UNSAFE;
GO
```

Next we install the serialization assembly. This can be installed with the SAFE permission set:

```
CREATE ASSEMBLY [WebServiceExample.XmlSerializers]
FROM 'C:\Apress\SqlAssemblies\Chapter11\WebServiceExample\
WebServiceExample.XmlSerializers.dll'
WITH PERMISSION_SET = SAFE;
GO
```

Finally, create the CLR stored procedure:

```
CREATE PROCEDURE uspGetCityData(@addressID int)
AS
EXTERNAL NAME WebServiceExample.[Apress.SqlAssemblies.Chapter11.
WebServiceExample].GetCityData
GO
```

Testing the Example

To test the example, run the stored procedure with an appropriate address ID from the Person.Address table, and then check the contents of the CityDetails table:

```
EXEC uspGetCityData 3
SELECT * FROM Person.CityDetails
```

You should see a couple of rows have been added, as shown in Figure 11-1.

	CityDetailsID	AddressID	Name	Latitude	Longitude	Population	Image
1	1	3	Bothell	-122.199996948242	47.7599983215332	0	0xFFD8FFE000104A46494600010100
2	2	3	Bothell Landing Park	-122.20972442627	47.7583351135254	0	0xFFD8FFE000104A46494600010100

Figure 11-1. *The contents of the CityDetails table after running the CLR stored procedure*

Since viewing the image data in hex format isn't very exciting, the code download contains the City Image Viewer—a small Windows application written in .NET 2.0 that you can use to view the images in this table; please see the readme.txt file for information on configuring this. Figure 11-2 shows an image displayed in this application.

Figure 11-2. *An image from the CityDetails table displayed in the City Image Viewer application*

Service Broker

One of the many new features in SQL Server 2005 is Service Broker—a message queuing system that's native to SQL Server. Service Broker allows us to send a message to a queue (which could be in a different database, or even in a different instance of SQL Server), which will be picked up and processed (typically by a stored procedure) at the other end. We can tell SQL Server to run the processing module every time a message arrives on the queue, or we can schedule it to run at regular intervals using SQL Server Agent, as well as running it on an ad hoc basis (e.g., from within a trigger).

The endpoints through which messages are sent to a queue are known as Service Broker *services*. When a message is received on a queue, the processing stored procedure can send a response message back to the initiating service, which can in turn reply to this response (and so on); this exchange of messages is called a *dialog conversation*. The types of messages that each service can send to the queue are stipulated by the *contract* for a given conversation.

SQL Server 2005 introduces a number of new T-SQL objects that are used to create Service Broker applications:

- *Message types*: Message types are used to define the content of messages that can be sent to a queue. Message types can be associated with an XML schema, in which case any message sent to the queue that doesn't conform to that schema won't be placed on the queue. Alternatively, we can specify that messages should contain well-formed XML, that the message body should be empty, or that no validation of messages should occur, in which case the message body can contain any data, including binary data.

- *Contracts*: A contract specifies the message types that can be sent to a queue by the initiating service, the receiving service, or either of these. The contract acts as an agreement between the two sides of a conversation.

- *Queues*: Messages are sent by a service to a particular queue, from which they can be picked up and either processed or forwarded to another queue. The two services in a conversation can be associated with a single queue, or they can be associated with separate queues (e.g., if the services are in different databases). A queue can also be associated with a stored procedure, which will be activated whenever a message arrives in the queue.

- *Services*: A service is an endpoint for a Service Broker conversation. Services associate queues with the contracts that define the conversations that can take place on that queue. Services are always associated with a single queue, but queues can have multiple services associated with them.

- *Endpoint*: If you want your Service Broker application to converse over two or more instances of SQL Server, you'll need to create a Service Broker endpoint that listens on a particular TCP port for incoming messages. There can only be one Service Broker endpoint per SQL Server instance.

- *Routes*: A route specifies how SQL Server should find a remote service. By default, SQL Server looks for the receiving service in a Service Broker conversation in the same instance, but if it's in another instance, you'll need explicitly to create a route providing the network address of the instance that hosts the remote service.

- *Remote service bindings*: Remote service bindings are used to provide authentication to a remote service. A remote service binding is associated with a certificate, which identifies the user to the remote service. The processing stored procedure on the service may then be executed in the security context of the database user associated with this certificate, or in the public role.

The .NET Service Broker Interface

Our brief overview of Service Broker so far may not seem to have much to do with SQL Server assemblies. The relevance, of course, is that both the initiating code, which begins a conversation by sending a message to the queue, and the processing code, which is fired when the message arrives on the queue, can be written in .NET.

To aid in writing Service Broker applications, the samples that are supplied with SQL Server include the Service Broker Interface, which includes .NET wrappers for Service Broker services and messages, as well as a class that encapsulates a Service Broker conversation. In addition to facilitating the writing of the code that processes messages in a queue, these wrappers provide a way to send a message to a Service Broker queue from inside or outside SQL Server.

Rather than reinvent the wheel, we'll use these classes in the following example, which will demonstrate the basics of creating a Service Broker application in .NET. In order to follow this example, you'll therefore need to install the SQL Server samples. To do this, select Programs ➤ Microsoft SQL Server 2005 ➤ Documentation and Tutorials ➤ Samples ➤ Microsoft SQL Server 2005 Samples from the Start menu, and follow the installation wizard.

The Service Broker Interface sample is one of the Service Broker samples under the Database Engine samples, and is installed in the folder `<Program Files>\Microsoft SQL Server\90\ Samples\Engine\ServiceBroker\ServiceBrokerInterface\cs`. You can build this sample using VS 2005, as the VS project and solution files are included in the installation. However, it's almost as easy to compile it from the command line, so we'll do it that way for the benefit of anyone without VS.

First, open up a command prompt and change to the folder for the Service Broker interface project. Depending on your drive letter, this will be something like

```
C:\Program Files\Microsoft SQL Server\90\Samples\Engine\ServiceBroker\
ServiceBrokerInterface\cs\ServiceBrokerInterface
```

The next task is to compile all the `.cs` files into a single DLL assembly:

```
csc /t:library /out:ServiceBrokerInterface.dll BrokerApplication.cs
BrokerMethodAttribute.cs Conversation.cs Message.cs Service.cs
ServiceException.cs
```

This creates a file called `ServiceBrokerInterface.dll`, which we can reference from our SQL assemblies to take advantage of the wrapper classes. We'll use a private copy of this to reference when we compile the assemblies for our example, so copy this file over to the folder where you'll be creating the C# source files for this example (e.g., `C:\Apress\SqlAssemblies\Chapter11\ServiceBrokerExample`).

Example Service Broker Application

Now we can start to write the code for this example. The example will gather usage statistics from SQL Server by calling the statistical functions such as `@@CONNECTIONS`, etc., and will write this information to a queue using a SQL Server Agent job that executes at regular intervals. Periodically, we'll then retrieve the messages from this queue, process the information to work out how much each statistic has changed, and store this information in a table. The overall effect is much like calling `sp_monitor`, but instead of simply sending the statistics back to the user, we store them for later examination.

The logic behind creating this as a Service Broker application, rather than simply writing the stats straight into the table, is that we reduce the workload of the more frequently executing stored procedure, so it doesn't need to perform any processing of the figures or insertions into the table. This can be scheduled to run at a later time, when the server is expected to be less busy. In reality, there's obviously an overhead to using Service Broker, so we'd need to be performing some more intensive calculations to completely justify this approach, but as Service Broker applications can become complex, a relatively simple example will demonstrate its usage more clearly.

The same stricture holds true for writing the message processing code in .NET rather than T-SQL: for a simple example such as this, the code is probably actually more complex in .NET. This is particularly true for the server-side example, where the messages are retrieved from the queue. However, if we were doing more complex processing when retrieving the messages, the justification for using .NET would be much clearer. It does have to be said that neither the T-SQL nor the .NET interfaces for Service Broker are particularly friendly at the moment, but that will likely change in future releases (a particular issue is that many methods require `SqlConnection` and `SqlTransaction` objects to be passed into them, even though these have already been supplied to the object).

The example consists of two assemblies: a client that will initiate the conversation by sending a message to the queue, and a server that will periodically process those messages. Even though we're using the Service Broker Interface, we also need to create the T-SQL objects used by the example: the services, queue, and message type. We'll also need to create the table where we'll store the stats data, and a T-SQL stored procedure that retrieves this data. We'll begin by writing the client service.

Writing the Client Service

The client consists of a standard stored procedure assembly that uses the Service Broker Interface to send a message to our queue. The procedure retrieves the current statistical data by executing a T-SQL sproc called `uspGetSystemStats` (we'll look at this later in the chapter), packs this up into an XML document, and sends it as a message to the queue.

The source code for this assembly is contained in a file named `ServiceBrokerClient.cs`. As always, we start with the `using` directives:

```
using System;
using System.Data;
using System.Data.SqlClient;
using System.Data.SqlTypes;
using System.IO;
using System.Text;
using Microsoft.SqlServer.Server;
using Microsoft.Samples.SqlServer;
```

Besides the usual SQL Server namespaces, note that we include `System.IO` and `System.Text`, which contain classes we need for writing the message body, and the `Microsoft.Samples.SqlServer` namespace, which is where all the classes in the Service Broker Interface reside.

The first task for our code is to retrieve the current statistics by executing the `uspGetSystemStats` procedure. This has a number of output parameters (all of type `int`) that are populated with the latest figures when the sproc is run, so after we've opened up the context connection and instantiated the `SqlCommand` that we're using to execute the sproc, we need to create a `SqlParameter` for each of these, and set its `Direction` to `ParameterDirection.Output`:

```
namespace Apress.SqlAssemblies.Chapter11
{
    public class ServiceBrokerClient
    {
        public static void WriteStatsToQueue()
        {
            using (SqlConnection cn = new SqlConnection("context connection=true"))
            {
                string sql = @"EXEC uspGetSystemStats @connections OUTPUT,
                        @cpuBusy OUTPUT, @idle OUTPUT, @ioBusy OUTPUT,
```

```
                        @packErrors OUTPUT, @packRecd OUTPUT, @packSent OUTPUT,
                        @timeticks OUTPUT, @totErrors OUTPUT, @totRead OUTPUT,
                        @totWrite OUTPUT";
    SqlCommand cmd = new SqlCommand(sql, cn);
    cn.Open();

    SqlParameter connParm = new SqlParameter("@connections", SqlDbType.Int);
    connParm.Direction = ParameterDirection.Output;
    SqlParameter cpuParm = new SqlParameter("@cpuBusy", SqlDbType.Int);
    cpuParm.Direction = ParameterDirection.Output;
    SqlParameter idleParm = new SqlParameter("@idle", SqlDbType.Int);
    idleParm.Direction = ParameterDirection.Output;
    SqlParameter ioParm = new SqlParameter("@ioBusy", SqlDbType.Int);
    ioParm.Direction = ParameterDirection.Output;
    SqlParameter packErrsParm = new SqlParameter("@packErrors",
                                        SqlDbType.Int);
    packErrsParm.Direction = ParameterDirection.Output;
    SqlParameter packRecdParm = new SqlParameter("@packRecd",
                                        SqlDbType.Int);
    packRecdParm.Direction = ParameterDirection.Output;
    SqlParameter packSentParm = new SqlParameter("@packSent",
                                        SqlDbType.Int);
    packSentParm.Direction = ParameterDirection.Output;
    SqlParameter ticksParm = new SqlParameter("@timeticks", SqlDbType.Int);
    ticksParm.Direction = ParameterDirection.Output;
    SqlParameter totErrsParm = new SqlParameter("@totErrors",
                                        SqlDbType.Int);
    totErrsParm.Direction = ParameterDirection.Output;
    SqlParameter totReadParm = new SqlParameter("@totRead", SqlDbType.Int);
    totReadParm.Direction = ParameterDirection.Output;
    SqlParameter totWriteParm = new SqlParameter("@totWrite",
                                        SqlDbType.Int);
    totWriteParm.Direction = ParameterDirection.Output;
```

Once we've created all these parameters, we need to add them to the SqlCommand object, which we can then execute. As the returned data is all contained in output parameters, we can use the ExecuteNonQuery method to do this:

```
    cmd.Parameters.AddRange(new SqlParameter[] { connParm, cpuParm,
            idleParm, ioParm, packErrsParm, packRecdParm, packSentParm,
            ticksParm, totErrsParm, totReadParm, totWriteParm });
    cmd.ExecuteNonQuery();
```

Once we've executed the procedure, we'll store the usage statistics in local variables. The values returned by @@CPU_BUSY, @@IDLE, and @@IO_BUSY are not absolute values, but represent the number of ticks that the CPU has been busy in terms of IO and CPU, or the number of ticks it has been idle. To turn these tick values into microseconds, we need to multiply by the number retrieved from the @@TIMETICKS function. These microsecond values could exceed the maximum possible value for an int, so we need to use longs instead for these variables; however, we can't cast directly from a SqlInt32 to a long, so we have to convert them to ints first:

```
long timeticks = (int)ticksParm.Value;
int connections = (int)connParm.Value;
long cpuBusy = timeticks * (int)cpuParm.Value;
long idle = timeticks * (int)idleParm.Value;
long ioBusy = timeticks * (int)ioParm.Value;
int packErrors = (int)packErrsParm.Value;
int packRecd = (int)packRecdParm.Value;
int packSent = (int)packSentParm.Value;
int totalErrors = (int)totErrsParm.Value;
int totalRead = (int)totReadParm.Value;
int totalWrite = (int)totWriteParm.Value;
```

We also need to get the current time so we know when the statistics were taken, which we can get from the static Now property of the DateTime struct. Since we'll be inserting this into an XML file, we must use the XSD format. Fortunately, the DateTime.ToString method has an overload that takes a formatting string. Once we've got all these values, we can use them to create the XML document that will form the body of our message. We build this by calling the string.Format method, which allows us to insert parameters into the string in exactly the same way as Console.WriteLine:

```
string time = DateTime.Now.ToString("yyyy-MM-ddTHH:mm:ss.ff+00:00");
string msgBody = string.Format(@"<?xml version='1.0'?>
<sysStatsMessage>
    <connections>{0}</connections>
    <cpuBusy>{1}</cpuBusy>
    <idle>{2}</idle>
    <ioBusy>{3}</ioBusy>
    <packErrors>{4}</packErrors>
    <packRecd>{5}</packRecd>
    <packSent>{6}</packSent>
    <totalErrors>{7}</totalErrors>
    <totalRead>{8}</totalRead>
    <totalWrite>{9}</totalWrite>
    <time>{10}</time>
</sysStatsMessage>", connections, cpuBusy, idle, ioBusy, packErrors, packRecd,
packSent, totalErrors, totalRead, totalWrite, time);
```

Now we have the message body, we can go about sending it. There are four basic steps to send a message on a new conversation using the Service Broker Interface:

1. Instantiate a Service object that represents the sending service.

2. Call the BeginDialog method on the Service to start the conversation. This returns a Conversation object.

3. Create a Message object to represent the message that you want to send.

4. Call the Send method of the Conversation, passing in the Message object.

So, first we create the Service:

```
Service client = new Service(
        "http://schemas.apress.com/sqlassemblies/StatsRequestService",
        cn, null);
```

The Service constructor takes three parameters: the name of the service (this is the name that we assign the service when we create it as a database object in T-SQL); the connection to the database that the service resides in (in our case, this is the context connection); and a SqlTransaction object representing the transaction that conversations on this service will belong to (we pass in null here, as we're only going to send one message and then close the conversation).

Next, we begin the dialog:

```
Conversation conv = client.BeginDialog(
        "http://schemas.apress.com/sqlassemblies/StatsProcessorService",
        "http://schemas.apress.com/sqlassemblies/StatsServiceContract",
        TimeSpan.FromMinutes(1), false, cn, null);
```

The BeginDialog method takes six parameters: the name of the receiving service; the name of the contract that governs the conversation; the time span after which the conversation will expire; a Boolean value indicating whether the messages should be encrypted (but note that encryption is never used when the initiating and receiving services are in the same SQL Server instance); the SqlConnection object for the connection to the host database; and the SqlTransaction object for the current transaction.

Once we've started the conversation, we can prepare the message to send. The message body has to be provided as a stream, so we need to read our XML document into a MemoryStream. One overload of the MemoryStream constructor takes a byte array, so we just read the XML document into a byte array using the ASCII Encoding object, and create a new MemoryStream from this. We can then instantiate a new Message object, passing in the name of the message type that this message belongs to, and the MemoryStream we've just created:

```
MemoryStream msgStm = new MemoryStream(
        Encoding.ASCII.GetBytes(msgBody));
Message msg = new Message(
        "http://schemas.apress.com/sqlassemblies/StatsRequestMessage",
        msgStm);
```

All that remains is to send the message, close the conversation, and clean up the open objects:

```
        conv.Send(msg, cn, null);
        conv.End(cn, null);
        msgStm.Close();
    }
  }
 }
}
```

Finally, compile this file into a DLL, referencing `BrokerApplication.dll`:

```
csc /t:library /r:ServiceBrokerInterface.dll ServiceBrokerClient.cs
```

Writing the Server

The second assembly will retrieve all the messages from the queue, process the data in them, and add a new row for each message to the `SystemStats` table that we'll create to store the data.

Whereas the client assembly just created a new instance of the `Service` class, we have a bit more work to do in the server: we need to subclass the `Service` class to override its `Run` method, which is called to process messages in the associated queue.

The code for this assembly is contained in the file `ServiceBrokerServer.cs`, and starts with the following `using` directives:

```
using System;
using System.Collections;
using System.Data;
using System.Data.SqlClient;
using System.Data.SqlTypes;
using System.Xml;
using Microsoft.SqlServer.Server;
using Microsoft.Samples.SqlServer;
```

As well as the usual SQL Server namespaces and the `Microsoft.Samples.SqlServer` namespace for the Service Broker Interface, we import `System.Xml` for reading the XML-formatted messages, and `System.Collections` for the `ArrayList` class.

The public constructor takes a `SqlConnection` object and simply calls the base constructor, passing in the `SqlConnection` and the appropriate value for the service name. Again we pass in null for the `SqlTransaction` and false to signify that the transaction shouldn't auto-commit.

```
namespace Apress.SqlAssemblies.Chapter11
{
    public class StatsProcessorService : Service
    {
        public StatsProcessorService(SqlConnection cn) : base(
                    "http://schemas.apress.com/sqlassemblies/StatsProcessorService",
                    cn, null)
        {
        }
    }
```

The bulk of the work in this assembly is performed in the `Run` method, which overrides the standard `Run` method of the `Service` class. Here, we perform three actions:

1. We read the latest running totals of the statistics from the `SystemStats` table, so that we know how much they've changed since the last time the method was called.

2. We retrieve each message from the queue, using the data to create an instance of a struct called SystemStats. Each of these SystemStats objects is added to an ArrayList so we can retrieve it later. We do it this way because the Service Broker Interface uses the context connection to retrieve messages from the queue, and we can't reuse to write our inserts to the table.

3. For each of our SystemStats objects, we work out how much each value has changed from the last message, and perform an insert into the SystemStats table, including both the change from the previous value and the running total.

We start by initializing a Message object to null; this will hold the messages as we read them from the queue. We also initialize a new ArrayList object to hold all the instances of the SystemStats struct. Then we declare variables to hold the last value of each of the statistics. We initialize these to zero, as we'll use zero if there aren't any rows in the SystemStats table:

```
public override void Run(bool autoCommit, SqlConnection cn, SqlTransaction tx)
{
    Message message = null;
    ArrayList statsArray = new ArrayList();

    int  lastConnections = 0;
    long lastCpuBusy = 0;
    long lastIdle = 0;
    long lastIoBusy = 0;
    int  lastPackErrors = 0;
    int  lastPackRecd = 0;
    int  lastPackSent = 0;
    int  lastTotalErrors = 0;
    int  lastTotalRead = 0;
    int  lastTotalWrite = 0;
```

Next we loop through all the messages in the queue. To do this, we need to retrieve the active conversations associated with the service. The GetConversation method of the base Service class returns the next active conversation if one exists, or null otherwise, so we need to keep calling GetConversation until it returns null:

```
    Conversation conv;
    while ((conv = GetConversation(cn, tx)) != null)
    {
```

Once we have a conversation, we call the Receive method on it to retrieve the next message in that conversation. Again, this returns null if there are no remaining messages, so we need to repeat the calls to Receive until it returns null:

```
        while ((message = conv.Receive()) != null)
        {
```

We're only interested in messages of our custom type (Service Broker also puts messages on the queue, e.g., to signify that the other side has ended the conversation), so we'll check the

Type property of the Message, and only create an instance of the SystemStats struct if this matches the name of our custom type:

```
if (message.Type ==
        "http://schemas.apress.com/sqlassemblies/StatsRequestMessage")
{
```

To read the message, we need to create a new XmlDocument, and load the body of the message into this (one overload of the XmlDocument.Load method takes a Stream). We then create a new instance of SystemStats and populate each of its fields with the data taken from the XML document. To cast the data to the appropriate type, we call the relevant static method of the XmlConvert object. When we've finished doing this, we add the object to the statsArray ArrayList:

```
XmlDocument msgDoc = new XmlDocument();
msgDoc.Load(message.Body);
SystemStats stats = new SystemStats();
stats.Connections = XmlConvert.ToInt32(msgDoc.SelectSingleNode(
                        "//connections").FirstChild.Value);
stats.CpuBusy = XmlConvert.ToInt64(msgDoc.SelectSingleNode(
                        "//cpuBusy").FirstChild.Value);
stats.Idle = XmlConvert.ToInt64(msgDoc.SelectSingleNode(
                        "//idle").FirstChild.Value);
stats.IoBusy = XmlConvert.ToInt64(msgDoc.SelectSingleNode(
                        "//ioBusy").FirstChild.Value);
stats.PackErrs = XmlConvert.ToInt32(msgDoc.SelectSingleNode(
                        "//packErrors").FirstChild.Value);
stats.PackRecd = XmlConvert.ToInt32(msgDoc.SelectSingleNode(
                        "//packRecd").FirstChild.Value);
stats.PackSent = XmlConvert.ToInt32(msgDoc.SelectSingleNode(
                        "//packSent").FirstChild.Value);
stats.TotalErrs = XmlConvert.ToInt32(msgDoc.SelectSingleNode(
                        "//totalErrors").FirstChild.Value);
stats.TotalRead = XmlConvert.ToInt32(msgDoc.SelectSingleNode(
                        "//totalRead").FirstChild.Value);
stats.TotalWrite = XmlConvert.ToInt32(msgDoc.SelectSingleNode(
                        "//totalWrite").FirstChild.Value);
stats.Time = XmlConvert.ToDateTime(msgDoc.SelectSingleNode(
                        "//time").FirstChild.Value,
                        XmlDateTimeSerializationMode.Local);
statsArray.Add(stats);
        }
    }
}
```

Once we've got all the data from the messages stored in our statsArray, we need to find out the running values from the last time a row was added to the SystemStats table. This is a simple SELECT statement, using the ORDER BY and TOP 1 clauses to indicate we're only in the row with the highest value for the Time column (i.e., the row that reflects the latest statistics added to the table). The command is created with the SqlConnection object that was passed into the Run method. We retrieve all of the running total columns into a SqlDataReader, and then set the local variables we declared earlier to these values; if the SqlDataReader doesn't have any rows, we'll use the default zero values with which we initialized the variables:

```
string sql = @"SELECT TOP 1 TotalConnections, TotalCpuBusy, TotalIdle,
                            TotalIoBusy, TotalPackErrors, TotalPackRecd,
                            TotalPackSent, TotalErrors, TotalRead,
                            TotalWrite
              FROM SystemStats
              ORDER BY Time DESC;";
SqlCommand cmd = new SqlCommand(sql, cn);

using (SqlDataReader reader = cmd.ExecuteReader())
{
    if (reader.HasRows)
    {
        reader.Read();
        lastConnections = (int)reader[0];
        lastCpuBusy = (long)reader[1];
        lastIdle = (long)reader[2];
        lastIoBusy = (long)reader[3];
        lastPackErrors = (int)reader[4];
        lastPackRecd = (int)reader[5];
        lastPackSent = (int)reader[6];
        lastTotalErrors = (int)reader[7];
        lastTotalRead = (int)reader[8];
        lastTotalWrite = (int)reader[9];
    }
}
```

Next, we need to create the insert command that we'll use to add a row to the SystemStats table for each set of statistics. Each column inserted needs to have a SqlParameter object created for it and added to the SqlCommand object:

```
string insertQuery = "INSERT INTO SystemStats VALUES (@time, @connections,
        @totalConnections, @cpuBusy, @totalCpuBusy, @idle, @totalIdle,
        @ioBusy, @totalIoBusy, @packErrors, @totalPackErrors, @packRecd,
        @totalPackRecd, @packSent, @totalPackSent, @numErrors,
        @totalErrors, @numReads, @totalRead, @numWrites, @totalWrite)";
SqlCommand insertCmd = new SqlCommand(insertQuery, this.Connection);

SqlParameter timeParam = new SqlParameter("@time", SqlDbType.DateTime);
SqlParameter connParam = new SqlParameter("@connections", SqlDbType.Int);
SqlParameter totalConnParam = new SqlParameter("@totalConnections",
                                               SqlDbType.Int);
SqlParameter cpuParam = new SqlParameter("@cpuBusy", SqlDbType.BigInt);
SqlParameter totalCpuParam = new SqlParameter("@totalCpuBusy",
                                              SqlDbType.BigInt);
```

```
        SqlParameter idleParam = new SqlParameter("@idle", SqlDbType.BigInt);
        SqlParameter totalIdleParam = new SqlParameter("@totalIdle",
                                                SqlDbType.BigInt);
        SqlParameter ioParam = new SqlParameter("@ioBusy", SqlDbType.BigInt);
        SqlParameter totalIoParam = new SqlParameter("@totalIoBusy",
                                                SqlDbType.BigInt);
        SqlParameter packErrsParam = new SqlParameter("@packErrors",
                                                SqlDbType.Int);
        SqlParameter totalPackErrsParam = new SqlParameter("@totalPackErrors",
                                                SqlDbType.Int);
        SqlParameter packRecdParam = new SqlParameter("@packRecd", SqlDbType.Int);
        SqlParameter totalPackRecdParam = new SqlParameter("@totalPackRecd",
                                                SqlDbType.Int);
        SqlParameter packSentParam = new SqlParameter("@packSent", SqlDbType.Int);
        SqlParameter totalPackSentParam = new SqlParameter("@totalPackSent",
                                                SqlDbType.Int);
        SqlParameter numErrsParam = new SqlParameter("@numErrors", SqlDbType.Int);
        SqlParameter totErrsParam = new SqlParameter("@totalErrors",
                                                SqlDbType.Int);
        SqlParameter numReadsParam = new SqlParameter("@numReads", SqlDbType.Int);
        SqlParameter totReadParam = new SqlParameter("@totalRead", SqlDbType.Int);
        SqlParameter numWritesParam = new SqlParameter("@numWrites",
                                                SqlDbType.Int);
        SqlParameter totWriteParam = new SqlParameter("@totalWrite",
                                                SqlDbType.Int);

        insertCmd.Parameters.AddRange(new SqlParameter[] { timeParam, connParam,
                totalConnParam, cpuParam, totalCpuParam, idleParam, totalIdleParam,
                ioParam, totalIoParam, packErrsParam, totalPackErrsParam,
                packRecdParam, totalPackRecdParam, packSentParam, totalPackSentParam,
                numErrsParam, totErrsParam, numReadsParam, totReadParam,
                numWritesParam, totWriteParam });
        insertCmd.Prepare();
```

Once we've prepared the command and parameters, we can iterate through our
statsArray and execute the command for each element in the ArrayList. We set the running
totals columns to the values taken directly from the message, but calculate the values for the
other columns by subtracting the last value for that statistic. When we've set the values of all
the parameters, we update the local variables that contain the last values with the values from
the SystemStats object we've just processed, and finally execute the insert command:

```
        foreach (SystemStats statsElement in statsArray)
        {
            timeParam.Value = statsElement.Time;
            connParam.Value = statsElement.Connections - lastConnections;
            totalConnParam.Value = statsElement.Connections;
            cpuParam.Value = statsElement.CpuBusy - lastCpuBusy;
```

```
            totalCpuParam.Value = statsElement.CpuBusy;
            idleParam.Value = statsElement.Idle - lastIdle;
            totalIdleParam.Value = statsElement.Idle;
            ioParam.Value = statsElement.IoBusy - lastIoBusy;
            totalIoParam.Value = statsElement.IoBusy;
            packErrsParam.Value = statsElement.PackErrs - lastPackErrors;
            totalPackErrsParam.Value = statsElement.PackErrs;
            packRecdParam.Value = statsElement.PackRecd - lastPackRecd;
            totalPackRecdParam.Value = statsElement.PackRecd;
            packSentParam.Value = statsElement.PackSent - lastPackSent;
            totalPackSentParam.Value = statsElement.PackSent;
            numErrsParam.Value = statsElement.TotalErrs - lastTotalErrors;
            totErrsParam.Value = statsElement.TotalErrs;
            numReadsParam.Value = statsElement.TotalRead - lastTotalRead;
            totReadParam.Value = statsElement.TotalRead;
            numWritesParam.Value = statsElement.TotalWrite - lastTotalWrite;
            totWriteParam.Value = statsElement.TotalWrite;

            lastConnections = statsElement.Connections;
            lastCpuBusy = statsElement.CpuBusy;
            lastIdle = statsElement.Idle;
            lastIoBusy = statsElement.IoBusy;
            lastPackErrors = statsElement.PackErrs;
            lastPackRecd = statsElement.PackRecd;
            lastPackSent = statsElement.PackSent;
            lastTotalErrors = statsElement.TotalErrs;
            lastTotalRead = statsElement.TotalRead;
            lastTotalWrite = statsElement.TotalWrite;
            insertCmd.ExecuteNonQuery();
        }
    }
```

Run is an instance method, so we can't execute that as a stored procedure; instead, we need to write another method which we'll use as the stored procedure method that can be called from SQL Server. In this method, we simply open up the context connection, create a new instance of the StatsProcessorService class, call its Run method, and close the connection again:

```
public static void ProcessMessages()
{
    using (SqlConnection cn = new SqlConnection("context connection=true"))
    {
        cn.Open();
        StatsProcessorService svc = new StatsProcessorService(cn);
        svc.Run(false, cn, null);
    }
}
```

Finally, we need to define our SystemStats struct that holds the data read in from each message. This is only used internally in the Run method, so we can define it as private:

```
private struct SystemStats
{
    public int Connections;
    public long CpuBusy;
    public long Idle;
    public long IoBusy;
    public int PackErrs;
    public int PackRecd;
    public int PackSent;
    public int TotalErrs;
    public int TotalRead;
    public int TotalWrite;
    public DateTime Time;
}
}
}
```

That completes the .NET source code for this example; compile it into a DLL, again referencing the BrokerApplication.dll that contains the Service Broker Interface:

```
csc /t:library /r:ServiceBrokerInterface.dll ServiceBrokerServer.cs
```

Deploying the Assemblies

That completes the .NET code for the example, but unfortunately we've still got a lot of T-SQL code to write. Not only do we have to deploy our assemblies to SQL Server, we also have to create the SystemStats table, the uspGetSystemStats T-SQL stored procedure, and a host of Service Broker objects. We'll add these all to the AssembliesTesting database, but they could really go anywhere.

Gathering and Storing Statistics

Let's start with the uspGetSystemStats procedure that collects the usage data and returns it as output parameters:

```
USE AssembliesTesting
GO

CREATE PROCEDURE uspGetSystemStats
(
    @connections int OUT,
    @cpuBusy     int OUT,
    @idle        int OUT,
    @ioBusy      int OUT,
    @packErrors  int OUT,
```

```
       @packRecd     int OUT,
       @packSent     int OUT,
       @timeticks    int OUT,
       @totErrors    int OUT,
       @totRead      int OUT,
       @totWrite     int OUT
)
AS
BEGIN
    SET @connections = @@CONNECTIONS;
    SET @cpuBusy = @@CPU_BUSY;
    SET @idle = @@IDLE;
    SET @ioBusy = @@IO_BUSY;
    SET @packErrors = @@PACKET_ERRORS;
    SET @packRecd = @@PACK_RECEIVED;
    SET @packSent = @@PACK_SENT;
    SET @timeticks = @@TIMETICKS;
    SET @totErrors = @@TOTAL_ERRORS;
    SET @totRead = @@TOTAL_READ;
    SET @totWrite = @@TOTAL_WRITE;
END;
GO
```

This is very simple—we just retrieve the values from each of the system statistical functions, and return it to the caller as an output parameter.

Next we create the SystemStats table in which to store these statistics:

```
CREATE TABLE SystemStats
(
    ID                int IDENTITY PRIMARY KEY,
    time              DateTime,
    Connections       int,
    TotalConnections  int,
    CpuBusy           bigint,
    TotalCpuBusy      bigint,
    Idle              bigint,
    TotalIdle         bigint,
    IoBusy            bigint,
    TotalIoBusy       bigint,
    PackErrors        int,
    TotalPackErrors   int,
    PackRecd          int,
    TotalPackRecd     int,
    PackSent          int,
    TotalPackSent     int,
    NumErrors         int,
    TotalErrors       int,
    NumReads          int,
```

```
    TotalRead      int,
    NumWrites      int,
    TotalWrite     int
);
GO
```

Creating the Service Broker Objects

Now we can move on to the Service Broker–related objects. First, we'll create the XML schema collection that we'll use to validate messages sent to our queue. This schema states that the messages must have a root element called <sysStatsMessage>, containing a child element for each of the values returned from the uspGetSystemStats procedure, plus one for the current time:

```
CREATE XML SCHEMA COLLECTION
    [http://schemas.apress.com/sqlassemblies/StatsRequestSchema]
AS N'<?xml version="1.0"?>
<xs:schema xmlns:xs="http://www.w3.org/2001/XMLSchema">
    <xs:element name="sysStatsMessage">
        <xs:complexType>
            <xs:sequence minOccurs="1" maxOccurs="1">
                <xs:element name="connections" type="xs:integer" />
                <xs:element name="cpuBusy" type="xs:integer" />
                <xs:element name="idle" type="xs:integer" />
                <xs:element name="ioBusy" type="xs:integer" />
                <xs:element name="packErrors" type="xs:integer" />
                <xs:element name="packRecd" type="xs:integer" />
                <xs:element name="packSent" type="xs:integer" />
                <xs:element name="totalErrors" type="xs:integer" />
                <xs:element name="totalRead" type="xs:integer" />
                <xs:element name="totalWrite" type="xs:integer" />
                <xs:element name="time" type="xs:dateTime" />
            </xs:sequence>
        </xs:complexType>
    </xs:element>
</xs:schema>';
```

Now we can create the message type based on this schema:

```
CREATE MESSAGE TYPE [http://schemas.apress.com/sqlassemblies/StatsRequestMessage]
VALIDATION = VALID_XML WITH SCHEMA COLLECTION
            [http://schemas.apress.com/sqlassemblies/StatsRequestSchema];
```

The VALIDATION clause specifies what type of content the messages of this type must contain. The possible values are as follows:

- VALID_XML WITH SCHEMA COLLECTION <schema name>: The message body must contain an XML document that is valid according to the named schema.

- WELL_FORMED_XML: The message body must contain well-formed XML, but won't be validated against any schema.

- EMPTY: The message body should be empty.

- NONE: No validation is performed, so the message body can contain any data in any format.

Next we create the contract that specifies what message types can be sent on this conversation. In our case, only the initiating service may send messages, and only of our StatsRequestMessage type:

```
CREATE CONTRACT [http://schemas.apress.com/sqlassemblies/StatsServiceContract]
(
    [http://schemas.apress.com/sqlassemblies/StatsRequestMessage] SENT BY INITIATOR
);
```

The contract contains a list of message types, followed by a SENT BY clause indicating which of the services can send messages of this type to the queue. The possible SENT BY values are INITIATOR, TARGET, or ANY. All contracts must contain at least one message type that can be sent by the initiator or ANY, as otherwise the conversation could never be started.

Next comes the queue:

```
CREATE QUEUE StatsServiceQueue
WITH STATUS = ON, RETENTION = OFF;
```

The STATUS = ON clause indicates that the queue will be activated immediately, and the RETENTION = OFF clause indicates that messages will be removed from the queue when they are retrieved by the processing service.

We could also specify an ACTIVATION clause that contains a PROCEDURE_NAME indicating the name of the stored procedure to run whenever a message arrives in the queue. However, for this example, we want to check the queue periodically and process multiple messages in one go.

The last Service Broker objects we need to create are the services themselves. For each service, we need to provide the name of the queue it's associated with, and the names of all the contracts for the conversations the service can participate in. Since our two services share the same queue and participate only in the same conversation, the CREATE SERVICE commands are identical but for the service names:

```
CREATE SERVICE [http://schemas.apress.com/sqlassemblies/StatsRequestService]
ON QUEUE StatsServiceQueue
(
    [http://schemas.apress.com/sqlassemblies/StatsServiceContract]
);

CREATE SERVICE [http://schemas.apress.com/sqlassemblies/StatsProcessorService]
ON QUEUE StatsServiceQueue
(
    [http://schemas.apress.com/sqlassemblies/StatsServiceContract]
);
GO
```

Deployment

All that remains is to deploy the assemblies and the CLR stored procedures. First come those for the client; the assembly can be created with the SAFE permission set:

```
CREATE ASSEMBLY ServiceBrokerClient
FROM
    'C:\Apress\SqlAssemblies\Chapter11\ServiceBrokerExample\ServiceBrokerClient.dll'
WITH PERMISSION_SET = SAFE;
GO


CREATE PROCEDURE uspWriteStatsToQueue
AS
EXTERNAL NAME ServiceBrokerClient.[Apress.SqlAssemblies.Chapter11.
ServiceBrokerClient].WriteStatsToQueue;
GO
```

Next come the server assembly and CLR sproc; the server assembly can also be installed with the SAFE permission set:

```
CREATE ASSEMBLY ServiceBrokerServer
FROM
    'C:\Apress\SqlAssemblies\Chapter11\ServiceBrokerExample\ServiceBrokerServer.dll'
WITH PERMISSION_SET = SAFE;
GO


CREATE PROCEDURE uspProcessMessages
AS
EXTERNAL NAME ServiceBrokerServer.[Apress.SqlAssemblies.Chapter11.
StatsProcessorService].ProcessMessages;
GO
```

Testing

We'll set the client service to run every half an hour so that reasonably frequent usage data is gathered, so we need to create a new SQL Server Agent job. Obviously, this means that you need to make sure your SQL Server Agent service is running!

In Object Explorer in Management Studio, right-click the Jobs node under SQL Server Agent and select New Job. This displays the New Job dialog, seen in Figure 11-3.

On the General tab, enter the name for the job (we've chosen StatCollection), and the owner, and move on to the Steps tab. Click the New button to add a new step for executing our client procedure to the job, and you will see the dialog shown in Figure 11-4.

Figure 11-3. *The General tab of the New Job dialog*

Figure 11-4. *Adding a step to the job*

Enter a name for the step, select Transact-SQL script from the Type drop-down list and AdventureWorks from the Database drop-down, and enter the following command.

```
EXEC uspWriteStatsToQueue
```

Click OK to close this dialog and return to the New Job dialog. Here, move to the Schedules tab, and click the New button to create a new schedule. You are now presented with the dialog seen in Figure 11-5.

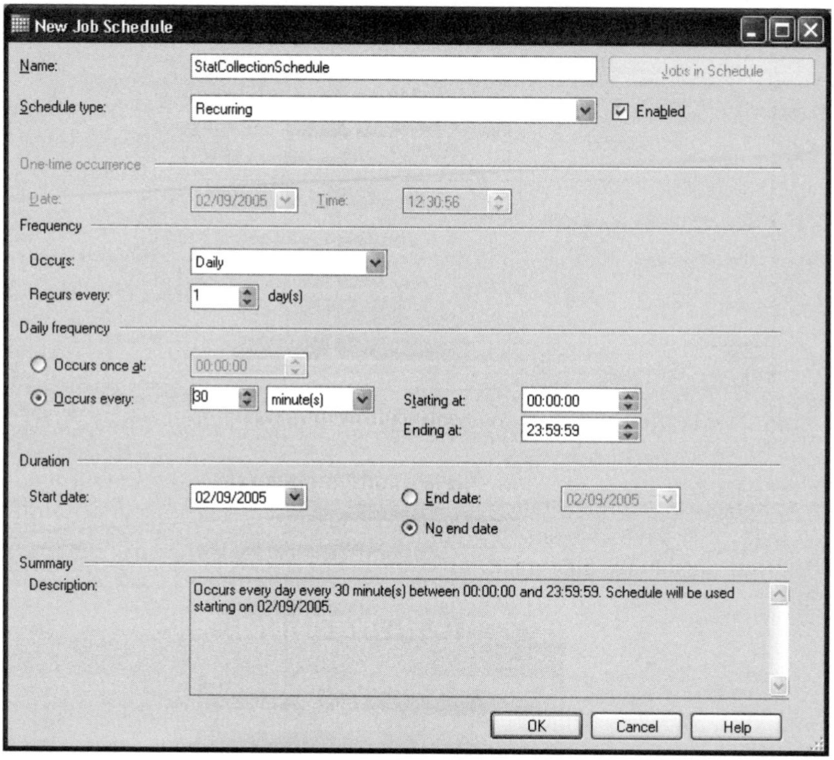

Figure 11-5. *Setting the schedule for the job*

Choose an appropriate schedule; Figure 11-5 shows the settings to run the job every half an hour. When you've finished, click OK to return to the New Job dialog, and then click OK there to create the job.

Note that the bug described in KB 241643 still exists in SQL Server 2005, so SQL Server Agent jobs won't run successfully on Windows 2000/2003 domains if the job is scheduled to run under a Windows login that doesn't belong to the Pre-Windows 2000 Compatible Access Group. For more details, please see the following web site:

```
http://support.microsoft.com/default.aspx?scid=kb;en-us;q241643
```

In real life, we'd also create a schedule to run the processing procedure at set times daily, but in a test scenario, you're unlikely to have the patience for that.

To test the application, you'll need either to wait an hour or so for the StatCollection job to execute a couple of times or to run the client sproc manually two or three times. Then execute the uspProcessMessages sproc to process the messages that should by now have been placed on the queue, and run a SELECT command on the SystemStats table to see the inserted rows:

```
EXEC uspProcessMessages
SELECT * FROM SystemStats;
```

You should see a resultset something like that shown in Figure 11-6.

	ID	time	Connections	TotalConnections	CpuBusy	TotalCpuBusy	Idle	TotalIdle	IoBusy	TotalIoI
1	5	2005-09-07 14:30:00.520	4964	4964	72250000	72250000	-887214388	-887214388	21843750	218437
2	6	2005-09-07 15:00:01.150	1119	6083	5312500	77562500	1750531250	863316862	2593750	244375
3	7	2005-09-07 15:30:09.240	798	6881	26718750	104281250	-2591811046	-1728494184	35781250	602187
4	8	2005-09-07 16:00:09.460	1333	8214	14187500	118468750	1731968750	3474566	11906250	721250
5	9	2005-09-07 16:30:02.040	1157	9371	6687500	125156250	1741437500	1744912066	2468750	745937

Figure 11-6. *The rows added to the SystemStats table*

Summary

This chapter was devoted entirely to two examples that demonstrate how SQL assemblies can be used to interact both with other .NET technologies (web services), but also with other SQL Server technologies (Service Broker). Both web services and Service Broker are huge topics, worthy of books in their own right, so we've only skimmed the surface here. However, we hope (and like to believe!) that over the course of this chapter, and this book, we've provided you with plenty of ideas for using .NET assemblies in SQL Server, and also given you a good idea of the potential and the limitations of this exciting new development.

Index

forums.apress.com

JOIN THE APRESS FORUMS AND BE PART OF OUR COMMUNITY. You'll find discussions that cover topics of interest to IT professionals, programmers, and enthusiasts just like you. If you post a query to one of our forums, you can expect that some of the best minds in the business—especially Apress authors, who all write with *The Expert's Voice™*—will chime in to help you. Why not aim to become one of our most valuable participants (MVPs) and win cool stuff? Here's a sampling of what you'll find:

DATABASES
Data drives everything.

Share information, exchange ideas, and discuss any database programming or administration issues.

INTERNET TECHNOLOGIES AND NETWORKING
Try living without plumbing (and eventually IPv6).

Talk about networking topics including protocols, design, administration, wireless, wired, storage, backup, certifications, trends, and new technologies.

JAVA
We've come a long way from the old Oak tree.

Hang out and discuss Java in whatever flavor you choose: J2SE, J2EE, J2ME, Jakarta, and so on.

MAC OS X
All about the Zen of OS X.

OS X is both the present and the future for Mac apps. Make suggestions, offer up ideas, or boast about your new hardware.

OPEN SOURCE
Source code is good; understanding (open) source is better.

Discuss open source technologies and related topics such as PHP, MySQL, Linux, Perl, Apache, Python, and more.

PROGRAMMING/BUSINESS
Unfortunately, it is.

Talk about the Apress line of books that cover software methodology, best practices, and how programmers interact with the "suits."

WEB DEVELOPMENT/DESIGN
Ugly doesn't cut it anymore, and CGI is absurd.

Help is in sight for your site. Find design solutions for your projects and get ideas for building an interactive Web site.

SECURITY
Lots of bad guys out there—the good guys need help.

Discuss computer and network security issues here. Just don't let anyone else know the answers!

TECHNOLOGY IN ACTION
Cool things. Fun things.

It's after hours. It's time to play. Whether you're into LEGO® MINDSTORMS™ or turning an old PC into a DVR, this is where technology turns into fun.

WINDOWS
No defenestration here.

Ask questions about all aspects of Windows programming, get help on Microsoft technologies covered in Apress books, or provide feedback on any Apress Windows book.

HOW TO PARTICIPATE:
Go to the Apress Forums site at **http://forums.apress.com/**.
Click the New User link.